THIS
WAR
REALLY
MATTERS

THIS WAR REALLY MATTERS

Inside the Fight for Defense Dollars

George C. Wilson

CQ PRESS

Washington, D.C.

CQ Press

A Division of Congressional Quarterly Inc.

1414 22nd St. N.W.

Washington, D.C. 20037

(202) 822-1475; (800) 638-1710

www.cqpress.com

Printed in the United States of America

03 02 01 00 99   5 4 3 2 1

Cover: Dennis Anderson

Library of Congress Cataloging-in-Publication Data

In process

ISBN 1-56802-460-6

To Nathan, Avery, and McKenzie,

with hopes you will know a peaceful world.

Contents

Foreword

This War Really Matters, by veteran defense correspondent George C. Wilson, is an insider's account of how the U.S. government tries to live up to its constitutional responsibility to provide for the common defense. It offers insight into the process of procuring and apportioning defense dollars by involving the readers in the process.

Throughout my career inside and outside government as a researcher, teacher, and practitioner, I wondered how such a diverse and vital activity as the budget process could be analyzed between the covers of a book without providing only a single individual's viewpoint or ending up a dull, monotonous tome. Wilson, whom I have known for decades as an outstanding reporter on defense issues, overcomes both problems. By framing the discussion within the 105th Congress (1997–1999), he presents a logical beginning, middle, and end. Readers are introduced to the major players in the process—their goals, biases, and role in moving the process forward. Wilson delves into the intricacies of budgeting while keeping readers firmly rooted to the narrative. He allows the players themselves to explain what they are doing and why, usually in their own words. In addition, Wilson has managed to persuade William S. Cohen, the secretary of defense, and Gen. Henry H. Shelton, chairman of the Joint Chiefs of Staff, to provide an inside account of how they changed President Clinton's mind on the core question of "how much money was enough" for national defense.

Readers will be intrigued and enlightened by the frankness of three top-ranking generals and an admiral as they point out the flaws they see in the defense budget process and candidly discuss the way their rival armed services waste taxpayers' dollars. Congressional politics are woven throughout the book. The discussion on the slipshod fiscal 1999 "emergency" appropriations bill gives an authoritative account of how legislative leaders operate behind closed doors.

This War Really Matters demystifies the process of buying tanks, ships, and missiles and explains the stresses of fielding today's all-volunteer force. It is the best book I know describing the defense dollar—and who gets what, when, and why. It is a useful manual for students taking courses in foreign policy, national security, public administration, and American government. As a case study it lends itself to a number of applications in the classroom, both as a text that analyzes a vital government process and as a supplement that encapsulates the larger themes of American government courses. For example, students will get a lesson in real-life politics as they are presented with firsthand accounts of how the legislative and executive branches hammer out compromises on national defense.

Whether introduced at the beginning of a course or used as a capstone to integrate the various components, *This War Really Matters* gives students a clear sense of how and why providing for the national defense is a political process. Because of its concise and readable format, the book fits neatly into any course segment. The individual perspectives of political and military leaders shed light on governmental processes that both students and the public need to understand.

This War Really Matters is a field manual on national politics for military professionals and should be required reading at war colleges. By learning from this book how things work at the top, military leaders can become more effective, no matter what their rank. Military officers should read the words of top Pentagon officials as they discuss the threats of the twenty-first century, as these beliefs and convictions drive the leaders' choices of weapons and military strategy. It is also instructive and healthy for military officers and the general public to read and understand what critics see as the dangers ahead if the nation sticks to its current course.

Although the 105th Congress is the focus of this work, the political dynamics that it portrays are timeless. Wilson has written a fascinating, inside account that will serve as a valuable teaching and learning tool.

Lawrence J. Korb

Acknowledgments

Most authors, certainly this one, become obsessed with the book they are writing. This makes the author a poor helpmate and often poor company. For putting up with such single-mindedness, I again salute and thank my wife, Joan Gibbons Wilson.

For leaning my way on so many occasions to provide time for writing the book, I thank my primary employer, Nancy J. Schwerzler, vice president and editor of Legi-Slate, the *Washington Post* on-line news service.

For supporting this project from start to finish, I thank Brenda W. Carter, the college market director at CQ Press. At the midway point, she deputized Charisse Kiino to develop the book and see it to publication. Ms. Kiino worked tirelessly and effectively to make the book—as the Army might put it—be all it can be. For skillful editing of the manuscript, I thank John L. Moore, a veteran Congressional Quarterly writer and editor.

For all their generous research help to me in my pursuit of information as an accredited member of the Congressional Press Gallery, I thank Greg Harness, librarian for the Library of Congress branch in the Senate, and his able staff of reference librarians, especially Nancy Kervin.

For their time and insights, and often their fortitude in speaking frankly, I thank everyone quoted in this book and many more I cannot mention for fear of jeopardizing their careers.

And for being constant inspirations through the years, including the years of work on this book, I thank two people: my reporter-editor-friend William Greider and John J. Ford. John, a former staff director of the House Armed Services Committee and rival softball pitcher when we both came to Washington decades ago, read the manuscript and made invaluable contributions.

THIS
WAR
REALLY
MATTERS

Introduction

YOUR HIRED HANDS in Washington—the president, secretary of defense, generals, admirals, senators, representatives—spend $500,000 of your tax dollars every minute to defend you and American interests. Ever since 1952, war or no war, this spending on national defense has totaled between $200 billion and $400 billion a year in comparable fiscal 2000 dollars. Some say this is too much. Others contend it is not enough.

The process of deciding how much is enough to spend for national defense is a political one. Although *Webster's New World Dictionary* defines politics as "the science and art of political government," politicians themselves consider politics the art of the possible. And they act accordingly.

In a democracy such as the United States, no president can put laws on the books without help. The chief executive must settle for what is politically possible. The same goes for a senator or representative. On big issues like national defense, the president and Congress must work together to get anything done.

True, a president can start a war on his own. But he cannot finish the war unless Congress appropriates the money for it. And, yes, a member of Congress can wheel and deal to force the Pentagon to build a ship or airplane in the member's home area to create jobs. The senator or representative can fight the closing of a local shipyard or air base. But no lawmaker can do this alone. He or she must engage in the art of the possible to achieve such goals.

Politicians work day and night throughout their political careers to hone skills in the art of the possible. They need knowledge, energy, power, charm, nerve, cunning, persistence, and luck to be successful.

Few generals or admirals can match politicians in these skills. But they have other weapons, notably expertise and experience in the military arts. These, plus the esteem that goes with volunteering to fight the nation's battles, give the military leaders credibility when a president or secretary of defense is weighing choices in apportioning a limited amount of defense dollars.

Even though they are armed with credibility, military leaders still must engage in the art of the possible to achieve their goals. How many tanks the Army can put on the battlefield; how many ships the Navy can send to sea; how many fighter planes the Air Force can fly; how fast Marines can get themselves to a distant trouble spot—all these things and more depend heavily on how skillful military leaders are in the art of the possible, a skill which they must acquire to maximize their effectiveness in government councils.

Although Americans provide the money for national defense, few of them know much about the bloodless but vital fight for their defense dollars. This book provides a ring side seat for watching this fight up close and personal. Where practical, the fighters speak in their own words taken off my tape recorder. *This War Really Matters* shows the art of the possible in action on the most vital issue: how best to protect the United States. The decisions made in national defense really do matter because many of them in this nuclear age affect almost every living thing on Planet Earth.

Despite those immense consequences, the process for deciding how much should be spent on national defense, and for what, is flawed. It is politicized by presidents, secretaries of defense, lawmakers, generals, admirals, and defense contractors. Building and arming an Army, Navy, Air Force, and Marine Corps for the next war must be largely guesswork because nobody knows what the next war is going to be like. This uncertainty makes it tempting for our civilian and military leaders to hang on to what won the previous war rather than acquire different strategies and weapons for the most likely next one.

Yet, for all its flaws, the process for providing soldiers and guns through the art of the possible has made the United States the strongest nation on earth. The more U.S. citizens understand how the process works, the more likely it is they will be emboldened to participate in it to make it better. This was one of the reasons I wrote *This War Really Matters*.

I chose to be a guide with a red umbrella taking the reader on a tour of the most significant battles in this little-understood war for minds and money. In the interest of letting the reader make his or her own assessment of the decision-making process for national defense, I hold back my own views until the last chapter of the book. Then I draw on my thirty-eight years' experience as a defense reporter to say what I think is right or wrong about the way the United States makes some of its most important decisions—those that involve the nation's ability to defend itself and its allies around the world.

This War Really Matters shows ordinary people struggling to make extraordinary choices within the boundaries of the art of the possible. One boundary is money. Even in the United States, the richest nation on earth, there is only so much money available for defense. Guns rightly compete with butter. Teaching its young people to learn and think strengthens a nation more than teaching them to shoot.

In drawing this up-close-and-personal portrait of the process as it is actually practiced on this little-explored political battlefield, I focused on the 105th Congress, which ran from 1997 through 1998. I could have chosen almost any post–cold war Congress. But the 105th, because it fell between the 1996 and 2000 presidential elections, was less distorted by seasonal electioneering. The process described between these covers typifies those that will be followed for years to come. In that sense, the book is timeless.

Chapter Summaries

Although I tried to make the defense budget process understandable, with parenthetical definitions of terms that might not be familiar, there is no denying that it is a complex process with many players and parts. For that reason I've provided the following chapter summaries, to help you the reader stay on track through the process and its chronological twists and turns.

The tour I have arranged moves from one event to another in the order they happened. I did this in hopes of holding your interest as we move along without skipping any of the important fights in the political war for defense dollars.

CHAPTER 1, "Firing the Opening Shot," describes the beginning of the Clinton administration's two-year war to win over minds for the president's national defense program. The reader meets Pentagon Comptroller John J. Hamre first as a person, then sees him in action as a Clinton point man. You learn that Hamre was an "accidental tourist" who ended up at the top tier of the Pentagon—much to his own surprise and his mother's consternation. The chapter portrays the public part of the selling of the Pentagon budget. The private part comes later.

This first chapter also describes how an ongoing government study can wet the powder of the would-be political combatants. In 1997, when the book opens, all sides feel obliged to hold their fire until the results of a giant study—called the Quadrennial Defense Review or QDR—are in hand.

Clinton's political shrewdness is revealed. Because the president named a Republican, former senator William S. Cohen of Maine, as his secretary of defense, GOP warriors in Congress have to shoot through Cohen to hit Clinton and his defense budget—something they are loath to do out of party loyalty and personal friendship.

Cohen's own political shrewdness is also underscored as he invites congressional critics to add money to the defense budget. This puts them on the spot. Cohen knows the critics are reluctant to increase the defense budget for fear they will be blamed for breaking Congress's promise to put top priority on balancing the federal budget.

Clinton as the chapter opens has set forth the nation's basic military strategy in his budget message, declaring that the Army, Navy, Air Force, and Marine Corps must be "capable of prevailing in two nearly simultaneous regional conflicts."

CHAPTER 2, "The Cautious Blueprint," profiles the evolution, implementation, and reception of the QDR blueprint in 1997. The QDR report was supposed to set forth the Clinton administration's military plans for the twenty-first century.

Members of Congress in 1996 had sensed that the strategy and forces designed for the cold war were not suitable for the different challenges of the new century. Outlaw nations no longer had the restraining hands of either the United States or the Soviet Union on their shoulders. During the cold war, the North Atlantic Treaty Organization (NATO), dominated by the United States, restrained one group of nations from provocative military action; the Warsaw Pact, dominated by the Soviet Union, kept another bloc of countries under control. But the collapse of the Soviet Union and the end of the cold war in 1989 took small and reckless nations off the leashes of the superpowers. This meant that the Pentagon, in drawing its blueprint for the twenty-first century, had to reckon with the possibility of rogue behavior—perhaps with nuclear and biological weapons—by potential enemies such as Iran, Iraq, Libya, and North Korea. At the same time, the generals and admirals were reluctant to give up their cold war weapons for fear Russia with its heavy forces might rise again.

The chapter outlines the QDR blueprint and describes the congressional reaction to it.

CHAPTER 3, "Looking Through the Military's End of the Telescope," goes inside the minds of modern-day military leaders. You see how they view the big questions of national defense, how their combat experience makes them passionate about their beliefs, and how and why they often become disgusted with their civilian bosses as they settle for the possible, not what the military proposed.

Although the Founders in writing the Constitution empowered civilians "to pay the debts and "provide for the common defense," U.S. presidents and secretaries of defense have learned that they need the support of the uniformed military to get their military policies approved by Congress. Clinton calculates in 1997 that he can persuade the Joint Chiefs of Staff—made up of a four-star general as chairman and the uniformed commanders of the military services—to go along with a no-growth defense budget in the interest of balancing the federal budget. The chapter shows that Clinton is right—but not for long.

With only so many defense dollars to go around, military chiefs constantly seek a bigger slice of the money pie. Leaders of the Army, for example, sincerely believe the country would be safer if they received some of the dollars going to the Air Force and Navy. The chapter provides an inside look at this military parochialism.

To identify the wellspring, I give military leaders space to recount war experiences that fired up their commitment and passion to get as many dollars for their troops as possible in the fight for defense dollars.

The credibility gap between military people who fought the nation's wars and civilians who stayed home is exposed in the generals' own words. During the 105th Congress, no civilian at the top of the national security pyramid had ever been in the active duty military, let alone experienced combat: not Clinton, not Cohen, not Hamre, not Secretary of State Madeleine K. Albright, not White House national security adviser Samuel Berger.

Yet the secretary of defense, to achieve the civilian control of the military mandated by the Constitution, must not be intimidated or captured by ribbon-bedecked generals and admirals. The secretary's job is to formulate the president's national defense program and then make sure it is carried out. The secretary, in the corporate sense, is the executive vice president of a division of the federal government reporting to the president. Similarly, the civilian secretaries of the Army, Navy, and Air Force are supposed to impose the will of the president and secretary of defense on their services. Civilian versus military collisions on military issues are unavoidable in the American form of government as each camp argues that its approach would provide the nation with the best defense.

One of Cohen's biggest challenges as the book opens in 1997 is to craft a QDR report that both the Joint Chiefs of Staff and Congress will support. He relies heavily on Army Gen. John M. Shalikashvili, the Joint Chiefs chairman and a master in the art of the possible, to win over the Chiefs for him. Cohen assigns himself to win over Congress.

CHAPTER 4, "Guns versus Butter," examines the classic dilemma of a democracy as it tries to budget enough money to keep the nation strong militarily without weakening it economically, socially, and culturally.

In 1997, the first year of the 105th Congress, the big guns-versus-butter fight was between defense and highways. A fragile budget-balancing agreement had been negotiated between the executive and legislative branches of the federal government before this debate over priorities began. Republicans and Democrats alike warn in this chapter that suddenly taking money away from guns for highways would weaken the national defense and bust through agreed-upon money ceilings.

The fight typifies the guns-versus-butter battles to be fought in future Congresses, especially those during times when the national economy is depressed. Lawmakers in such an economic environment most likely would choose butter over guns in apportioning tax dollars.

CHAPTER 5, "Spurning the Holy Grail," describes how leaders of the hawkish House National Security Committee begin building a case for scrapping or end-running the 1997 budget agreement. The chapter explains the inside politics of this fight for more defense dollars. Republican leaders in the Senate and House do not want to take the blame for breaking the budget agreement. They try to get Clinton to do it. The politically shrewd Clinton refuses. Republican leaders decide to use the Joint Chiefs of Staff as their lever for raising the defense budget. They plan to put the Chiefs on national television to lament the lack of money in Clinton's defense budget.

CHAPTER 6, "Heating Up the Iron," shows how one political party can use military leaders to embarrass the other and advance its agenda at the same time. Republicans in a 1998 Senate hearing succeed in pressuring the Joint Chiefs of Staff to distance themselves from the very same Clinton defense budget they had endorsed at the beginning of the year. The testimony presents Clinton with the choice of opposing the Chiefs' call for more money, thereby putting the Republicans and military leaders on one side and Democrats on another, or welcoming last-minute additions to his defense budget. A booming economy, including surplus money to help balance the federal budget, and the chance to help Democrats in the 1998 congressional elections make going along with the Chiefs the easy choice for Clinton. His acceptance makes it difficult for the Republicans to charge Clinton and his party with being weak on defense. The Senate hearing marks a turning point in the inside fight for defense dollars.

CHAPTER 7, "Realpolitik Behind the Scenes," shows how a successful politician is like a successful running back: when either sees daylight, he runs for it. Rep. Jack R. Murtha, a wily Pennsylvania Democrat on the House Appropriations Committees, sees daylight in the catch-all money bill Congress is frantically cobbling together in the closing days of the 105th Congress. He runs for that daylight, providing a case history of how the art of the possible plays out behind the scenes. The chapter shows how a member of Congress who has allies in the Pentagon can push and pull the White House in his desired direction.

CHAPTER 8, "Is There a Better Way?" gives the Republican chairman and ranking Democrat on the House Appropriations Committee an opportunity to critique the process of providing money for defense. Both men contend that the House and Senate Budget committees, which set money ceilings for the Pentagon and other government departments, have outlived their usefulness. Wisconsin Democrat David R. Obey, a respected liberal and perhaps the angriest man in the House on defense issues, issues a searing indictment of the military-industrial-political complex. He not only faults the current system but holds forth on how it could be improved. He argues that the system is broken and that Congress ought to fix it, but doubts it will because of the cozy relationship between lawmakers and defense contractors. Obey's friend Robert Livingston, the committee chairman, partly disagrees with the Democrat's analysis.

CHAPTER 9, "The Turnaround," tells how the secretary of defense and the chairman of the Joint Chiefs of Staff combined efforts to change the mind of the president on how much is enough for national defense in 1998. In exclusive interviews, Secretary Cohen and Chairman Hugh H. Shelton disclose how they persuaded the president to abandon his 1997 plan to provide no more than $250 billion a year, plus an amount to offset inflation. Behind the scenes maneuvering by Cohen, including a stream of written entreaties to Clinton as well as face-to-face lobbying, is detailed in a rare account of how the art of the possible is practiced at the top of the U.S. government.

CHAPTER 10, "Shooting the Messenger: A Case History," reconstructs what turned out to be one of Clinton's most grievous, self-inflicted wounds on the defense battlefield. In the interest of winning California and Texas in his 1996 re-election bid, Clinton in 1995 promised to save civilian jobs at Air Force bases in those states even if the bases were recommended for closure by a non-partisan commission. His idea was to entice private defense contractors to take over the work formerly done at the two bases by the Air Force. The contractor, under Clinton's scheme, would hire the men and women who had worked for the Air Force, thereby keeping the jobs that would have been lost if the bases were simply closed down. Clinton called it "privatization in place."

Clinton's plan touched off howls of protests. Members of Congress charged he was politicizing the supposedly non-political process of deciding which surplus military bases should be put out of business to save billions of dollars. The lawmakers passed laws restricting Clinton's freedom of action on privatization.

After Clinton was re-elected in 1996, the political furor over privatization died down, only to erupt again in 1998 when a confidential Pentagon memo about White House efforts to privatize a California military base leaked to Congress and the press. Disclosures in the memo doomed Clinton's chances of persuading Congress to approve additional base closings during his term of office. White House officials whose remarks caused the political uproar blamed the writer of the memo, the acting secretary of the Air Force. The acting secretary had been pressed hard by administration appointees to help make good on Clinton's promises to California and

Texas. The chapter gives the reader a close-up look at the internecine fight for defense dollars.

What happens to the acting secretary, who was only passing along what a White House official said to him, is a classic case of government leaders shooting the messenger instead of accepting the bad news. This case is different from most of its kind, however, because it has a happy ending.

IN CHAPTER 11, "Peering into the Future," the reader sees what's ahead through the eyes of Secretary Cohen, General Shelton, and others who spent years puzzling over the who, when, where, and how of military threats the United States was likely to face in the early decades of the twenty-first century. In exclusive interviews, Pentagon leaders disclose their innermost worries—worries that will fuel the fight over defense dollars well into the future.

IN CHAPTER 12, "Summing Up," I put down my guide umbrella and set forth my own views about the process of deciding how to spend $500,000 a minute to protect the United States. I offer my ideas for improving the process.

George C. Wilson

1

Firing the Opening Shot

"GOT THE CHARTS?" Defense Department Comptroller John Julian Hamre asked his military aide, Army Col. Derald Emory, as they stood in Hamre's outer office on the third floor of the Pentagon.

"You've got plenty of charts," Emory replied.

With that assurance, Hamre (pronounced HAM-ree) threaded through the cluster of petitioners who are almost always in the outer offices of the Pentagon's powerful. Their offices are along the outermost corridor, the E-ring.

The E-ring is part of the 17.5 miles of hallway connecting the concentric rings of the grim, five-story, bureaucratic fortress that wags call Fort Fumble. The five-sided building sits on 280 acres of flood plain on the Virginia side of the Potomac River—one reason the basement leaks. Messengers use bicycles to get from one place to the other within the tan edifice whose joyless exterior is relieved by the jungle gyms in the day care center in the Pentagon's distant front yard.

Hamre this fifth day of February 1997 was headed, with me in tow, for the Bear Pit one floor below. The Bear Pit was what former defense secretary Caspar W. Weinberger had called the small auditorium where defense officials fielded often-hostile questions from reporters.

Just outside Hamre's office we passed a glass-encased display containing an invoice from an early defense contractor, Paul Revere. The patriotic silversmith had requested eleven pounds, one shilling for expenses he incurred in riding through the night in April 1775 shouting, "The British are coming!" Hamre's predecessor as chief bean counter for the spartan military-industrial complex of that day paid Revere only ten pounds, four shillings—one of the few cost underruns in the history of American defense contracting.

As Hamre walked along the E-ring, tourists being guided through the Pentagon by a shouting sergeant took little notice of the fifty-two-year-old, six-feet-four-inch, 230-pound man in the dark suit hurrying past them. If they had stopped to engage him in conversation, they would have been warmed by interested eyes looking at them through thick glasses. Hamre probably would have treated them to a bit of his sharp-pointed wit before hurrying on toward the Bear Pit. I had been treated to that Hamre wit just before we left his inner office on this February day. Identifying a glum portrait as James Warren, Hamre said: "He was the second officer commissioned in the Continental Army. George Washington was the first one. Warren was the Army's first paymaster. He threatened to quit that job unless the generals stopped wrangling. Here we are two hundred years later, and the only thing that has changed is that we have thirty-seven more states."

Hamre's tongue could also fire armor-piercing words, like the time he demolished an Army request for more light divisions by terming them "pre-positioned prisoners of war."

There was nothing in Hamre's appearance, except for the dark suit, to suggest to the tourists that the man passing by was the world's most powerful bean counter with the three official titles of Department of Defense comptroller, under secretary of defense, and chief financial officer. No green eye shade. No holster full of pens. No scowling face. He could have been taken for a college professor, something Hamre had wanted to be, who had donned a dark suit to fit in with the environment. Or perhaps his open face would have suggested a clergyman, something his mother had wanted her son John to be—just like his maternal grandfather.

John Hamre this winter afternoon was neither tree-loving academic nor stiff-collared cleric. Instead he was the designated point man for the largest and most dangerous enterprise in the world, the United States Department of Defense. Largest not only because it employed more than 2.3 million people but also because it spent so much money—about $500,000 a minute, day and night. The thousands of weapons the Department of Defense had at its disposal, especially the nuclear ones, could incinerate almost every living thing on the planet and poison the air, water, and land for generations.

Point man Hamre's mission this day was to persuade the stockholders of the Department of Defense, the American people, that they should let their giant corporation spend more than a trillion of their tax dollars in the six-year period running from October 1, 1997, through September 30, 2003—fiscal years 1998 through 2003. After subtracting what inflation would eat up, this total would come to about $250 billion a year, or $475,647 a minute for every minute of every year for the foreseeable future.

Hamre knew that some stockholders through their hired hands in Congress, senators and representatives, would say that was too much. After all, the cold war ended with the fall of the Berlin Wall in 1989 and no enemy was in sight to take the Soviet Union's place. Hamre also knew that others would say $250 billion a year was not enough, given the madmen threatening the United States, such as those running Iraq and North Korea.

How MUCH military spending was enough to protect the American people and their interests abroad was part of a larger political war Hamre and other government and military leaders would have to fight during the 105th Congress and beyond. How should defense dollars, regardless of how many, be spent? The United States, no matter how rich; the American military, no matter how powerful; could not fix everything in the world that needed fixing. Choices had to be made.

Should American soldiers, sailors, airmen, and marines be deployed to distant hot spots such as Kosovo in the Balkans to right wrongs even if no U.S. economic nor political interests were at stake? Madeleine K. Albright, secretary of state and former UN ambassador, was hawkish on the question of deploying American soldiers abroad. Members of the Joint Chiefs of Staff, the highest military body in the land, were dovish. Their attitude had been that way since the days of Gen. Colin L. Powell, who served as chairman of the Joint Chiefs from 1989 to 1993. "My constant, unwelcome message at all the meetings on Bosnia was simply that we should not commit military forces until we had a clear political objective," Powell wrote in his autobiography, *My American Journey.* "[Defense Secretary Les] Aspin shared this view. The debate exploded at one session when Madeleine Albright, our ambassador to the UN (United Nations), asked me in frustration: 'What's the point of having this superb military that you're always talking about if we can't use it?' I thought I would have an aneurysm. American GIs were not toy soldiers to be moved around on some sort of global chess board." Army Gen. John M. Shalikashvili, Powell's successor as Joint Chiefs chairman, espoused Powell's view but expressed himself more diplomatically in high councils.

Another question facing Hamre and other crafters and overseers of the new defense budget was what weapons to buy for the post–cold war world. The Soviet Union was no more. But it had sold much of its heavy weaponry, such as tanks and sophisticated aircraft, to potential U.S. enemies, notably Iraq, Iran, and North Korea. The U.S. Army, Navy, and Air Force—arguing that they might still have to fight against Soviet weapons—resisted giving up their own cold war weapons. At the same time they kept pressuring their civilian leaders to buy new generations of weapons even though no superpower threatened the United States. The Defense Department could not afford both to keep the old and build the new. Something had to give if the defense budget were to remain in bounds to help balance the total federal budget. But Hamre knew that most members of Congress would side with the generals and admirals when it came to weaponry. The Republican Party enjoyed majorities in both the House and Senate in the 105th Congress. Its members could raise Clinton's defense budget to try to make the president look weak on defense before the 1998 congressional elections. The Clinton countercharge would be that the Republicans unbalanced the budget, something they did not want to be accused of doing.

Nobody in the United States knew the who, what, when, where, or why of the next war. The people entrusted to divine the next war and prepare for it had no divining rods. All the president, secretary of defense, secretary of state, generals, admirals, and members of Congress could do was make guesses about what kind of military forces to field and how to arm them. Then they had to get their best guesses financed by Congress. The process of obtaining the money was political. It required everyone involved to engage in the art of the possible, not the ideal.

The perception that the Pentagon was not looking over the horizon and preparing the nation for the likeliest wars bothered members of Congress. So much so that in 1996 Congress passed legislation requiring the Pentagon to reassess what it was doing. Specifically, the National Defense Authorization Act enacted on September 23, 1996, said:

> In order to ensure that the force structure of the armed forces is adequate to meet the challenges to the national security interests of the United States in the 21st century . . . and to assess the appropriate force structure of the armed forces through the year 2010 and beyond (if practicable), it is important to provide for the conduct of an independent, nonpartisan review of the force structure that is more comprehensive than prior assessments of the force structure, extends beyond the quadrennial defense review and explores innovative and forward-thinking ways of meeting such challenges. . . .

Toward this end, the law continued,

> . . . the Secretary of Defense, in consultation with the chairman of the Joint Chiefs of Staff, shall complete in 1997 a review of the defense program of the United States. . . . The review shall include a comprehensive examination of the defense strategy, force structure, force modernization plans, infrastructure, budget plan and other elements of the defense program and policies with a view toward determining and expressing the defense strategy of the United States and establishing a revised defense program through the year 2005.

The law further stated that an outside body of defense experts was to review and make recommendations regarding the report to come out of the Quadrennial Defense Review conducted by the secretary of defense and chairman of the Joint Chiefs of Staff. This outside group was to be called the National Defense Panel.

Waiting for the Defense Review

The congressionally mandated Quadrennial Defense Review, or QDR, was just getting under way as Hamre headed for the Bear Pit to try to persuade the country and Congress through the press that the Pentagon's latest six-year budget plan would indeed prepare the nation for the next war, not the previous one. Former secretary of defense William J. Perry had designed the six-year budget Hamre was about to unveil. Perry's replacement, former Republican senator William S. Cohen of Maine, had been in the Pentagon's top job only a month. So he could do little more than read the Perry budget he inherited and bless it. Cohen decided to wait until the QDR report was in hand in the spring of 1997 before making any major changes in the Perry blueprint.

As Hamre and I walked along toward the Bear Pit, I chided him about a rumor flying around the Pentagon: "I hear Cohen might choose you as his deputy secretary of defense."

"You heard that, huh?" Hamre responded dismissively. "That's embarrassing. The secretary regards me as a staffer." Hamre had been a staffer for the Senate Armed Services Committee while Cohen served on the committee. The rumor would turn out to be true, much to the delight of Hamre's parents out in Clark, South Dakota. Their boy really seemed to be getting someplace in Washington, even though that was not what his mother, Ruth Larson Hamre, daughter of a Lutheran minister, had in mind for her bright son. John's father, Melvin Sanders Hamre, a rural banker, was unreservedly pleased with his son's progress, knowing John was doing something he liked.

John Hamre had grown up happily on the prairie heartland. He earned honor grades at Clark High School, played in the band, found himself too awkward for sports but not for school plays, never smoked nor drank, and, by his own definition, was "a typical 1960s nerd." After high school, he went to Augustana College in Sioux Falls and then to Harvard Divinity School in 1973, pleasing his mother but not himself. He stayed only one year. "I decided the church did not need another insecure pastor."

Hoping to teach at some leafy campus, Hamre credentialed himself for that life by earning his doctorate at Johns Hopkins University School of

Advanced International Studies (SAIS) in Washington, D.C. But upon his graduation in 1978 no college nor university sought the new doctor. Nor did the State Department. The idealistic young Hamre did not want to fulfill the destiny that had been scratched onto a bathroom wall at Hopkins: "SAIS is the West Point of the multi-national corporation." Why make Mobil Oil even richer? he asked himself.

Having been rebuffed by academe, Hamre applied for and received a job at the Congressional Budget Office (CBO), a think tank for Congress. To his amazement, he discovered he loved the work of analyzing national defense issues. Georgia Democrat Sam Nunn, chairman of the Senate Armed Services Committee, came to admire Hamre's reports and hired him away from CBO in 1984. The two clicked. Nunn recommended Hamre to his counterpart, Wisconsin Democrat Les Aspin, chairman of the House Armed Services Committee, in 1993 when Aspin was about to become President Bill Clinton's first secretary of defense. Aspin, who knew Hamre from working with him in Congress, was happy to name Hamre as his chief bean counter.

Although Aspin had been an inspiring economics teacher at Marquette University and put forward more bold ideas on national defense than any other lawmaker while in the House of Representatives, at the Pentagon he could not seem to make the trains run on time. At least that was the complaint of the generals. He also took the blame publicly for failing to send armor to Mogadishu, Somalia, in 1993 as the U.S. command there had requested before eighteen American troopers were killed in street fighting. For these and other reasons, Clinton fired Aspin in 1994 and appointed Aspin's better organized deputy, William Perry, as the nineteenth secretary of defense. Perry kept Hamre on as comptroller. So did Cohen when he succeeded Perry on January 24, 1997.

Beginning the Sell

When Hamre and I reached an office on the second floor of the Pentagon a few hundred feet short of the Bear Pit, Hamre turned off the E-ring corridor. Inside the office was Kenneth H. Bacon, a former *Wall Street*

Journal reporter who was now assistant secretary of defense for public affairs. Bacon's mission was to control, or at least try to shape, whatever Hamre and other defense officials said in public so their words would reflect favorably on the Clinton administration. The bow-tied Bacon had joined Washington's army of spinners. Hamre went alone into Bacon's office to go over what he would say to reporters waiting in the Bear Pit. Hamre was to speak "on background," meaning that reporters could quote what he said but not tell readers who said it. "Why play this shell game on the public that is paying the Pentagon's bills?" I asked Bacon later.

"We give reporters a background briefing to help walk them through the budget," Bacon replied. "What's important? What are our themes? What are we stressing this year? How does it differ from last year? What are the problems we anticipate? Successes we hope for? We've always done that on background because people cannot run the stories anyway [before the specified release time], and we basically wanted to leave the quotes to the secretary. We don't want to undercut the secretary" by having the quotes of a deputy steal his thunder.

"We see this as really helping the press master the budget," Bacon said. "So when the secretary makes his pitch, the reporters ask better informed questions. They don't have to ask questions like, 'Mr. Secretary, can you tell me again what the Army budget is?' They've got all that on background. The quotes are, as they should be, the top political appointee of the department explaining what our agenda is. This is standard government public relations—to focus light on your boss."

I asked Bacon whether the White House spin masters dictated how President Clinton's defense budget should be presented to keep it "on message" or left him alone as he crafted the briefings. "They generally leave us alone," he replied. "They regard us with a combination of envy and fear. With envy because we have so much more money to spend than other agencies do. With fear because they know that in the current fiscal climate —whereas almost all the other agencies are being cut by Congress—we in the last few years have gotten increases in the midst of this austerity drive to balance the budget. There is always the fear that we can manipulate the process so if we don't win in the White House Office of Management and

Budget [OMB], we can win on the Hill" [Capitol Hill, where Congress rules].

Bacon's game plan called for Cohen to brief reporters the next day on the record so television stations could send his face and words around the world. He hoped that by then Hamre and other defense officials would have answered the nitty-gritty questions of the trade press reporters and other specialists, saving Cohen the possible embarrassment of not knowing an answer.

"Standing room only, sir," an exultant Army Col. Richard Bridges, a Bacon deputy, told Hamre about the Bear Pit he was about to enter. Looking on during this exchange outside Bacon's office was a dark-haired young woman at the gatekeeper desk. Her name was Monica S. Lewinsky. Nobody knew at this moment that this former White House intern, who had been exiled to the Pentagon, would become one of the most famous, or infamous, women in the world in a few months.

Hamre entered the Bear Pit with characteristic zeal. He thought reporters asked better questions than senators and representatives and enjoyed the verbal fencing. Standing at the podium he looked over the crowd of reporters sitting row upon row in metal, card-table chairs and broke the ice with this opener: "I apologize to all of you. I'm coming down with this flu bug that's going around. So if I have to dash off the stage, it means phase two has cut in."

Hamre went on to confess that procurement—the hardware account that pays for new tanks, planes, aircraft carriers, and missiles—had not risen as high as he had projected in his budget briefing a year earlier.

"Scout's honor," said the one-time Eagle Scout from America's heartland. "I was not lying to you. But my guess is that my credibility with you is lower than a snake's belly in a wagon rut."

Hamre explained that the armed services, much to his surprise and dismay as the Pentagon's chief financial officer, had raided their own procurement accounts at the last minute to pay for running the industrial underpinning of the military—shipyards, aircraft repair depots, and similar facilities. The military's operations and maintenance accounts also held the money for operating trucks, ships, and planes.

"Are we going to have slippage like this again every year?" Hamre asked rhetorically in lamenting that he and others had been unable to ramp up hardware dollars from the $42.6 billion in the fiscal 1998 budget to the $60.0 billion a year the military's Joint Chiefs of Staff said they needed by 2001 to maintain the technical edge over all potential U.S. enemies. "We've got to do something about getting costs out of the infrastructure," Hamre said. By infrastructure, he meant the network of military bases and repair depots spread around the country. President Clinton wanted to close or shrink many of the bases to save money, but Congress was balking on grounds that he had politicized the process in 1995 to get himself reelected in 1996. *(See Chapter 10.)*

"Secretary Perry gave [us] precise instructions" about how this fiscal 1998 budget (for the year October 1, 1997, through September 30, 1998) should be built, Hamre told the reporters. " 'Your first priority is readiness, your second priority will be quality of life, third priority is, well, complete the downsizing without breaking anything, and then, finally, if you've got any money left over, put as much as you can into modernization.' "

Readiness is Pentagonese for giving the soldier the training and weapons he needs to fight and win tomorrow morning. "We're absolutely confident we'll be able to sustain our readiness rates through this budget," Hamre said in a prediction that would prove dead wrong. *Quality of life* is how well the soldier and his family live: their house, available doctors, hospitals, day care centers, schools. *Downsizing* is the process of shrinking the armed forces by not replacing those who leave and forcing others off the payroll. The active duty force shrank from 2.2 million to 1.5 million between 1989 and 1997, or a cut of 32 percent. *Modernization* is the umbrella term for buying new guns, tanks, missiles, ships, and aircraft.

Cohen's Objectives

Cohen took the same podium the day after Hamre's "on background" briefing. As TV lights glared and cameras whirred, Cohen told the reporters that "top priority number one for me" in making choices as secretary of defense will be to "continue to attract and retain high quality personnel" needed to run the high-tech U.S. military force. Since President Richard Nixon and Congress allowed draft calls to stop in 1973, the armed forces have been required to fill their billets with volunteers. Enticing young men and women to sign up for military service when they had other options loomed as one of Cohen's biggest challenges as the new defense secretary.

Even before Cohen had gone on television to unveil President Clinton's new defense budget, a number of Republicans had assailed it as too timid. Some called it a "tread-water" defense plan because it failed to restructure the military to meet the different threats of the post–cold war world. Were these Republican critics right? one reporter asked Republican Cohen during his February 6, 1997, televised presentation of the new budget.

"Is it enough?" Cohen replied. "We'll have to wait and see in terms of whether or not there will be additions on the part of the Hill. As far as our mission is concerned today, we can satisfy that. We can carry out the mission that is required as of today. Will that mission change? Will we have a different strategy? Will we have a different force structure? The entire purpose of the QDR is to examine whether or not for future years we have to change in any substantial way the way in which we're doing business to protect the country's interests."

Cohen noted that Congress was split between those who wanted to increase defense spending and those who wanted to reduce it to help balance the federal budget. As a Republican championing the defense budget of a Democratic president, Cohen said he saw his mission as building in Congress and the country "a bipartisan consensus for a [defense] budget that we can sustain over a long period of time."

"As we look into the future," Cohen continued, "the battlefield is obviously going to become much more complicated. It's going to require the best systems we can possibly take advantage of as far as technology is concerned. So we can't afford to defer any longer the ramp-up as far as modernization is concerned." Reaching the $60-billion-a-year figure by fiscal 2001, as the Joint Chiefs of Staff requested, "is going to be a very hard climb," Cohen said. "In order to get there, we've got to make changes elsewhere," including running the Pentagon more like a private business and closing down excess military bases.

Asked how much should be spent on a missile-catching umbrella for the fifty states, Cohen replied, "I favor defense against a limited missile strike. I've been in the forefront for a national missile defense capability against accidental launches, or a limited type of strike, in order to protect the people of this country." Cohen defended the president's modest missile defense increases in the fiscal 1998 budget as well as his "three-plus-three" policy of trying to perfect antimissile systems in the three-year period ending in 2000 and then taking the next three years to deploy them if the threat justified that expensive step. A homeland missile defense could cost as much as $90 billion, according to the Congressional Budget Office where Hamre used to work.

President Clinton's fiscal 1998 defense budget presented by Hamre and Cohen continued to finance weapons designed for the cold war. It was not much smaller than President Jimmy Carter's cold war budget for fiscal 1979—$250.7 billion compared with $271.6 billion in dollars adjusted for inflation to make them comparable. However, the Clinton request for $250.7 billion was way under the dollar peak of President Ronald Reagan's buildup, $414.5 billion for fiscal 1985 in dollars comparative to 1998.

Pentagon reporter Thomas E. Ricks in his story on the new defense budget told his *Wall Street Journal* readers:

> Above all, the Clinton administration's proposed fiscal 1998 defense budget of $250.7 billion seems designed to avoid domestic political controversy. It emphasizes military readiness, sidesteps difficult questions and seeks to minimize disagreements with Congress—most notably by increased spending on ballistic missile defenses. The budget may be even more significant for what it doesn't do. Nowhere in the thousands of pages of budget material released by the Office of the Secretary of Defense and the services is there a hint of how the Pentagon plans to solve a future budget crunch. Current plans call for the military to retain its size, with a slight budget decline in real terms over the next five years, while somehow boosting weapons spending nearly 50 percent. That squeeze is the central issue facing the pending Quadrennial Defense Review. . . .

A week after his gentle questioning by reporters in the Bear Pit, Cohen found himself in an even friendlier environment: the hearing room of his old outfit, the Senate Armed Services Committee. His former colleagues heaped praise upon him even though many thought the defense budget he was championing was too small. Yet, this once powerful Senate committee and its House counterpart, the National Security Committee [formerly House Armed Services], were virtually powerless to raise the top line of the defense budget. Congress in 1974 had ceded that power to House and Senate Budget committees. They set the money ceilings for the Pentagon and other government departments. The Senate Armed Services Committee, House National Security Committee, and Senate and House Appropriations committees were limited to redistributing money under the ceilings, or caps, set by the Budget committees.

Using this redistribution power, however, lawmakers were still able to switch money around to provide jobs in their states by directing money to questionable defense projects—a practice called *pork-barrel* spending. The top congressional Republicans, Senate Majority Leader Trent Lott of Mississippi and House Speaker Newt Gingrich of Georgia, were among the many politicians in the 105th Congress who considered it their right to add pork to the defense budget. Lott reportedly threatened to keep the Navy budget from going through the Senate if the Navy did not throw work to the Ingalls shipyard in his home state, while Gingrich changed the defense budget to compel the Air Force to buy more C-130J transport planes than it wanted from Lockheed Martin Corp. in Georgia. Arizona Republican John McCain, a member of the Senate Armed Services Committee, exposed the pork-barrel politics at every opportunity. But his disclosures failed to stop lawmakers from treating the defense budget like a jobs bill for their home areas whenever they could by practicing the art of the possible.

Cohen was about to enter this melee as he sat down to testify in a cavernous hearing room of the Hart Senate Office Building. "As I begin my tenure," Cohen told his former colleagues, "a key goal of mine is to forge a good working relationship with this committee and with the Congress as a whole." This was music to the ears of the older members who had found themselves at swordspoint with previous defense secretaries, most notably Robert S. McNamara, whose tenure spanned most of the Vietnam War. "While I was not involved in preparing President Clinton's fiscal year 1998 defense budget request," Cohen continued,

I do recommend that the Congress fully support it as it will sustain America's military might and our active engagement around the world. Having said this, however, let me also note that over the next few months I will be reviewing major Department of Defense plans and programs in connection with the Quadrennial Defense Review. Our central goal in the QDR will be to ensure a proper match of strategy, programs and resources. I expect important results from the QDR, but it is still too early to predict those results. . . . This year promises to be a pivotal year in the continuing task of adapting America's defense posture to the uncertainties of the post–cold war period.

When it came, however, the QDR report proved to be tame.

2

The Cautious Blueprint

THE LONG-AWAITED Quadrennial Defense Review amounted to a self-examination by the Defense Department. Even so, Secretary Cohen and Joint Chiefs Chairman Shalikashvili did not brush off the congressionally mandated reassessment of where the armed services of the nation were going, and why. Their orders for a broad review spawned hundreds of meetings in late 1996 and early 1997 where the participants argued heatedly over how the armed forces should be structured for the twenty-first century.

All through the paper exercises, however, there was the knowledge that nobody at the top wanted radical change, such as eliminating the decorative but unnecessary secretaries of the Army, Navy, and Air Force or triggering screams of protest from Congress by canceling a major weapon. Cohen, Deputy Secretary Hamre, Shalikashvili, and Air Force Gen. Joseph W. Ralston, the Joint Chiefs vice chairman who orchestrated the QDR, were not radical men. Their guidance did not encourage drastic change. They were evolutionaries, not revolutionaries.

Given this philosophy at the top of the Pentagon and President Clinton's detachment from the review, it was not surprising that the QDR report that emerged from all those Pentagon meetings was bland. It basically said that the civilian hierarchy of the Pentagon and the armed forces should stick to their current courses; steady as she goes was the order of the sixty-nine-page QDR report released on May 19, 1997.

Although Cohen had been sworn into office on January 24, 1997, giving him only three months to be involved in the QDR, he endorsed its recommendations and rejected the charge that the armed services were preparing for the previous war, not the most likely next one.

"It is a commonly held, but erroneous, notion that America's military establishment and forces are trapped hopelessly in the past, still structured and struggling to fight yesterday's wars," Cohen said in the report introduction.

As we examine how we intend to prepare America's armed forces for an uncertain future, it is important to look at how we got to where we are, and where we are going.

During most of the Cold War years, the United States pursued a strategy of containing the Soviet Union. In 1985, America appropriated about $400 billion for the Department of Defense (in constant fiscal 1997 dollars), which constituted 28 percent of our national budget and 7 percent of our Gross National Product. We had more than 2.2 million men and women under arms, with about 500,000 overseas, 1.1 million in the Reserve forces and 1.1 million civilians in the Department of Defense. Defense companies employed 3.7 million more and about $120 billion of our budget went to procurement contracts.

Since 1985, America has responded to the vast global changes by reducing its defense budget by some 38 percent, its force structure by 33 percent and its procurement programs by 63 percent. Today, the budget of the Department of Defense is $250 billion, 15 percent of our national budget and an estimated 3.2 percent of our Gross National Product. We now have 1.45 million men and women under arms, 200,000 overseas, 900,000 in the reserves and 800,000 civilians employed by the Department [of Defense]. Today, $44 billion is devoted to the acquisition of weaponry from a smaller defense industrial base employing 2.2 million workers.

In making these reductions, we have carefully protected the readiness of our military to carry out its currently assigned missions. But it has become clear that we are failing to acquire the modern technology and systems that will be essential for our forces to successfully protect our national security interests in the future.

Through base closings and more efficient buying practices, Cohen said, the Pentagon must save billions of dollars to invest in new weaponry while staying under the $250 billion budget ceiling.

The Department's plans are fiscally responsible. They are built on the premise that, barring a major crisis, national defense spending is likely to remain relatively constant in the future. There is a bipartisan consensus in America to balance the federal budget by the year 2002 in order to ensure the nation's economic health, which in turn is central to our fundamental national strength and security. The direct implication of this fiscal reality is that Congress and the American people expect the Department to implement our defense program within a constrained resource environment. The fiscal reality did not drive the defense strategy we adopted, but it did affect our choices for its implementation and focused our attention on the need to reform our organization and methods of conducting business. . . .

Two-War Capability

"We have determined that U.S. forces must be capable of fighting and winning two major theater wars nearly simultaneously," Cohen's introduction said. To do that, the report recommended an active duty force of 1.36 million men and women backed up by 835,000 people in the reserves.

Although Cohen did not go into it, such a force was less than half the size of the one the United States fielded to wage the cold war and also fight the so-called little war in Vietnam. The disparity prompted critics to contend that the Two-MRC (major regional contingencies) strategy— enough force to fight Iraq and China at nearly the same time—could not be fulfilled with the downsized forces the United States had on active duty in 1997.

By the end of the twentieth century, the military had shrunk considerably over three decades. There had been 3.55 million men and women on active duty in 1968, the height of the Vietnam War, compared with 1.50 million in 1997. To field a Vietnam-sized force, the United States almost certainly would have to take the politically unpopular steps of activating the National Guard and other reserve forces and resuming draft calls. Reserve units, with minor exceptions, stayed home during the Vietnam War and became havens for draft resisters. Draft calls were suspended in 1973. Since then the armed services have had to fill their billets entirely with volunteers or go short.

Cohen, after his broad endorsement of the QDR report, ticked off what he considered its major recommendations:

Air Force. Reduce its active duty strength by twenty-seven thousand people but keep fielding twelve active wings and eight reserve ones. The report recommended reducing the Air Force buy of F-22 fighter planes from 438 to 339 aircraft.

Army. Retain its ten active divisions but get fifteen thousand active duty soldiers off their payroll. Reduce the number of people in the National Guard and reserve units by forty-five thousand.

Navy. Retain twelve aircraft carriers plus enough warships to escort them along with twelve Amphibious Ready Groups, which take marines to global hot spots. To save money, the number of cruisers and destroyers would be reduced from 128 to 116 ships and the attack submarine force from 73 to 50. Cohen recommended reducing the buy of Navy F/A-18 E and F fighter bombers from 1,000 to 548 aircraft unless the Joint Strike Fighter were delayed. Then the F/A-18 E and F buy could rise to 785.

Marine Corps. Retain three Marine Expeditionary Forces, accelerate production of the prized V-22 Osprey but reduce the total buy from 425 to 360.

Shalikashvili in a letter to Cohen endorsing the findings in the QDR report said that "the recommended changes will strengthen our armed forces and provide our nation over the long term with the strong defense programs needed to protect America's interests well into the next century." The Joint Chiefs chairman seemed to anticipate that he would be criticized for asking the armed forces to conduct business as usual with fewer people and aging weapons, for he included this caveat in his QDR endorsement:

> However, for the QDR to have the desired effect, we must ensure that the savings it identifies be redirected to preserve our procurement accounts, to fix recently emerging readiness problems and to do all that is necessary to maintain faith with our people, both military and civilian.
>
> The Department faces an unprecedented challenge: transforming our

military capabilities while supporting our role as the world's only remaining superpower. The key will be to manage the rate of change to achieve future capabilities without degrading present readiness. The QDR sets us on the correct path.

The body of the QDR report saw no nation capable of seriously challenging the U.S. military for up to fifteen years, declaring:

> The United States is the world's only superpower today, and it is expected to remain so throughout the 1997–2015 period. . . . The demand for smaller-scale contingency operations is expected to remain high over the next 15 to 20 years. U.S. participation in smaller-scale contingency operations must be selective, depending largely on the interests at stake and the risk of major aggression elsewhere. However, these operations will still likely pose the most frequent challenge for U.S. forces through 2015 and may require significant commitments of forces, both active and reserve.

Congressional Reaction

Cohen presented the QDR report to the Senate Armed Services and House National Security committees in back-to-back hearings on May 20 and May 21, 1997.

After lavishly praising the job their former colleague was doing as secretary of defense, several members of the Senate Armed Services Committee assailed the QDR report as calling for business as usual rather than needed change.

"This report is largely a status quo product that cautiously makes no changes to the organization of the current force and only minor changes to the size of that force," said Sen. Joseph I. Lieberman, Connecticut Democrat, in typifying that criticism.

"Perhaps more important, although new security threats were identified —including threats from terrorists, information warriors, and weapons of mass destruction—there is inadequate clarity about how to meet those needs. The explosion in technology could totally change the way antagonists will fight us. I believe we need to act more boldly and broadly now to stop doing business as usual so we can better respond to these challenges."

The senator expressed hope that the National Defense Panel, an outside group that was to critique the QDR report, would be bold.

Sen. John McCain, the Arizona Republican who sponsored the legislation establishing the QDR and National Defense Panel, told Cohen he was "concerned" that the downsized forces recommended in the QDR report "could not, with the same degree of flexibility and the same small number of casualties, fight another Desert Storm type war."

Members of the House National Security Committee were less gentle than their Senate counterparts when Cohen formally presented the QDR report to them in the Carl Vinson hearing room in the Rayburn House Office Building.

"What we have is a QDR that will be presented as all things to all people," complained Chairman Floyd Spence, South Carolina Republican, in rasping tones. Surgery performed on Spence in 1982 left his voice raspy. Doctors, unable to kill a life-threatening virus in his lungs, removed them and sewed in transplants. The former University of South Carolina track star often greeted people with, "Glad to be here." He meant it. He considered his survival from the double lung transplant a miracle.

The QDR blueprint, Spence continued to scold, "calls for an expansive military strategy, including accelerated modernization, all of which is to be paid for from within declining budgets through some end-strength cuts [in the size of the armed services], a few more closed bases, a revolution in business affairs [by having the Pentagon adopt the cost-saving practices of private industry], and a reduction in the out-year procurement" of some of the big weapons.

"It would seem to me that the QDR's most glaring shortcoming is its demand on the one hand that America accept difficult trade-offs. Yet on the other hand the review fails to provide a clearly defined baseline from which to assess the risks and tradeoffs in an environment of fiscal restraint. What are the risks associated with this specific path you recommended? Without a formal, comprehensive understanding of how the department arrived at the QDR, without access to the reviews [and] analytical underpinnings, Congress will have no ability to ascertain how viable the QDR really is."

The QDR blueprint asks the armed services to do more with less,

Spence told Cohen. It is "under-resourced. Reductions in forces, in budgets, and equipment just since 1991 [when the Persian Gulf War ended] lead me to conclude that we could not even do one Persian Gulf operation again today—certainly not with the same effectiveness we did the last one, and that was just a few short years ago.

"In responding to questions about whether the QDR was budget- or strategy-driven, the official [Pentagon] answer seemed to be that it was strategy-driven but infused with a large dose of budget reality. But if budget reality translates into a real decline in defense spending, then the expansive QDR strategy is either overly ambitious relative to projected budgets or it has been tailored to fit within projected budgets. I suspect time will show it as consistent with projected budgets while in reality underfunded."

Rep. Ronald V. Dellums of California, ranking Democrat on the committee, assailed the QDR report as timid, declaring it was merely "another incremental step away from the cold war force" at a time when there "cannot be a global peer competitor with the United States for a decade, perhaps even further."

Rep. Ike Skelton of Missouri, the committee's second-ranking Democrat, faulted Cohen for expecting the armed services to carry out the same old two-war strategy with far fewer forces.

Declaring that the two wars the Pentagon had in mind would be against Iraq and North Korea, Skelton said: "The interesting thing about that is that we've fought both those wars. We don't have to guess too much about what we need in those two wars. In Desert Storm [the Persian Gulf War of 1990–1991, in which the United States pushed Iraqi forces out of Kuwait], we utilized eight divisions" out of the eighteen the Army had at the time. "We're down to ten. We had twenty-four fighter air wings. We're now down to thirteen. We had 546 naval vessels. We're now down to 346. We used seven divisions in Korea. Eight and seven are fifteen."

As Cohen sat at the long witness table listening to these and other attacks on his blueprint, he had no choice but to stare into the sign fastened to the facing wall of the second bank of desks in the House committee room. The oak-framed metal sign bore this engraved message: "U.S. CONSTITUTION ART. 1 -sec. 8. THE CONGRESS SHALL HAVE POWER . . . TO

Raise and Support Armies . . . Provide and Maintain a Navy . . . Make Rules for the Government and Regulation of the Land and Naval Forces." Former committee chairman L. Mendel Rivers, South Carolina Democrat, had installed the sign to humble Robert S. McNamara, who ran the Pentagon from January 1961 to February 1968—a period that encompassed the Vietnam War. Rivers felt that McNamara was arrogantly ignoring Congress on defense questions of the day. He even demanded that McNamara read the sign aloud before testifying before the committee. McNamara resisted, saying he could read the sign. River insisted. The angered defense secretary read the words out loud.

Cohen's Rebuttal

Rebutting criticism from some committee members, Cohen denied that he had given contradictory instructions to the authors of the QDR report. He said he told them to keep strategy at the forefront but also instructed, " 'Do not come back with a number of recommendations that are clearly unrealistic. We have to present something that is real and tangible to the Congress. Let's operate in a budget-constrained environment, because that's the reality on Capitol Hill. I just left [Capitol Hill]. I know what the sentiment is.'

"And frankly," Cohen said of Spence's complaint about a mismatch between the recommended QDR strategy and the money the Pentagon was requesting to carry it out, "I don't see strong support on a bipartisan basis for increasing defense spending in the absence of a major conflict in the foreseeable future. I think we will be fortunate if we can hold it at roughly $250 billion, where it is today, in constant dollars. And I wanted the military to operate with that assumption in the background. Look at the strategy first, and let's go through the analysis, but also we have to be real ourselves. The last thing I needed to do was to present an analysis, ignore what the budget realities are likely to be, and present a document that says, 'We need roughly $275 billion, $300 billion.' It would be a waste of your time to look at that because the reality is that the Congress is never going to support that, absent a major conflict."

"I don't think the American people will support large amounts more" than $250 billion a year for defense. "If they will, General Shali will take it. They don't see a Soviet Union. They see a Russia that has been seriously crippled by its economic woes. They see a Russia that has been declining in terms of its conventional capability. They don't see a peer competitor as such. And the pressure is always on a democracy to take it out of defense. I am trying to hold the line where we are; to say, 'Yes, we can do this with some minimal increase in risk.' In fact, when I talk to Republican and Democratic leaders, they say, 'We want you to turn the Pentagon into a triangle [a facetious allusion to the building's shape]. We want you to reduce it much further. We want you to go from a major force of the, quote, cold war, down to today's reality.'"

The 1997 agreement between President Bill Clinton and Congress to balance the federal budget by 2002 virtually ruled out big hikes in military spending, Cohen told Spence. "I think I have a pretty good understanding of how Congress operates," said Cohen, who served in both the Senate and the House. "The pressure is going to be on year after year: take it out of defense. And so that is something that all of us have to be concerned about."

Despite spending his adulthood feeling and reading the political pulse, including serving as mayor of his native Bangor, Maine, and spending twenty-four years in Congress, Cohen's reading of the congressional pulse on this twenty-first day of May 1997 would prove to be dead wrong. He misjudged the political impact of budget surpluses and military readiness problems. His former Republican colleagues would soon insist on providing more money to pay for guns and soldiers. Cohen's misreading of the congressional mood was such that he felt compelled to warn against cutting defense further, telling Spence:

> Mr. Chairman, you asked about risks and trade-offs. Here's the trade-off for you: You can cut deeply into the force structure [Army divisions, Navy battle groups, Air Force squadrons, Marine expeditionary forces] by saying the cold war is long past; let's start dealing with the future; let's just cut the size of that force down. And you can do that. But if you do that, then you give up that ability to shape the environment. You can't have those forward deployed forces; you can't have one hundred thousand in

the Asia Pacific region or in Europe. So you have a smaller force which is less extensive in its operations. You then have a certain dynamic that sets in in other countries. They say, "Well, maybe you're not quite as reliable. Maybe we have to do militarizing on our own. Maybe we should start building up our own capabilities. Maybe we should strike a different alternative as far as our alliances[are concerned]. Maybe our chances are better in going with other allies than you." That's a risk. If you think I'm exaggerating, dismiss it.

Cohen said money could be freed up for defense if Congress approved closing more surplus military bases. Since the end of the cold war, he said, the divisions, fleets, and air wings that make up "force structure" have been cut by one-third while bases, repair depots, laboratories, and other Pentagon facilities have been cut only one fifth. "We have got excess capacity. So we can either choose to carry it and not be able to use some of those savings to put into the revolution in military affairs" or eliminate the excess capacity to forestall additional cuts in force structure. "And I can't make that decision. You make that decision. And unless you authorize BRAC [base realignment and closure] proceedings, it doesn't happen."

Shalikashvili told the committee that "the Quadrennial Defense Review, in my judgment, provides a rational, prudent, and well-thought-out approach to keep our armed forces strong and the American interest protected for many years to come. I support its recommendations."

QDR Detractors

In contrast to the remarks of Cohen and Shalikashvili, the QDR report was lambasted by others, including Franklin C. Spinney, the Pentagon's most outspoken heretic; outside groups; and some of the high-ranking officers who were deeply involved with what Congress had hoped would be a no-holds-barred QDR.

Spinney, a tactical aircraft specialist within Cohen's own Program Analysis and Evaluation office at the Pentagon, fearlessly issued a critique of the QDR under his own name. He wrote that the report was "headed for the dustbin of history because it is not connected to the real world."

He said its authors failed to reckon with a number of budget realities, including the fact that "the unit costs of buying and operating the new weapons will continue to increase much faster than the budgets for those weapons, even if budgets exceed Cold War levels early in the next century." The new-high tech weapons, like the Navy F/A-18 E and F fighter bomber and Air Force F-22 fighter, will cost so much that the armed services will have only enough money to buy a few of them, Spinney predicted. Older airplanes will have to be repaired over and over again to fill the vacancies in tomorrow's squadrons, the analyst warned.

"The increasing maintenance burden of old technologies will drive up operating costs at the same time we are trying to increase the modernization budget, balance the federal budget and manage the growing demand for Medicare and Social Security," Spinney wrote. "Something will have to give. And if past is prologue, they will be forced to reduce readiness and trash our combat forces to save the modernization program."

The Center for Strategic and Budgetary Assessments, a nongovernment think tank, estimated that cost, not strategy, dictated the QDR blueprint. "In this area, too," said the center, "the QDR falls short." Even if the economies recommended in QDR were carried out, the center said, the rest of the blueprint calls for military activities that would cost $20 billion more a year than projected Pentagon budgets could cover at the coming turn of the century. "The QDR provides ample evidence that DoD has yet to transcend its Cold War planning framework," the center said.

The National Defense Panel, which had four retired flag officers among its nine members, released a bland, ninety-four-page critique of the QDR report in December 1997. The panel made a few ripples by suggesting in these roundabout words that the Two-MRC strategy was obsolete:

> Defense choices invariably entail risk. The only question is where we take the risk. A significant share of today's Defense Department resources is focused on the unlikely contingency that two major wars will occur at almost the same time. The Panel views this two-military-theater-of-war construct as, in reality, a force-sizing function. We are concerned that, for some, this has become a means of justifying current forces. This approach focuses significant resources on a low probability scenario which consumes funds that could be used to reduce risk to our long-term security. The

Panel believes priority must go to the future. We recognize that in the near term the United States cannot ignore the threats posed by Iran and Iraq in the Persian Gulf and North Korea in Northeast Asia. However, our current forces with the support of allies should be capable of dealing with both contingencies.

The Awkward Middle Ground

Military men and women take an oath to support the Constitution, which calls for civilian control over the military. Most all of them who reach the top of their profession fervently believe in civilian control. They would not have it any other way. They do not want any part of military coups or other undemocratic practices so prevalent in "banana republics." At the same time, military officers are required to speak frankly when a member of Congress asks for their personal opinions. They are obliged to express those opinions even if they are contrary to those held by the president and the civilian secretary of defense.

The obligation of top military officers to give their views on a defense budget or a new airplane often pushes them into a gray area. If one feels he or she cannot support the defense budget that the civilian bosses wrought, the officer is obliged to resign before attacking it. Otherwise, he or she sits beside the secretary of defense at congressional hearings, and, by presence and words shows support for the total budget. However, when asked by a member of Congress about a specific part of the budget, such as whether the commander believes there is enough money in it for the F-22 fighter, the officer may give an opinion that differs from that of the civilian bosses. Although that is not so politically damaging as faulting the whole defense budget of the president, such opinions give critics ammunition for attacking it. The Joint Chiefs are therefore put in a damned-if-they-do and damned-if-they-don't position. They are often caught in the middle. This was the case with the QDR and the Chiefs. They did not dispute its endorsement by Chairman Shalikashvili, but several of the Chiefs and their top deputies had qualms both about the process of the QDR and the end result. They understandably felt that their combat experience outweighed the book smarts of their superiors who had never been in the military, including Clinton, Cohen, and Hamre. Many of the top officers involved with the QDR came away disappointed, frustrated, or angry. They felt passionately about the issues, many of which never got addressed in their view. Yet no military leader considered the QDR bad enough to resign over in 1997. But the vast paper exercise did make many of these officers more determined to fight harder for the needs of their services in 1998.

Looking Through the Military's End of the Telescope

"I HAD HIGH HOPES for the QDR," Air Force Gen. Ronald R. Fogleman told me in reconstructing how the Quadrennial Defense Review fell in his estimation even before release of the report in May 1997. Fogleman's first efforts to make the QDR a significant blueprint for restructuring the United States military for the twenty-first century came in 1996 when he was Air Force chief of staff—the nation's top airman—and William J. Perry was secretary of defense.

"All of us had great confidence in Bill Perry," said Fogleman. "In my view, for the QDR to be a success, there was going to have to be some fairly significant realignment among the services," meaning defense dollars and military missions would have to be apportioned differently among the four military services—the Army, Navy, Air Force, and Marine Corps.

Each member of the Joint Chiefs of Staff felt his service deserved a bigger slice of the Pentagon's money pie. This feeling ran deeper than parochialism. Each Chief believed his service could do much more to meet the radically different challenges of the post–cold war world if only it had more money. Congressional leaders recoiled from the idea of boldly changing the apportionment of defense dollars. When politicians sense the nation confronts a tough problem, such as restructuring the American military for the different threats of the near and not-so-near future, they look for expert advice. They know they do not have the expertise to decide how big the Army should be, for example, or whether the Air Force should be allowed to spend almost $200 million on each F-22 fighter plane. The QDR amounted to Congress's contracting the Pentagon to design military forces for the twenty-first century. Fogleman and other heads of the armed services immersed themselves in the QDR to shape the design.

Although Fogleman realized that the QDR amounted to the Pentagon's investigating itself, he dared hope that the Pentagon would stop apportioning defense dollars among the armed services the same old way: 29 percent of the total for the Air Force, 24 percent for the Army, and 32 percent for the Navy and Marine Corps. [The corps is part of the Navy Department.] The rest went to defense-wide activities, such as missile defense.

"I went to Perry in November [1996], which was kind of the two-year point in my tour [as Air Force chief of staff], to give my midterm report." Fogleman told Perry he was exploring unconventional concepts to see if they had any potential for the Air Force of the future.

"Perry was the kind of guy who would say, 'I understand why you need to do that. You need to understand this.' He would never put any handcuffs on you. He was comfortable to know."

Toward the end of this midterm discussion, Fogleman said, he told Perry, "If you will get engaged in this QDR and come give us your vision in the Tank [the room in the Pentagon where the Joint Chiefs of Staff meet], the services will do what you want us to do because you have that kind of respect. But if you do not do that, I don't have much hope for the QDR." Perry left office shortly after that 1996 conversation and never had a chance to provide the leadership and vision that Fogleman sought.

Shalikashvili: "No Billy Mitchells"

"In September 1996 Shali [Gen. John M. Shalikashvili, chairman of the Joint Chiefs of Staff] saw that if the uniformed services took the initiative they could get out ahead and sort of control what happened to the QDR.

That's why he started the strategy review and all this good stuff and kind of caught the [civilian] Office of the Secretary of Defense crowd by surprise. Ted Warner [assistant secretary of defense for strategy and threat reduction], Bill Lynn [director of program analysis and evaluation], and a bunch of those guys worked like hell to try to catch up. But the uniformed guys had seized the initiative on this thing.

"While all this was going on, it was starting to look to all the Chiefs as if there might be some movement" to break the grip of the cold war on Pentagon thinking and reapportion the money pie in light of the changed responsibilities of the armed services. But Fogleman said his own hopes for this were dashed by an Army major general whom Shalikashvili sent to his office. "He sat there on that couch in my office and said, 'I have a message for you from the chairman [of the Joint Chiefs, Shalikashvili]. The chairman would like to have the QDR turn out to be as close to status quo as we can make this thing work. His message is, 'We don't need any Billy Mitchells.'"

[Army Brig. Gen. Billy Mitchell revolutionized the use of air power during World War I. In 1923 the fiery general demonstrated the lethality of air power and embarrassed the Navy into developing an aircraft carrier by using bombers to sink two obsolete warships off Cape Hatteras. Mitchell subsequently was demoted to colonel, and, in 1925, was court-martialed for insubordination.]

"I told this guy," Fogleman continued, 'Tell the chairman I understand the message.' And from that point on, I went from expecting that something good might come out of the QDR to working to minimize the damage from it.

"To tell you the truth, what I think the chairman [Shalikashvili] was trying to say when he said the objective is to come as close to the status quo as possible was that we can't afford to lose any more forces. We want to preserve what we've got. I don't think he was trying to be obstructionist, but the message was clear that we're not going to do any great dramatic shifts in this thing."

Fogleman said that when Perry left and William S. Cohen took over as defense secretary on January 24, 1997, Cohen felt that he "needed to do something" to put his own mark on the QDR. "But by this time the uniformed guys had the message: status quo. Even so, Cohen and the OSD (Office of the Secretary of Defense) were trying to do something to show, 'By God, I'm in charge and I made some kind of move.' That's when I went from thinking something good might happen because of the QDR to, 'Man, I just don't want something bad to happen.' Because you've got these guys who are a bunch of amateurs trying to move pieces on the chessboard just for the hell of moving pieces so they can claim some great political victory.

"I don't think the QDR did any good. I think it did harm in the end because programs got perturbated [changed around] for no logical military reason," such as reducing the buy of the F-22 from 438 to 339 fighters. "I went in [to Cohen] and said, 'Mr. Secretary, this doesn't save you any money because you're cutting off the end of the production line. And when you cut off the end of the production it also drives the cost up in the front of the production run'" because the savings from volume production and the rise in the learning curve on the factory floor are lost.

"But he wanted to make a political statement that he was doing something," so he went ahead and cut the orders for both the Air Force F-22 and Navy F/A-18 E and F fighter bomber.

Fogleman said Cohen's guidance on the QDR was contradictory. On the one hand, he directed his military leaders to think boldly. On the other hand, he said in effect do not spend more money than we're going to get from the White House and Congress. Fogleman said that Cohen told the Chiefs in one meeting early in 1997 in the Tank that they should let strategy, not dollars, drive their QDR recommendations. But his top deputies, Warner and Lynn, kept insisting all through the QDR that the Chiefs needed to come up with ways to save money. What did the civilians really want from the Chiefs? Fogleman wondered.

"I didn't have the good sense to keep my mouth shut. I said, 'Mr. Secretary, I've been around a long time. You told us this wasn't going to be a budget cut drill. This smells like a cut drill; tastes like a cut drill; looks like a cut drill. If you want to do a cut drill, give us a bogie [a specific amount of money to be cut from the budget] and allow the services to reach it. We know how to do it.'

"He was kind of taken back by my outburst but essentially said, 'OK.

You guys come in next Thursday and give us your proposals.' So we all went off and started moving things in the margin" to save major programs from big cuts. "I moved the Air Force chess pieces in such a way that we were going to do more out-sourcing" and take other steps that Fogleman thought would save as much money as reducing F-22 production.

"We came back in [to the Tank]" and presented the plans of the military Chiefs for making the required savings. "While the dollars were right," Fogleman said, "the political message wasn't there" because neither the Air Force nor the Navy had cut their high profile tactical aircraft programs, the F-22 and F/A-18 E and F. "I had made an offer to slip the JSF (Joint Strike Fighter) program two years to the right" to save money. "That brought Krulak [Marine Corps commandant Charles C. Krulak] out of the chair because he's counting on getting the JSF.

"Cohen went off and huddled with his staff." At first, "much of what we nominated" for cuts "was accepted. But then it went beyond that and perturbated things we had tried to protect. I asked the question" of Cohen's deputies overseeing the QDR, " 'If this is not a cut drill, what are you going to do with the money that you allegedly save? I mean, Congress didn't tell us to cut the budget. Nobody has told us to cut the budget. You're generating a bishop's fund, basically.' [A bishop's fund is money a bishop can distribute as he wishes.]

"Everybody acknowledged that they were going to try to take money out of everywhere and pump it into procurement. But yet they were cutting procurement programs like the F-22 and F/A-18. This is where I had the philosophical problem with what was going on. I wrote Cohen a letter in which I said, basically, 'Mr. Secretary, I cannot concur' " with a series of cuts his office made, notably reducing the buy of F-22s. "Basically I said, 'If you're going to cut the F-22 procurement and we're really looking long range, we are going to have to buy something in addition to that small buy of F-22s to replace F-15E fighters and the F-111 bombers.' "

Cohen's behavior on the QDR "to me was a blatant case of asking for military advice and letting it be overridden by the political consideration of making a statement: 'I cut something,' particularly the tacair [tactical aircraft like the F-22 and F/18 E and F] programs."

Civilian-Military Conflict

Fogleman said he was also bothered during the QDR by civilians with absolutely no military experience rejecting the considered advice of military people who had been in combat and had held command posts where they learned first hand what the armed services did and did not need; what worked and what did not. "Bill Lynn is a neat guy but he ain't never flown the trail," said warrior Fogleman of the Cohen deputy who replaced John Hamre as comptroller during the QDR. Lynn did not serve in the military. "And yet this is the guy up there whispering in the secretary's ear, cut this; cut that. Is military judgment and advice worth anything?"

Fogleman said that under Cohen, in contrast to Perry, he did not feel he could dissent vigorously without being penalized in the minds of his civilian bosses. "Your position was not looked upon as a legitimate disagreement from a professional but as an act of disloyalty. 'Jeez. He's not being a team player.'"

Fogleman turned out to be a team player on the QDR in the sense that he did not oppose it publicly while in office. He believed strongly in civilian rule of the military. He resigned as Air Force chief of staff and became a civilian on September 1, 1997, to protest, among other things, Cohen's second-guessing him on whom, if anybody, should be held responsible for the terrorist bombing of Air Force barracks at Khobar Towers, Saudi Arabia, in June 1996. Fogleman said his reaction to the final QDR report was one of sadness; a sense of missed opportunity; a feeling of dread about the armed services' future suffering because no one had had the fortitude to impose "true strategic change" on the U.S. military at the end of the twentieth century.

With no nation powerful enough to challenge the American military before around 2015, Fogleman said, the mistakes made and opportunities missed during the QDR will not show up dramatically for years. "We truly don't have an enemy. We'll muddle through," but the military "will continue to erode."

Fogleman told me that $250 billion a year plus enough to offset inflation should be plenty, if not too much, to finance the activities of the armed services in the post–cold war world, barring a war. The problem was not the

$250 billion top line of the defense budget, he said, but money-wasting activities under it. Given that view, I asked him how he would change his three brother services to get maximum bang out of the taxpayer's buck in the post–cold war era. This is what he said, service by service:

Army. It has allowed itself to become too heavy to be deployed quickly to post–cold war trouble spots. "The time lines" in the war plans are unrealistic and should be changed. The Army could never get its heavy armor in Texas to Iran, for example, to meet the deadline in the war plans. The Army wastes millions of dollars trying to meet that goal, which never should have been set in the first place. It would be cheaper and more productive to scrap the time lines for the active Army's heavy outfits and rely on air power to stop or blunt the enemy's initial attacks. Air power, the Air Force four-star general contended, might stop the conflict outright. At a minimum, early use of air power would buy the Army the time it needed to get its heavy stuff on scene for a reasonable cost.

Navy. "I think aircraft carriers are tremendously inefficient things when you look at how few are at sea at any one time, but they have tremendous utility. So I wouldn't hit the Navy too hard" except for reducing its total number of deployable carriers from twelve to eight plus one carrier for training. Fogleman would accept the gaps in global coverage that the reduced carrier force would create.

"The only reason the Navy drives its people into the ground is that we allow the CINCs" [commanders in chief of specific areas of the world, such as the Pacific and Middle East regions] to dictate how many carriers shall be in their region for how long. "Hey, if I have an Air Expeditionary Force [an Air Force quick response team of fighters and bombers designed to stop an attack within a few hours of its launching], why the hell do I need to have a carrier at all times" plying the waters off a global hot spot?

"We don't need all those Navy P-3 aircraft out there. Those guys were out there to hunt down Soviet submarines. There aren't any more submarines out there, so they're inventing new missions for the P-3s." The diminished hostile submarine threat also means the Navy does not need to keep buying $2 billion attack submarines to keep its fleet at fifty boats, Fogleman added.

Marine Corps. "The Marine Corps is too big [173,000 men and women on active duty in 1998]. The first thing I would do is take the marines out of Okinawa. If you go look at the marines in Okinawa, they serve no military function. They don't need to be in Okinawa to meet any time line of any war plan. I'd bring them back to California" where the marines have a big base at Camp Pendleton outside of San Diego. "The reason they don't want to bring them back to California is that everyone would look at them and say, 'Why do you need these twenty thousand?'" Bringing the corps down to about one hundred fifty thousand would be "about the right number and wouldn't hurt them a lick."

Combat: The Shaping Experience

I told Fogleman and other military leaders I interviewed over a tape recorder that many of the people, if not most, reading this book will not have been in combat—an experience that shapes the survivor's views on everything, including what kind of troops and weapons the United States should develop and field. There is a gap between those who have been in combat and those who have not. That gap was wide between military leaders and civilians during the 105th Congress. To help the reader understand why operational experience can be such a shaping experience and can open gaps between military and civilian leaders, I asked military leaders immersed in the QDR to describe some of their most memorable combat experiences. Fogleman went back to the Vietnam War for his.

Air: General Fogleman

"On my first tour in Southeast Asia, in 1968–69, I was flying F-100s [Air Force fighter bombers] with the all-volunteer Super FACs (Forward Air Controllers) based in Phu Cat, who flew into North Vietnam and Laos where the antiaircraft threat was so great that a normal slow-moving FAC could not survive." [Forward air controllers spot targets and guide other aircraft into them with radioed directions. Fogleman's fast-flying outfit was called Misty FACs, one in which adventure, daring, caring, and death were hallmarks.]

"In the history of the unit, there were 161 of us. I was the eighty-third guy to sign in. When I signed in, twenty-eight had been shot down." Fogleman himself had been shot down in September 1968, shortly before becoming a Misty FAC. He and the other Mistys knew first hand how important it was for aviators going into battle to feel that every effort would be made to rescue them if they got shot down. The Mistys also had perfected under fire the tactics that maximized the chance of plucking a downed airman out of the jaws of capture or death. "We were real good at rescuing each other," Fogleman recalled.

Fogleman and his fellow Mistys flew in low over Laos and North Vietnam in search of hidden surface-to-air missiles and trucks used to carry war supplies north to south. One tactic was to fly low over streams to see if one was carrying mud stirred up by trucks running across it. If so, the Misty pilots would trace the mud trail back to the crossing point and search in both directions from there to find the trucks' assembly area.

Once the Mistys found the trucks, they would radio fighter bombers to come and bomb them. Misty pilots, who did not carry bombs, would lead the arriving bombers into the target area and fire rockets into the parked trucks to pinpoint their location.

"I saw a lot of aircraft shot down [on these missions]. One of the most gratifying things was to see a chute and know the guy got out. You hear his emergency [locator] beacon. You see his chute in a tree or on the ground. You hear him talking on the survival radio. You know there are bad guys in the area.

"You call in the A-1" fighter bombers to strafe and bomb enemy forces that may be closing in on the downed pilot while U.S. rescue helicopters are flying toward the area. Rescue forces often had to leave a pilot on the ground when darkness closed in.

"You can't imagine the feeling of spending the night" back at the base worrying about the downed pilot. "Your last call to this guy was, 'Buick One. Go off the air. I'll see you in the morning.'"

The next morning "you would go across where this guy was and light your afterburner," throwing down a sonic boom to wake up the pilot if he was sleeping and uncaptured. "You go kaboom, and then you wait," hoping to hear the pilot's voice come through the F-100's cockpit radio.

"You'd wait. And then you'd hear this, 'Misty. Buick One.'

"Sometimes I would have five flights of fighters stacked up there" to destroy antiaircraft guns near the downed pilot. The whole idea was to try to make it safe enough for rescue helicopters to risk flying into the area to snatch the pilot off the ground before enemy troops could reach him. The rescue forces took great losses but always tried to save the downed airman. Knowing that would-be rescuers would go all out for them gave them courage and hope in even the most desperate circumstances, Fogleman said.

"I remember one rescue mission we were flying when we had the guy up on the radio. An A-1 swept in. A bad guy on the ground hosed off a clip of .37 millimeter shells which went over his wing.

"I'm up high, so I called and said, 'Spad [the nickname for the old propeller driven A-1 bomber], you just had a clip of .37 fired at you.'

"'I saw it,' responded the A-1 pilot, "'I want to make one more pass.'

"So this guy turns around and comes back across and that gunner puts five rounds in the cockpit. This guy pressed the mike button and said, 'Spad One is hit. I'm going in.' Then there was a big fireball.

"At that point, I said, 'This is Misty One-One. I'm now the on-scene commander. Pull the rescue forces back. I'm going to put in strikes.' Then you just start killing guns and try not to kill the survivor. When you think you've got it sanitized, you say, 'OK. Spad Two. You're free to come in'" to choreograph the rescue by helicopters.

"This was life or death struggle. It was the trust that you had in one another that made Misty pilots willing to go out on these missions time after time despite the high risks. "You knew if you were down, they would come after you."

Fogleman and his comrades did rescue the downed pilot in the episode he reconstructed, but they often took the risks in vain. One such case was when his flight instructor from pilot training was talking across the Laotian sky to him when the former instructor got hit by antiaircraft fire. "We were talking on the radio and then this guy gets killed."

Ground: General Garner

Lt. Gen. Jay Montgomery Garner was directing the Army part of the QDR, and, like Fogleman, was chafing under its inside politics in 1997 when I first interviewed him. His office was on the third floor of the Pentagon just around the corner from that of Gen. Dennis J. Reimer, Army chief of staff. I relayed to Garner that Hamre had told me that the Army could save lots of money if it kicked uniformed clerks and other non–trigger-pullers off its payroll and let civilians do their work.

"I like John Hamre, but he doesn't know what he's talking about!" Garner snapped in a classic example of different views being formed by different experiences. Garner and Hamre looked at the Army through opposite ends of the telescope as far as Garner was concerned.

"He's never served [in the military]," Garner said of Hamre. He went to seminary, didn't like it, and now he practices theology here. He can't be convinced with facts.

"Tell any of those kids in a division that they aren't trigger pullers. John Hamre did his little bean counting. He asked, 'How many infantrymen are there in the Army? That's X. How many tankers are there in the Army? That's Y. Do I want to consider some artillerymen? Well, maybe. Let me consider the cannon artillerymen. That's Z. Let me divide that out. These are the trigger pullers. Everybody else operates a computer.'

"Tell the kids who were on the Patriot [antiaircraft and antimissile] sites during Desert Storm [the Persian Gulf War of 1990–1991] that they weren't trigger pullers. Tell the sappers, the engineers who go out to clear a mine field, that they aren't trigger pullers. Tell the medic who goes out there to get some wounded that he's not a trigger puller. Tell the mechanic who's trying to recover a tank during a fire fight that he's not a trigger puller. You can't make those kinds of statements. It's denigrating to the rest of the force for him to make that kind of remark.

"Let me tell you a little story that will show you why Hamre is so wrong. On my last tour in Vietnam in the Highlands I was in a big fire fight. I had a Dust Off [a helicopter ambulance] come in with a medic on it. I handed him a wounded American. The medic put his arms out and took this wounded sergeant in his arms. And as the medic took him in, he got hit in the chest by a .51 caliber machine gun bullet and fell back in the chopper. Now that medic to John Hamre is not a trigger puller."

Garner, a warm person with a history degree from Florida State University, not a cold martinet with a U.S. Military Academy ring, suffered through the QDR. He considered it both misguided and nonguided. He said the services' politicking for a bigger slice of the money pie, including his own for the Army, often depressed him. He thought the inside politics demeaned the medic and others he had seen die in the field. He felt the stringy Kurdish boy—who, as a way of thanking Garner for saving his family in the mountains of Iraq had drawn sketches of American soldiers doing good deeds—would have been disillusioned by all the politicking by his heroes.

When Garner and I first talked about the QDR in 1997, the active duty Army numbered 492,000 men and women. This contrasted with the 6.0 million men and women the Army had on active duty at the end of World War II in 1945 and the 1.6 million it had on active duty at the height of the Vietnam War in 1968. The Army would break if civilian leaders kept giving it more work while continuing to reduce it below 492,000, Garner said.

It is unfair to the people in the Army to make them do more with less, Garner maintained. He said the Army needed and deserved more than its traditional 24 percent of the total Pentagon budget. "That doesn't work any more," he said. "Since 1990 we've deployed the U.S. military twenty-seven times. The Army has done the majority of that. The Army is well over 50 percent of the total force that was deployed those twenty-seven times. We're doing that with an Army that has come down about 40 percent in those same six years. In the forty years prior to that, we deployed only ten times. The frequent deployments have put a tremendous operational tempo, a lot of stress, on the units."

Unless the Army receives a larger share of the budget, Garner said, it will have to continue to rob Peter to pay Paul within its own money accounts. More people will have to be kicked off the payroll, operating tempo will have to be slowed down, maintenance of barracks and trucks will have to be postponed, and research on tomorrow's weapons will have to be reduced. To buy the new helicopters and guns it needs for the twenty-first century, Garner said, the Army—unless it gets an unexpected extra dollop of big money—will have to eat part of itself as it did in the 1970s.

Sooner or later, Garner predicted, the Army even under budgets bigger than $250 billion a year plus inflation will have to choose and finance certain key weapons and cancel others to save money. He said he and Gen. Walter T. "Dutch" Kerwin Jr. did this in 1975 with great success. At the time Garner was a staff officer in the Army's Office of Operations and Plans and Kerwin was vice chief of staff, the second-highest rank in the Army.

"We thought the Russians were at least a generation and a half ahead of us in terms of weapons," Garner recalled. "And so what we did was put everything we had into modernization. We said there's enough warning time, so we'll take the shortage in the readiness of the force in the short term because we've got enough warning time to build the force up.

"We did the Big Five: the XM-1, which became the Abrams M-1 tank; the mechanized infantry fighting vehicle, which became the Bradley troop carrier; the Black Hawk [troop carrying] helicopter; the Cheyenne, which became the Apache armed helicopter; and the SAM D antiaircraft missile, which became the Patriot antiaircraft and antirocket missile [employed against Iraq's flying Scud missiles during the Persian Gulf War in 1990–1991.] We circled the wagons around those chosen few weapons and beat the hell out of anybody who tried to interfere with their development."

With the Army struggling to recruit and hold enough people to fill its billets, Garner said, its leaders have been right to put people ahead of new weapons in divvying up the service's money. To get the people money for housing, schools, hospitals, and day care centers, Garner said, "You go to the modernization account," which holds money to buy new weapons. "Over the last six years, we've taken billions of dollars out of modernization to keep the force ready and to keep the quality of life up. But what we really did was sacrifice future readiness by sticking with old trucks and weapons rather than buying new. So as we go into this QDR, we've got a big deficit in modernization accounts because the Army was under-resourced by DoD [Department of Defense]."

Garner echoed Fogleman's lament about confusing, contradictory, and shortsighted guidance during the QDR. "The uniform side says to the civilians, 'Just a minute. Tell us what you want to do with the military, and

I'll tell you what it looks like,'" Garner said. "What's the national military strategy going to be? We'll build you a force. If that force is too big, you can take it down to what you want to, and we'll assess risks for you. You've got to state the things that you want our force to do for the nation.'

"In my judgment, OSD below the secretary hasn't done this. They say, 'Hmm. I've only got so much money, so what can I do for that? And by the way, I want most of it to be for modernization [buying new tanks, ships, and aircraft] because that provides work to make everybody over in Congress happy.' So there's a big, big pull between the civilians trying to direct the QDR, with some saying they want a resource-based force and others saying they want a strategy-based force."

Another problem with the QDR, Garner said, was the lack of agreement on how far in the future to look in designing the twenty-first century Army. The intelligence agencies, he noted, were not trying to describe threats beyond the year 2010. Yet, Garner said, as the assistant chief of staff directing the Army's QDR, he was told to look all the way out to the year 2015—an impossibility.

Garner also shared Fogleman's belief that an annual Pentagon budget of $250 billion plus inflation should be plenty of money for the armed services in the post–cold war period. "If I were a congressman on the Hill, I might even take a little more out. The problem is the way the money is divvied up. If I had a blank sheet of paper and I wasn't going to get rolled by political pressure so I could pull it off, I could save a lot of defense dollars.

"I'd say, 'Army, I don't want you building tanks incrementally by continually upgrading the M-1 beyond what you need for the threats, the overmatches. You figure out what your next tank is going to look like and invest in it so it will be ready around 2010.'" [Army statistics suggest that the service built far more M-1 tanks than it could use. Of the total 8,101 M-1s the Army bought for $5.6 million each, only 2,530 were with its active duty units and almost as many, 2,006, were in storage.] Except for the Crusader mobile artillery piece and Comanche helicopter, "the way you're spending money now on weapons amounts to putting patchwork on legacy systems" designed for the cold war. "Save that patchwork money to build the Army of the future like we did with the Big Five in 1975.

"You could fix the Army by giving it from 2.5 to 3 percent more of the total defense budget, or about 27 percent of it. If you do that, you've put the Army on an azimuth to getting well over the next ten to fifteen years. The way we're going, the Army is going to be the bill payer for modernization of itself and the other services. To get more money for weapons, DoD is going to say, 'We've got a great big Army out here, so let's take it down some more in personnel and put the savings into modernization.'

"The reasoning will be that with all these precision weapons, I won't have to put forces on the ground. I engage the enemy from the sea or from the air with so much precision that the enemy will lose his will to fight. A lot of that is being said by the Air Force.

"I believe in precision engagement, don't get me wrong. But we've gone too far over. It has begun to be our total focus. Precision engagement is now thought of as the dominant dimension of warfare. We've forgotten about maneuver, and that you've got to be there to control populations. We've never caused an enemy to give up because we bombed him. [Garner was speaking before the 1999 NATO bombing campaign against Yugoslav president Slobodan Milosevic, which for the first time caused a national leader to capitulate.]

"If you're fighting me, and you have this great Air Force and this great Navy with all these precision weapons, I'm going to find a way for you not to use them. I'm going to fight you in the city so you're going to have to kill the city to kill me. Or I'm going to take refugees and put them on my platforms [like tanks and ships]. I'm going to let you kill civilians and see how that flies on CNN. Doing that gives you a big problem. You've got to send some infantrymen in there and separate people from weapons platforms in order to kill the weapons platforms. You've got a tough, tough game. Those asymmetries are not being considered adequately as DoD divvies up the money. The Army is shortchanged."

How do you explain that the Army through the years has received fewer dollars per active duty person than the other armed services? I asked. After all, its Patton-like armored sweeps across the desert during the Persian Gulf War in 1991 glamorized the Army. Why didn't this result in more money for the Army? And more people have served in the Army than any other service, producing the largest alumni to champion Army causes.

"Washington is a Navy town, and it always has been," Garner replied in noting how many recent presidents—John F. Kennedy, Richard M. Nixon, Gerald R. Ford, Jimmy Carter—and other influential persons had been in the Navy. Garner added that the Air Force outflanked the Army because of its power within the Defense Department hierarchy. He said, for example, that Air Force general Joseph W. Ralston, vice chairman of the Joint Chiefs of Staff, was really running the military part of the QDR day by day.

"There is no constituency outside the Army staff for the Army except in the hands of a few congressmen," Garner contended. "On Capitol Hill, the glamorous part of the ground forces is the Marine Corps. So the Army is a service without really much of a constituency."

But wait a minute, I pressed during one of several discussions. The top soldier in the whole country, the chairman of the Joint Chiefs of Staff, General Shalikashvili, is an Army man.

"Never helps," Garner replied. "An Army chairman of the Chiefs says how bad can I stick my service to prove that I'm a purple guy? If you make a Navy or Air Force guy the chairman, he's the most parochial SOB you've ever seen in your life. An Army guy has grown up in an interservice environment. We in the Army depend on the other services to get from here to there, for close air support, and for a lot of other things. We're taught to be team players. Everything the Army does is on a team basis, not an individual basis. So when you get an Army guy as chairman, he's a team player. He's been in a joint environment and he says, 'Oh my God, they don't think I'm purple so let me stick my service to show I'm purple.'

"In order for this nation to be successful, it has to have an Army that's able to execute. I'm working my butt off on this QDR to help put the Army on a glide path to be ready for the next event. I'm not talking about tomorrow. I'm talking about 2010, 2015. My fear is that there's a feeling in OSD, and to a degree in the Congress, that the Army is a cold war relic. People who believe that don't see that everything we're doing today requires an Army to do it.

"The Marine Corps has had the Marine Expeditionary Unit [MEU] floating off the coast of Bosnia now for four years. Our leaders haven't used it yet in Bosnia because the MEU can't do it. The marines are great for what they're structured for. [The marines traditionally have been fast-strike assault troops. Seldom do they stay for long periods in the occupied area and govern as the Army did in Japan after World War II and in Bosnia in 1997. An exception was the marines' long-term presence in Haiti from 1915 to 1934.] The marines aren't structured for the stuff that is going on in the world today," Garner contended. [In 1999, however, the marines would be deployed to Kosovo as peacekeepers.]

"The Air Force is wonderful. We went in there and we bombed the hell out of the bad guys in Bosnia. They said, 'Screw you. I'm still doing what I'm doing.' You had to put the Army in there to make the bad guys in Bosnia behave. Ninety five percent of the solutions for the nation require an Army to do them.

"Despite its importance, the decision makers have shortchanged the Army to the point it is now on the razor's edge. We've got a personnel and operational tempo so high that the troops are fatigued. My fear is that the Army is going to break under that. What I'm trying to do is reshape that Army and get it ready for the future. I want a modernization program that really reflects on how you use information to make yourself more survivable, to make your weapons more lethal. I want the Army to have such situational awareness that every shooter shoots, every leader leads, and every supporter supports."

To do that, Garner continued, the Army either will have to break the mindset of senior officers or wait until they are replaced by a new generation of officers who are comfortable with computers and other high-tech equipment. "Generals," said General Garner, "have a tough time changing the mentality of the Army because they cannot relate to young officers. When they talk to lieutenants, they reflect back to when they were lieutenants. There's no relationship. The lieutenant today has his head in the game more than a lieutenant colonel had his head in the game in the Army I entered in 1962."

Garner said keeping these smart young officers in the Army to prevent or wage the new kind of warfare was one of his service's biggest challenges. "Despite being more involved, today's lieutenants have no logical reason to stay in the Army. They can make so much more money on the outside. They can have so much better family life on the outside. They can create an environment for themselves that is so much better on the outside. The only thing that would keep them in the Army is dedication and the camaraderie and the bonding that we have with one another. The two ways we can keep these lieutenants in the Army is to make their work challenging and physical. You give them opportunities to personally excel. You create college availability. You make them feel proud; feel good about themselves."

Returning to how he would change the other armed services if he were in charge of restructuring the American military for the early twenty-first century, Garner said:

"I'd say, 'Navy, I'm not going to build another attack submarine. I'm going to slip that to the right [postpone it].'

"I'd say, 'Air Force, in the tactical fighter program, I'm going to take about a seven- to ten-year slip.' I see no peer competitor out there who can knock down the aircraft we already have flying. I believe in the F-22, I believe in the Joint Strike Fighter, so I'm going keep pursuing that technology. But I'm going to slip both programs to the right, to later dates, to save money in the near term. With nobody out there, that's an acceptable risk at a time our civilian bosses are saying readiness is nonnegotiable.

"'Marines, your V-22 [troop-carrying, tiltrotor aircraft that takes off like a helicopter, flies like an airplane, and costs about $80 million each] is the equivalent of the Air Force leather jacket. You don't need that. You go take the Air Force Special Operations Black Hawk. And the money you've got left over, you improve your ability to come over the horizon in a surface vehicle.

"'Reserves, I'm going to take you down in size some more and restructure your units to fit today's needs.' The heavy National Guard divisions don't serve a purpose. I would make them light divisions where they could do more work for the governor and share in the Operations Other Than War real stuff that the active component is doing there.

"'DoD agencies, I'm going to cut you down or eliminate you.' There is no mechanism in place to make agencies like the Defense Finance and Accounting System, Defense Logistics Agency, Ballistic Missile Defense Organization, and the Defense Security Assistance Agency efficient. They just pass their inefficiencies on to the armed services and we have to pay for them. If I couldn't eliminate them, I would at least put them on an operating account where they had to give so much service for a fixed amount of money."

Sea: Admiral Pilling

Donald Lee Pilling looked like an admiral, talked like an admiral, and was an admiral when we talked in 1997 and 1998 about the QDR and the Navy he envisioned for the twenty-first century. But he thought with the breadth of the Cambridge University scholar he had been, making him stand out from the officers of an institution that, though bearing the name United States Navy, is really several un-united navies. There is the surface navy made up of destroyers and cruisers; the aviation navy featuring aircraft carriers and pilots; the submarine navy consisting of "boomers," nuclear submarines that carry long-range missiles through the depths, and attack subs designed to kill enemy submarines with torpedoes. Each of these navies competes with the others for missions, money, and glory. And off to the side and fiercely independent is the Navy's amphibious infantry, the United States Marine Corps. The corps officially is part of the Navy but tries not to acknowledge it.

In early 1997, when Pilling and I first talked about the QDR and the future United States Navy, he was the vice admiral running the QDR. In November of that year he was promoted to the four-star position of vice chief of naval operations, the second-highest-ranking officer in the Navy and the prime architect of the twenty-first-century Navy. We talked several times while he was working on that blueprint.

Like Fogleman of the Air Force and Garner of the Army, Pilling said it was difficult to finance his service on its slice of the Pentagon's money pie, even though the Navy was getting the biggest piece. Navy leaders by 1997 had completely given up on the goal of former Navy secretary John F. Lehman Jr. to assemble an active duty fleet of six hundred surface ships and submarines. They were struggling as the twentieth century closed to keep a fleet of three hundred ships on active duty.

"I'm worried about the resource levels in the future," Pilling told me. "How can you afford to keep naval capabilities at levels you want under tighter budgets? The solution to that is to reduce the number of people on ships because people are very expensive." New ships will be automated as much as militarily practical to reduce crew sizes. Reducing manning will be an ongoing effort during the "recapitalization" of the fleet. *Recapitalization* in that context means building new ships to replace old ones so the Navy can continue to have at least three hundred modern ships and submarines in its fleet indefinitely. Pilling said his objective was to reduce the crew on the next generation of destroyer, DDG-21, from the usual three hundred to three-hundred-fifty sailors to ninety five.

"If we can buy eight to ten ships a year, that will keep us above three hundred ships," Pilling said. "That's sort of where our redline is. If we can stay on track with our surface combatants, our carrier and submarine construction, and do something like build and charter the logistic force," meaning letting private companies build and operate cargo ships under a Navy lease, "we think we can stay above three hundred ships through the year 2015.

"On the aviation side," instead of continuing to buy sixty or seventy planes a year "we need to get up to one hundred fifty planes a year and stay there" to keep the air arm modern. There was not enough money in sight for the Navy to do that as the twentieth century neared its end.

Asked to look over the horizon at the future Navy, Pilling, who earned a doctorate in mathematics from Britain's Cambridge University, said: "I was brought up in the cold war where we thought about going out and hunting Russian submarines." He said coastal areas will remain important but that the Navy will still be "thinking about how to influence what's going on on the other side of the beach." For example, he envisioned Navy ships firing cruise missiles deep inland while still providing fire support for marines storming beaches. The Navy will be able to strengthen the U.S. president's hand in the future and influence the behavior of foreign adversaries because of its long, deft, and fast-responding reach, Pilling predicted.

"If you can precisely target" from ships standing far out at sea and "you have knowledge of the guy's infrastructure, then you can bring him to his knees fairly quickly from an infrastructure perspective," Pilling said. Destroying an enemy's communications, air fields, and ports would be like cutting off the blood circulation within a human being. Navy planners during the QDR were deeply engaged in "nodal analysis" to determine the most vital places to hit the enemy with long-distance weapons early in a conflict.

"It's a different way of thinking," the admiral said. The strategy requires expensive, multipurpose ships that could be the sailing artillery for the marines in distant trouble spots. The old war plans called for taking on Soviet ships and submarines in their front- and backyards, keeping the sea lanes open, and, if it came to that, dropping nuclear bombs on the Soviet homeland.

The Navy's twenty-first-century blueprint called for aircraft carriers costing $5 billion each to continue to be the queens of the fleet. With the Soviet Navy rusting out of existence, Pilling and fellow Navy leaders were planning a Navy trained and equipped to answer "911" calls, large and small, from the sea. One big reason the Navy received more money than the other services was its usefulness to presidents trying to flex American muscle where neither the Army nor Air Force had nearby bases. Carrier bombers could threaten almost any nation from their seagoing landing fields. Although the Air Force could attack a global hot spot from U.S. bases with long-range bombers, before they could launch the State Department often had to negotiate rights to fly through the airspace of neighboring countries.

The biggest cloud on the Navy's horizon at the end of the twentieth century was the possibility of pricing itself out of the competition for missions in the post–cold war world. With each new ship and submarine costing several billions, the Navy was in danger of having only enough money to buy a few of them. No matter how sophisticated and lethal one carrier or one attack submarine might be, it could not be in two places at once. Pilling acknowledged that rising costs jeopardized the Navy's plan to finance a fleet of at least three hundred ships and submarines within a limited budget.

Like Generals Fogleman and Garner, Admiral Pilling felt a sense of urgency about keeping the tip of his service's spear sharp. Unlike Fogleman's Air Force and Garner's Army, the Navy embraced the policy of "tiered readiness," keeping forward-deployed ships ready to fight but tolerating a low state of readiness for forces that were back home training for the next mission. To help explain why he insisted to his civilian bosses during the QDR that the forward-deployed part of the Navy must be kept ever-ready for emergencies, Pilling recalled the urgency of rescuing Scott O'Grady, the Air Force captain shot down by a Serbian SA-6 missile while flying his F-16 fighter plane over Bosnia on June 2, 1995. Pilling's story began with an early-morning call on June 5 from Adm. Leighton W. "Snuffy" Smith Jr., commander of U.S. Naval Forces in Europe.

"We think we have Grady," Smith told Pilling. "We've talked to him" by radio while he was hiding in the woods of Bosnia where unfriendly Serbs were searching for him. "We've got to figure how to get him out before the sun comes up."

Pilling at the time was the three-star commander of the Sixth Fleet with headquarters in Gaeta, Italy.

He hurried from his bedroom ashore to his flagship tied up at Gaeta. It had secure communications connecting him with every corner of the world. Smith in London and Pilling in Italy combined efforts to organize the rescue attempt. Capt. Christopher Cole, skipper of the amphibious assault ship USS *Kearsarge* (LHD-3), which was plying the Adriatic Sea with marines and helicopters aboard, was ordered to steam east at "best speed."

"We want you to execute a TRAP (Tactical Recovery Aircraft and Personnel) to go after Scott O'Grady," Smith told Col. Martin Berndt, commander of the Twenty-fourth Marine Expeditionary Unit, on the *Kearsarge.* "Here's the longitude and latitude. Prepare for a TRAP to get Scott O'Grady."

Smith, Pilling, Berndt, and top U.S. military commanders all over the region swung into action to rescue this one, twenty-nine-year-old pilot hiding in a woody patch of Bosnia. The hands-on rescuers, if everything worked, would be Berndt and his forty-two-man TRAP rescue force. They boarded two CH-53E helicopters and headed toward O'Grady, even though they knew they would be taking on the high risk of operating on unfriendly ground in broad daylight. They succeeded, drawing the praise of President Clinton and the gratitude of O'Grady and his family. O'Grady's sister wrote to one marine that their rescue mission was "one moment of perfection in a world of imperfection."

Pilling said there are at least two lessons to be learned from the O'Grady rescue. One, he said, is that to be successful forward-deployed forces must be kept ready to swing into action at a moment's notice. Another is that civilian leaders should not expect the Navy to cover the same number of global hot spots with a fleet of three-hundred-plus ships as it covered during the cold war with almost six hundred. Pilling lamented that during the QDR he had neglected to give that second lesson enough thrust in meetings with his civilian bosses. Pilling felt civilian leaders did not appreciate the strain imposed by using the Navy as if it still had almost six hundred ships, not three hundred. He lamented that the do-more-with-less syndrome was impelling many men and women to leave the Navy in 1997 and 1998.

"You've got to give us some relief," Pilling said. "You remember that in the late 1970s people voted with their feet" and left the armed services in droves because they felt they were overworked and under appreciated. "My biggest fear is that we may lose our people again." [At the close of 1998, the Navy had eighteen thousand unfilled jobs, partly because it failed to recruit and train enough new people to take over from those who had quit.]

Marines: General Krulak

The United States Marine Corps is the smallest, and many would say the loudest, outfit in the U.S. military. The corps is also widely credited with being the most effective of the services in playing the Washington power game of getting influential players to champion its causes. Would-be macho senators and representatives fall all over themselves to help the corps in hopes of winning its respect. Marines regard their leader, the commandant, with a reverence unmatched by rival services—whether they like him or not. The commandant is a benevolent, and sometimes non-benevolent, dictator of a tight brotherhood. To quote Sen. John McCain, Arizona Republican, a former Navy captain and Vietnam War prisoner, "the corps is just different, that's all."

Marine commandants through the years usually have stood out from their grayish, play-it-safe comrades on the Joint Chiefs of Staff. This was indeed true during the 105th Congress when Gen. Charles C. Krulak, son of a marine general, was the thirty-first commandant of the corps. Unlike the generals and admiral heading the other services, Krulak was not holding onto weapons designed for the cold war with the tenacity of Linus hanging onto his security blanket. He saw a brand new world confronting marines and insisted that the corps change so it could fight in it successfully. This was the new world Krulak described to me in interviews in 1997 and 1998 and in other forums:

"In the battles I see being fought for at least the next twenty years, chaos will reign. Set-piece battles a la Desert Storm will probably be not what you see. You will see the stepchild of Chechen," the fiercely independent community near the Caspian Sea. Chechen, which has a crucially important oil terminal at Baku, fought off Russian troops after the breakup of the Soviet Union.

The fighting will be in "the cities and slums, places that the Marine Corps, the Army, and the Air Force" have avoided in devising their tactics, Krulak continued. "Our present doctrine is not to go into the cities. Why? Because it's so deadly. All you have to do is look at Leningrad, Hue City, Groznyy." Rubble piled up in cities will make smart weapons useless. Enemy riflemen hidden in crowds will have to be singled out. Artillery barrages by the acre will not get at tomorrow's enemy.

"What we're trying to do is say: 'OK; 70 percent of the world's population in the year 2010 will live in either cities or urban slums within three hundred miles of the coastline. Obviously, then, the Marine Corps doctrine of avoiding the cities is not going to work. The enemy is not going to allow it. Their center of gravity is going to be in cities.'" If Iraqi troops had made Kuwait City their center of gravity during the Gulf War "instead of sitting out in the desert where they were vulnerable to our technology, it would have been a very bloody experience. So what we're trying to do is come up with tactics, techniques, procedures, training, education, and equipment that will allow us to fight in that environment."

The commandant said the corps already has learned through its Urban Warrior experiments that simple changes in combat gear can save marines' lives, such as putting handles on flak jackets so one battling marine can pull another through a window in a downtown building. Protecting the urban warrior's elbows and knees with roller bladers' pads reduced injuries. Marines advancing through simulated city sewers found during Urban Warfare experiments that they could not keep in touch with each other by radio. Marines need communications that will work in sewers, Krulak said. They also need weapons that disable civilian mobs without killing them. The "three block wars" of the future will not be won with $5 billion aircraft carriers or $180 million F-22 fighter planes, Krulak predicted.

But Krulak, the would-be revolutionist, said breaking old habits turned out to be tougher than he had anticipated, especially when it came to taking on defense contractors and their champions in Congress. "Do you remember a guy named Eisenhower?" Krulak asked me in one interview in 1998. "He hit the problem right on the head" when he talked about the military-industrial complex.

President Dwight D. Eisenhower in a farewell address to the nation on January 17, 1961, said that

> until the latest of our world conflicts [World War II], the United States had no armaments industry. American makers of plowshares could, with time and as required, make swords as well. But now we can no longer risk emergency improvisation of national defense; we have been compelled to create a permanent armaments industry of vast proportions. Added to this, three and a half million men and women are directly engaged in the defense establishment. We annually spend on military security more than the net income of all United States corporations.
>
> The conjunction of an immense military establishment and a large arms industry is new in the American experience. The total influence—economic, political, even spiritual—is felt in every city, every State house, every office of the federal government. We recognize the imperative need for this development. Yet we must not fail to comprehend its grave implications. Our toil, resources and livelihood are all involved; so is the very structure of our society.
>
> In the councils of government, we must guard against the acquisition of unwarranted influence, whether sought or unsought, by the military-industrial complex. The potential for the disastrous rise of misplaced power exists and will persist.
>
> We must never let the weight of this combination endanger our liber-

ties or democratic processes. We should take nothing for granted. Only an alert and knowledgeable citizenry can compel the proper meshing of the huge industrial and military machinery of defense with our peaceful methods and goals so that security and liberty may prosper together. . . .

Krulak told me that Eisenhower's warning came back to him when, as one of his first money-saving attempts as commandant, he tried to cancel the obsolete Hawk antiaircraft missile manufactured by the Raytheon Corp. "I wanted to do away with Hawk the second I became commandant" on June 30, 1995. "Do you know how long it took me? It took me into my fourth year. Four years! You know how long it took to not buy MLRS [the multiple launch rocket system manufactured by the merged companies of Lockheed Martin and Vought Systems Corp.]?" "Forever." Although the rocket maker's headquarters were in Dallas, Texas, it had offices in several other states as well, including Georgia and California, which during Krulak's tour as commandant were represented in Congress by powerful politicians, including Republican House Speaker Newt Gingrich of Georgia.

"There's a lot of power out there," Krulak said. "When you say, 'I'm going to stop a program,' the political-military-industrial complex rolls in there and says, 'No you aren't.' So there's a real problem with industry, with the political side," when it comes to canceling weapons or changing the mindset of political and military leaders who felt more comfortable with preparing for the known cold war threat than they do for the unknown threats ahead, the commandant said.

Rather than have the corps try to walk slowly across that long, obstacle-strewn bridge stretching between the cold war and what Krulak termed the "three-block war" of the future, the commandant told me, he wanted it to vault to the bank on the other side. "You're at a strategic inflection point where things are changing so rapidly that you can literally steal a march on the future," he said. But too many politicians and military leaders are "not willing to do that, so they keep on with the legacy systems" designed for toe-to-toe combat with the heavy cold war forces of the former Warsaw Pact countries.

"It's a cultural problem," Krulak said of the resistance to change, adding that the other, bigger services will have a tougher time solving it than the

relatively small corps. "The Marine Corps has always been more innovative," he contended.

The innovative program that Krulak was trying hardest to protect during the QDR was the tiltrotor V-22 Osprey troop transport. Thanks to en-
gines and propellers that can be rotated upward or downward, the V-22
can take off and land like a helicopter and speed along in level flight like a
conventional airplane. But this advanced technology was costly. One V-22
was projected to cost $80 million, counting research and development,
over the planned production run. This cost compared with $7.5 million
for the Army's troop carrying Black Hawk helicopter. Krulak and his allies
contended that the V-22's ability to fly off a ship or any patch of ground
and speed troops to a hot spot would justify the plane's cost and revolutionize warfare.

If the Army does not follow the Marine Corps's lead in buying the V-22
as part of becoming lighter, faster, and more responsive, Krulak maintained, "they're going to be out of the damn ball game." General Reimer, the
Army chief of staff, rebutted this assertion in a separate interview, declaring: "I don't want the V-22. It can't carry anything." The V-22 is designed
to carry twenty-four marines for up to 2,100 miles with one refueling.

Although the V-22 survived the QDR, Krulak said that he is "worried
about getting the V-22 in the time that we need it. We can't wait until 2017
to get that aircraft. We're not only going to have an all V-22 fleet, but so is
the Army. Mark my word; take it to the bank. The Army will not be able
to *not* buy the V-22 because they will be out of the ball game without it.
The Marine Corps takes everything. We are going to move away from
heavy armor. We're going to go to a light-strike capability. Everything is
going to be transportable by the V-22 or CH-53 [heavy lift helicopter]. We're
getting the amphibious shipping" the corps needs to strike from the sea.

If you were in charge of a QDR with a mandate to restructure boldly
the Army, Navy, and Air Force, I asked Krulak, what would you recommend that each of the other services do? Here was the commandant's
reply:

Air Force. "If I were [Air Force] chief of staff, I would start looking a
lot harder at space. I mean that is his future. I'd go after a space and information operations command that ties together the biggest dangers we

have, somebody controlling the territory above us and somebody that's controlling the information. We're going to need more than a CINC [commander in chief of a specific geographical region, like the Middle East] to do that. We're going to need a service with a powerful service headquarters to keep a focus on that. If I were the Air Force, I'd go for it.

"Tomorrow morning I'd cancel the F-22 [air superiority fighter; the Air Force as of 1998 intended to buy 341 F-22s for a total of $63.8 billion, or $187 million each counting research and development costs]. I don't believe in the silver-bullet technology. I assume it's going to be boots on the ground that will decide the three-block wars of the future. There's no question in my mind."

Rather than buy the F-22 designed during the cold war to battle sophisticated Soviet fighters, Krulak said, he would execute "a massive buy of that state of the art stealth" to be incorporated in the Joint Strike Fighter the Pentagon was developing. "If everybody said [of the Joint Strike Fighter], 'This is it,' the money you'd save would be phenomenal." But Krulak doubted that the military-industrial-political complex would allow the Air Force to cancel the F-22 even if it wanted to do so. "How are you going to say we're not going to build this aircraft and all of sudden twenty thousand people are out of work?"

Army. "The Army needs to watch its soul. Its soul is the chain-mail fist of American diplomacy. They've got to be careful as they go to the Army-after-next that they don't lose the ability to crush somebody on the battlefield. I think they need to lighten up [their weapons and gear] in a smarter way than they are now planning."

Krulak said the Army in rushing to digitize its fighting units, a transformation where officers and senior enlisted people try to run a battle by watching it unfold on their consoles in computerized vehicles and command posts, will disconnect its forces from the less sophisticated forces of allied countries. "Let me tell you, every single coalition partner is petrified. When this digitized corps hits the field, who operates it? Also, I don't think the Army can afford it, and I don't think they've got the concept" down right. "What they've done is laminate this technology onto nineteenth-century concepts. That concept is the heavy division, the Bradleys" preparing to stop the no-longer-existing Warsaw Pact forces at Fulda Gap [the former West German border]. "I'm saying to them, 'Who's out there in the next twenty years? Who is it? Tell me.' There's not going to be major regional conflict" for about twenty years. "It's going to be three-block wars. The Army by not structuring itself to intercede quickly with easily deployable forces is "in trouble." He predicted that any general chosen to take over in the Army's 1999 change of command will "move very quickly" to make his forces lighter and faster so that they could reach a distant trouble spot in time to do some good.

Navy. "The Navy potentially is the biggest winner of all" in the competition for dollars and missions "if they had the guts" to restructure for the different challenges of the future, Krulak said. "They are honest to God the most relevant force we've got. They are sovereign territory. Any place they go they have unbelievable mobility: strategic, operational, and tactical. They bring to the fight capabilities that nobody else can bring.

"But they've got to have a whole new mindset" to build "a butt-kicking force that can literally manage instability. They've got to get an aircraft that's capable of fighting and winning in the twenty-first century, and that's not what they're getting" with the F/A-18 E and F. [Krulak angered Navy leaders by refusing to buy the F/18 E and F. He opted for waiting for the Joint Strike Fighter, a version of which will be designed to take off and land in a short space. Krulak feared that if the corps bought the E and F, the Navy would put all the marine squadrons flying them on aircraft carriers. Marine air, as Krulak saw it, would cease being a separate entity with unique capabilities to support marines on the ground.]

Krulak saw a costly disconnect between the Navy's long-decked, $5 billion CVX aircraft carrier and the short take off and landing aircraft expected be operational when the new carrier goes to sea in about 2015. The new carrier is "going to last for fifty years. So it's going to be a carrier for 2065. What kind of planes are going to be flying off of that?" Navy planners are displaying "almost an unwillingness to leave a comfort area" of familiar, costly, long-deck carriers.

Talking about all the armed forces, including his own, Krulak said that "it is the responsibility of the services to think ahead; to move forward; to take advantage of this inflection point and literally make some hard choices within themselves. We owe that to the American people. We've got to be able to sacrifice. We've got to be able to change. To get the modern force for the American people, you can't just stick your hand out. I'm saying we've got to do our part, too, and doing our part is to experiment, evaluate, and change. We owe it to the taxpayer. Chuck Spinney [Franklin C. Spinney, an outspoken aircraft specialist in the Pentagon's Office of Program Analysis and Evaluation] is valid in saying you guys [the Joint Chiefs of Staff] are just asking for more damn money for legacy systems."

Like Garner of the Army, Fogleman of the Air Force, and Pilling of the Navy, Krulak lamented that the top Pentagon civilians overseeing and shaping the QDR did not know the realities and needs of combat because they had not experienced it. Krulak's sense of mission, outspokenness, and impatience can be explained in part by what he went through in Vietnam. I went to the marines' Command and Staff College at Quantico, Virginia, to hear him recount one of his own searing battlefield experiences to the students there.

"I want to talk about something that rarely gets talked about," Krulak began in the crowded but silent auditorium. "It's something about who we are and what we should be as members of the professional arms. It is your willingness to do the right thing. Your willingness to speak up and tell the emperor he doesn't have any clothes on that really sets you apart from your contemporaries. And when it gets to my level, and you're looking around for that person who's going to sit outside your door, you look above all for a man or a woman of integrity who possesses the highest sense of moral courage. So that's what we're going to talk about today.

"In the spring of 1966 the 324th Bravo North Vietnamese Army Division moved south from the border of North Vietnam and China. It pulled itself through the country and moved along the demilitarized zone that separated North Vietnam and South Vietnam. Their mission was to lead the first direct invasion of the South by the North. A hell of an outfit. It was the same division that spearheaded the attack against the French in Dien Bien Phu. And here they are, ready to go again. The plan was pretty obvious: drive right through the DMZ; take Dongha, Quantri, and on to Hue City. Interesting that just a few years later that's what they did. Here they were, 1966; the spring; ready to go.

"The United States Marine Corps supported by the Army, the Air Force, and the Navy, moved eleven battalions up along the demilitarized zone. They took part in a battle that has subsequently been called Hastings. I was just one of those dumb lads—I was a first lieutenant—commanding Golf Company, Second Battalion, First Marines. We had a very simple mission. We were to land in a landing zone that was nothing more than dried-out rice paddies about six football fields in length, three football fields in width. It had a dried-out stream bed down one side and was surrounded by jungle-covered mountains. The mission was just to take this young rifle company, very small, we had about 151 people, get into this valley and move up onto a ridge line and just put ourselves in a blocking position to stop the North Vietnamese from moving southward into South Vietnam.

"At zero dark thirty in the morning [just before dawn] the helicopters landed, all at one time. Boomp. Into the zone. They pulled out. As they pulled out, we were taken under heavy small arms, automatic weapons, mortars, artillery fire. I mean it was bad news. Bad news.

"Two thirds of that company scooted off and got in this dried-out stream bed that gave us some cover and some concealment. One platoon, which had landed too far to the west, tried to make it across that open field [to the stream bed] and couldn't. They came under such intense fire. One of the squads found itself directly in the line of fire of North Vietnamese Army .50 caliber machine guns. Within a matter of seconds, we had what appeared to be three marines killed and four seriously wounded.

"And as I sat there on the lip of this stream bed, it was very obvious to me as the commanding officer that this gun was going to kill every one of the marines in that squad; was going to shift over to the next squad and kill everyone there, and shift to the third and kill everyone there. And I was going to lose a platoon of marines like that. [Snaps his fingers.]

"So I get on the hook [field telephone]. And I'm talking to my first platoon commander, and I'm pushing him up this dried-out stream bed as fast as I can. I've got my other platoon putting down a base of fire, trying to keep guns not only of those on the machine gun but a whole bunch of bad guys in the tree line right off of this rice paddy .

"As all of this was going on, I'm sitting there talking and dadgone rounds are hitting the deck and bullets are flying all over the place and people are yelling, smoke going. You talk about the fog of war. It was bad!

"My radio operator grabs me by the shirtsleeve, points out into the rice paddy, and says, 'Look at Lance Corporal Grable!' [not the marine's real name].

"I looked down into this rice paddy, and here was a young lance corporal, the acting squad leader of that squad that was in such deep trouble. He had jumped to his feet. In 1966 we still had the M-14. He had the M-14 rifle right in his hip and took off toward this machine gun as fast as he could. He was running right at them. He went about fifteen meters and then cut to the right, still firing. The machine gun picks up off of the squad and starts tracking this marine.

"The squad feels the firing lift. I mean they scoot. They grab their dead and wounded and scoot up behind the protection of the rice paddy dike. The other two squads do the same thing. You could just see them, like little spiders.

"The problem was the young lance corporal didn't look back. He didn't see any of that happen. He just kept on fighting. You could see the rounds. They would get close to him, and he would cut the other way. He'd fire out one magazine, kick that magazine out, shove another one in. Back and forth. He must have run three hundred meters to make another twenty-five until finally, whack! He was picked up like a rag doll and thrown back.

"In the time all this took place, his platoon was in a safe position. The other platoon I had been working with had got up on the flank of that gun. I got back on the horn. I told that platoon that when I pop a green star cluster [flare] I want the base of fire to shift and I want you to assault across [to knock out the machine gun]. Let's get ready to go. Everybody gives me the thumbs up.

"Boom! Up goes that green star cluster.

"Sure enough, the platoon starts the assault. Sure enough, the base of fire shifts. About that time I'm grabbed on the sleeve again. This time the radio operator didn't say anything to me. He just pointed out to the rice paddy.

"Here's this marine; this lance corporal. He gets back up on his feet.

This time he does what he was told in boot camp. He puts that weapon right in his shoulder. He gets good sight picture; he gets good sight alignment; he gets good trigger squeeze. And he walks right down the line of fire."

Krulak can't continue. The silent audience watches the anguish of the top Marine in the United States pound his fist into his palm and fight back tears for a full thirty seconds. The tears come. Krulak forces himself to continue the story in a croaking voice.

"Three minutes later, the [machine gun] fire lifts. We go up to where he is and then pick him up off the gun and open up his flak jacket. He's got five bullet holes in him. They came out his back. All that was left was a little bit of the spine that was held together by a flak jacket. Around the gun were nine dead North Vietnamese soldiers.

"This great hero—he was a hell of a marine. That's courage.

"But the other side of the story is that this was a black marine. A black marine. 1966. He could not even buy a hamburger in his own home town. Yet he gave his life for his fellow marines. Didn't look around there and say, 'OK, how many of them are white or black? Or what gender are they? Or what religion are they?' or whatever. Gave his life for his fellow marines. Somewhere inside of him was this sense to do the right thing against all the odds of coming up in a society that turned its back on him. He had within him the idea of doing the right thing. Great marine. A fine moment in your commandant's life."

Krulak held his enraptured audience through two more verbal profiles of marines who had done the right thing under tremendous stress. "The question for us," he told the young officers, "is how do you get that ability to do the right thing? Where does it come from?"

Krulak, in struggling to answer his own question, said "Lance Corporal Grable" and the two other marines he had portrayed had the common characteristic of selflessness. "Think about that, selfless," the commandant continued. "You and I have chosen something called the profession of arms. It is as much of a profession as a medical doctor or a lawyer. The difference is that we don't have malpractice insurance. When we foul up it costs big time. When we joined the profession of arms we took an oath. And part of that oath was to well and faithfully discharge the duties of the office of which we were about to enter. Well. Not adequately. But well. Faithfully. Not inconsistently but faithfully. That oath is not just a simple checking of the blocks. That should mean everything to us. Because when we wholeheartedly execute our responsibility to lead the sons and daughters of America into harm's way; when we have the moral courage to do the right thing; when we choose the more difficult path because it's the right path—then, and only then, do we start to stoke the fires of sacrifice and love.

"You and I are expected to possess moral courage. We expect it of our soldiers, our sailors, our airmen, and marines. I can tell you this nation and its people demand it of us. It's during the time that you are at this school, during the time that you have a moment to breathe that you need to consciously reach back and find your moral touchstone to ensure that who you are and what you stand for are as much a part of your professional reputation as your ability to fly a plane, drive a ship, or lead troops.

"When it's your responsibility to tell your boss that the new weapon initiative that you're working on didn't hack it, you need to have the moral courage to do the right thing. When your best friend is involved in an extramarital relationship with somebody else, you need to do the right thing. When one of your subordinates has a great idea and you'd like to claim that for yourself, you need to do the right thing. When you're on the joint staff and somebody wearing your same uniform says, 'I want you to be a little more parochial,' but it doesn't make any sense to you, you need to do the right thing. And when you kick it into the grandstand, and believe me, you are going to kick it into the grandstand, I mean I've punted balls out of the stadium, you've got to have the moral courage to immediately tell your boss that you did it. Unlike wine, bad news doesn't get better with age. The quicker you stand up and say here's what happened, the better off you're going to be. It takes moral courage to hold your ideals above yourself."

The marines in the audience seemed to take in his words and lock them in their hearts. The emotional heat in the auditorium reminded me of a revival meeting without the yelling. The cynicism of Washington thirty miles to the north seemed to have been killed like a virus by Krulak's speech. I understood more fully why these true believers became infuriated by politicians and reporters who did not share their values or priorities.

Afterward, I went through the record of Vietnam War dead trying to find the record of "Marine Lance Corporal Grable." He was not listed as having been killed in the battle Krulak described. I went back to Krulak. He said he had used the name Grable as pseudonym for another marine who had done what he had described but came from a family that did not want his name used. Krulak said otherwise his account of the battle was accurate.

Postscript

Because I am one who believes no pancake is so flat that it does not have two sides, I invited General Shalikashvili to respond to the flag officers' various criticisms of the QDR. Shalikashvili through his deputy, Vice Chairman Joseph Ralston, ran the QDR for Secretary Cohen before retiring in 1997. Here were Shalikashvili's responses to the main criticisms the military officers I had interviewed at length:

Status Quo. Although Shalikashvili said he did not remember if he had sent a deputy to warn Fogleman and the other Chiefs against acting like Billy Mitchell in drafting their parts of the QDR report, he said this could have been the case. "My admonition was that we need to do what we need to do to remain capable of defending our country and winning our nation's wars. I didn't want to get an award for innovation's sake. I didn't want anyone gambling with our nation's security just so we could be called great innovators. I looked at the QDR not as a one-shot thing but a process that would be continuous. Thus, I thought we should set a direction for the future and make appropriate adjustments every four years.

"What is so easy to do in the think tanks is not so easy to do in reality. Tell me how overnight you can go from one kind of force to another kind of force. The military doesn't make sharp left or right turns. You need more gentle turns. The cost is enormous [in human and dollar terms if the turns are too sharp]. I wanted to make the correct but not abrupt turns. What we did was right" for evolving the American military into a force that could handle both familiar and unfamiliar contingencies. However, he said, "we were too optimistic in assuming U.S. forces could be kept ready and procurement steadily increased to approximately $60 billion a year on budgets of $270 billion a year plus inflation. [He was referring to the higher defense budgets that followed 1997's.]

F-22 Procurement Cuts. "I recommended these cuts to Secretary Cohen." Shalikashvili said the reduction was needed to lower the bow wave of procurement in future years. He added that he did not favor canceling the F-22 despite its high cost because the Air Force needed "such an advanced fighter" for the future. Also, the technology developed for the F-22 would help develop the Joint Strike Fighter, he said. "There is a crossover. If you don't go to the F-22, you can't get to the Joint Strike Fighter without significantly higher costs. But this was not about politics, it was about reducing the procurement bow wave while saving the Joint Strike Fighter."

In a separate interview, Secretary Cohen denied he was trying to make a political statement by reducing the procurement of the F-22 and F/A-18 E and F. "I was just trying to make everything fit" into a budget that had a fixed top line, he said.

Lighter Forces. "It's a mirage that you can do with light forces" what you can do with heavy forces in demanding situations, Shalikashvili said. "We know what would have happened to the Eighty-second Airborne Division" if it had to fight heavy Iraqi forces during Desert Storm. The U.S. Army may have to fight the heavy Soviet tanks used by Iraq and North Korea some time in the future, so it is not prudent to discard heavy armor now, Shalikashvili said. "The tank is still the most effective weapon against another tank."

As for the M-1 tank, he said it is "one of the best tanks in the world." Making a lighter tank sounds good, he said, but no one has shown how this could be done without losing some of the lethality of the M-1. "And by the way, tanks in any number would still have to be transported to the trouble spot by ship," he added, "so reducing the weight of a tank from sixty tons to forty tons, let's say, is not crucial for transport. We're in a never-never land" in this part of the light-versus-heavy debate.

Two-MRC Readiness. "People were saying that it was highly unlikely that we would ever have to fight two major regional contingencies [MRCs] at once. That's true. But not impossible. Until you tell me that it's impossible, should I gamble the nation's security?" He said it is possible the United States would have to go to war against North Korea and Iraq at the same time. "I see North Korea the more likely as they begin to implode. People say, 'Gee, the U.S. armed forces are already so small that they can't do those things,' [such as fighting two wars almost simultaneously]. Not true. Although we are over 30 percent smaller, our capability has not decreased in relative terms against potential enemies because those adversaries themselves are even smaller and weaker than they were during the cold war. Because of our combat capabilities, today we are better off relative to anyone who would wish us ill than at any time in my thirty-nine years in the military, but that doesn't mean that we don't have problems. We do, and they need our full attention. It's certainly too early to conclude that we will not have to engage in two MRCs. It would have been irresponsible" to make that assumption while conducting the QDR in 1997.

Missile Defense. To decide to deploy a missile defense before the technology is proved effective "seems to me to be less than a prudent way to go. Find out that it works before deciding to deploy."

4

Guns versus Butter

KING ARTHUR'S LEGENDARY Knights of the Round Table went on a quest for the glittering Holy Grail and its supposed magic powers. While some glimpsed the Grail, none managed to seize and hold on to it. This was also the experience of members of Congress who sought a legislative holy grail in the form of a bipartisan agreement that would control federal taxing and spending for five years at a time. In the spring of 1997 this grail appeared to be in reach at long last.

"This is a moment that many of us have been waiting for for a long time," Rep. John R. Kasich told his colleagues in May 1997. The boyish-looking, lanky Republican from Ohio, then chairman of the House Budget Committee, had crafted what he considered to be a legislative holy grail. Officially titled House Concurrent Resolution 84, the measure set down in black and white what the Defense Department and other government entities could spend every year for the next five years, fiscal 1998 through 2002.

If both chambers of Congress adopted House Concurrent Resolution 84, it would be a gentlemen's agreement—not a law—to honor the money ceilings, or caps. House and Senate rules would enforce it. Lawmakers who tried to bust through the agreed-upon caps would be accused of breaking the gentlemen's agreement, of defying the will of the majority as expressed in 1997. It would take 60 votes, three fifths of the 100-vote Senate to override the agreement and exceed its budget ceilings. The House had a powerful Rules Committee that could protect the resolution if it were approved.

In urging the House to adopt House Concurrent Resolution 84, Kasich said it would do three things at once: limit federal spending, reduce taxes, and balance the federal budget by 2002. Rep. John M. Spratt Jr. of South Carolina, the Budget Committee's ranking minority member, had some qualms about the resolution but urged his Democratic colleagues to vote for it anyway.

"This is a divided government," Spratt said, reminding his party members that although a fellow Democrat, Bill Clinton, was president Republicans were in control of Congress. "And to do a deal," he said, "none of us gets to do it alone. We have a choice between gridlock and compromise. And what we have before us is just that. It is a compromise. It is not a perfect solution. It is the art of the possible. But if we let the perfect be the enemy of the good, we will not get anything done on the deficit this year.

"This compromise differs from most compromises by design, by conscious design," Spratt continued, "because what we sought in negotiating it was to let each party claim some clear victory. Rather than come out with just gray results, compromise to the point that they lost their identify and pleased nobody, this package allows the Republicans a clear victory: it allows them the chance to do significant tax cuts. It allows Democrats, my party, the chance to do initiatives in children's health care, in education, that we could not do if we tried to do it alone."

House Republican Majority Whip Tom DeLay of Texas also urged members to vote aye. "In my view," he said, "this budget resolution is kind of like Tiger Woods and his tee shot. It is not too far to the right nor is it too far to the left, and it takes us a lot further than we previously thought we could go. For the first time in modern memory the president of one party and a Congress controlled by the other party have agreed to balance the budget and to cut taxes in a very specific budget resolution."

"Highway King" Not Impressed

Although Kasich and his allies pleaded with House members not to derail the budget resolution by adding pet programs to it, they were braced for the likelihood that Pennsylvania Republican Bud Shuster, chairman of the House Transportation and Infrastructure Committee, would try to do just that. His chairmanship enabled him to lavish highway money on his home areas and those of his friends. "I hope they put on my tombstone, 'He helped build America,'" Shuster once said.

The acknowledged highway king of the House sought to replace Kasich's budget resolution with one that took $5.65 billion out of the defense budget and earmarked it for highway construction—a clear guns-versus-butter choice that would measure the congressional support for the defense budget in 1997 and the holy grail of a balanced budget agreement.

"Our infrastructure is crumbling," Shuster said in making his pitch to put butter over guns. "Thirty percent of our interstate [highway] system needs to be rebuilt; 25 percent of our bridges are deficient. There are forty-one thousand people killed on our highways every year. And we are told that 30 percent of those deaths are caused by inadequate construction of the highways. We can reconstruct the interstate system. And we can create thousands of good jobs, for every $1 billion spent in transportation means forty-two thousand jobs."

National Security Committee member Ike Skelton, Missouri Democrat, warned that taking $5.65 billion out of the defense budget equated to reducing the All Volunteer Force by fifty thousand people a year for five years. He pleaded with his colleagues to give priority to "that lone soldier who is out there standing on top of the hill in Bosnia because his commander in chief sent him there. We want to encourage him. We want to keep him trained. We want to take care of his family. And when he returns, we do not want him to have to go back on additional unnecessary deployments because of the lack of fellow soldiers."

Spratt reinforced Skelton, declaring, "We have held national defense to a level that I think is barely sufficient" in the Kasich resolution. "I would like to see more there. I do not like the Quadrennial Review [the Quadrennial Defense Review or QDR ordered by Congress in 1986]. But I certainly do not want to go any lower in what we have allocated for defense in this budget."

Rep. William J. Coyne, Pennsylvania Democrat, countered with a remark that went to the heart of the guns-versus-butter argument: "The greatest threat facing our nation today is an economic threat, not a military one. This budget [set forth in the Kasich resolution] spends too much money on our armed forces and not enough on the infrastructure and the work force that will determine the winners and losers in the coming global economic competition. The budget resolution we adopt today should spend less on our military forces and more on investment in our physical and intellectual capital."

At 3:11 A.M. on May 21, 1997, the House by only a two-vote margin, 216 to 214, rejected the Shuster substitute, giving guns a razor-thin victory over butter. Seven minutes later the House adopted House Concurrent Resolution 84 by a vote of 333 to 99. The weary Kasich and his allies left the chamber in the predawn dark only a few hours before Defense Secretary William Cohen was to appear before the House National Security Committee to defend the QDR. Cohen considered the Shuster vote a true measure of the narrowness of support of defense spending in peacetime and told bleary-eyed House members just that the morning after Kasich's two-vote victory.

The Senate adopted its version of House Concurrent Resolution 84 by a vote of 78 to 22 on May 23, 1997. The focus was on whether the tax cuts in the measure were too little or too much. The question of how much was enough for national defense was not debated. The Senate-passed resolution contained the same amounts for the Pentagon for fiscal 1998 through 2002 as did the House measure.

The Afterglow

Following the vote, senators applauded what they considered a historic action to balance the budget. Senate Republican Majority Leader Trent Lott of Mississippi singled out Sen. Pete V. Domenici of New Mexico, the Republican chairman of the Senate Budget Committee, for high praise, declaring: "I know he feels a rush of emotion right now. He has been working on trying to get us to this type of budget resolution for twenty-five years. I think he has done a great job. I commend him and thank him for the great work he has done."

Senators rose again from their schoolboy-sized wooden desks to applaud Domenici. The Italian immigrant grocer's son swelled with pride.

While the House and Senate versions of the House concurrent resolution were similar, they were not identical. A joint conference of senior members of the House and Senate Budget committees was called to iron out differences in the two measures. Then the House and Senate conferees sent identical resolutions to their respective chambers for what was to be the final vote on this long-sought holy grail.

Senate Democrat Ernest F. Hollings of South Carolina, who for decades had been trying to impose fiscal discipline on the government only to see his efforts crushed time after time, said the 1997 budget resolution was "a fraud" because it addressed only the balancing of annual tax income with annual government spending. He said it did little to reduce the national debt, which economists projected to reach $6.31 trillion by fiscal year 2001.

"It is time we stop lying to the American people and tell the truth and show the page," Hollings roared on the Senate floor. To make the government numbers look good to would-be budget balancers, Hollings charged, the crafters of the budget resolution "use Social Security monies. They use the military retirees' money, civilian retirees' pension funds, the unemployment compensation monies, the highway trust funds—and we are not building highways" with that money. "That is scandalous. That is a breach of trust.

"Just three weeks ago, Denny McLain, the all-star championship pitcher for the Detroit Tigers, was sentenced to eight years in prison because as head of a corporation he used the pension funds to pay a corporate debt. Here we are using trust funds to pay the government debt. In private, outside-the-Beltway America you get a prison sentence for this. Here in the wonderful Congress, heavens above, you get the 'Good Government Award'; you get consensus; you get bipartisanship; you get one grand fraud."

Despite Hollings's opposition, the Senate adopted the conference version of the budget resolution by a vote of 76 to 22 on June 5, 1997. The House followed suit, passing the measure 327 to 97 the same day.

With House Concurrent Resolution 84 now the expressed will of Congress, chairmen of the congressional committees that authorized and appropriated money for the Pentagon and other government departments had to write bills that did not break through the ceilings in the resolution. Cuts made to reach permissible limits below the resolution's ceilings were called rescissions.

For the defense budget, the House and Senate Armed Services committees are the authorizing bodies. (In the 105th Congress the House called it the National Security Committee.) The committees recommend to their respective chambers how much money the Pentagon should be allowed to spend on what weapons and how many people should be kept on active duty by each of the armed services. The House and Senate Appropriations committees recommend how much money the Treasury Department should actually deposit in the Pentagon's bank account in a given year and how much of that can be spent. The appropriations for various Pentagon projects can be less, but not more, than the amounts authorized by the National Security and Armed Services committees. Members of the authorizing committees are called authorizers while those on appropriations committees are called appropriators.

Would It Last?

Holding together the uneasy coalition of defense hawks, defense doves, tax cutters, and budget balancers beyond 1997 loomed as the big challenge as Kasich and others celebrated their success in getting House Concurrent Resolution 84 adopted .

"Today is only the ratification of the agreement," said Rep. Earl Pomeroy, North Dakota Democrat, when the final version of the 1997 budget resolution cleared the House and Senate. "Will it work? Will it hold? Or will it fall apart as the committees of jurisdiction simply refuse to live within the bounds of this agreement?"

For a while, it appeared as if the lawmakers would give higher status to the 1997 gentlemen's agreement. The House and Senate hardened the money ceilings by passing the Budget Balancing Act of 1997, a law instead of the nonbinding House Concurrent Resolution 84. The holy grail had been captured—at least for 1997. Chairman Floyd Spence of the House National Security Committee was among those who wanted to let go of the Budget Balancing Act and authorize more money for the Pentagon than these ceilings set in the resolution:

Fiscal year	Budget Authority*	Outlays
	(In billions of dollars)	
1998	$268.2	$266
1999	270.8	265.8
2000	274.8	268.4
2001	281.3	270.1
2002	289.1	272.6

[*Budget authority* is the amount of money Congress adds to the Pentagon bank account for a single year. *Outlays* are the amounts the Pentagon can actually spend from its account in a given year. The numbers differ because the Pentagon seldom spends all of one year's appropriation in the same year it is voted. The unspent money stays in the Pentagon's bank account where it can be spent in later years.]

House Concurrent Resolution 84 as adopted by both the House and Senate also set down the amount of money the federal government should take in for the five-year period fiscal 1998 through 2002. Those numbers had the effect of setting floors, not ceilings, for government income year by year. Lawmakers therefore could not cut taxes to such an extent that the government's total income for a given year would be beneath those floors.

Title III of the resolution expressed the philosophy of the House and Senate on spending and tax cuts, including these "sense of Congress" declarations:

The Congress and the president have a basic moral and ethical responsibility to future generations to repay the federal debt, including the money borrowed from the Social Security Trust Fund.

The Congress and the president should enact a law which creates a regimen for paying off the federal debt within 30 years.

If spending growth were held to a level one percentage point lower than projected growth in revenues, then the federal debt could be repaid within 30 years.

This resolution assumes that a substantial majority of the tax cut benefits provided in the tax reconciliation bill will go to middle class working families earning less than approximately $100,000 per year and the tax cuts in the tax reconciliation bill will not cause revenue losses to increase significantly in years after 2007. . . .

The House expressed its objectives and concerns about the nation's financial future in Section 306 of the resolution, declaring:

Achieving a balanced budget by fiscal year 2002 is only the first step necessary to restore our nation's economic prosperity.

The imminent retirement of the baby-boom generation will greatly increase the demand for government services.

This burden will be borne by a relatively smaller work force resulting in an unprecedented inter-generational transfer of financial resources.

The rising demand for retirement and medical benefits will quickly jeopardize the solvency of the Medicare, Social Security and Federal Retirement Trust Funds.

The Congressional Budget Office has estimated that marginal tax rates [the highest ones] would have to increase by 50 percent over the next five years to cover the long-term projected costs of retirement and health benefits.

The Senate broadcast its alarms in Section 311 of the resolution, declaring:

Entitlement spending [money the government is contractually bound to pay out, such as Social Security, Medicare, and Medicaid checks] continues to grow dramatically as a percent of total federal spending, rising from 56 percent of the budget in 1987 to an estimated 73 percent of the budget in 2007.

This growth in mandatory spending poses a long term threat to the United States economy because it crowds out spending for investments in education, infrastructure, defense, law enforcement and other programs that enhance economic growth.

In 1994, the Bipartisan Commission on Entitlement and Tax Reform concluded that if no changes are made to current entitlement laws, all federal revenues will be spent on entitlement programs and interest on the debt by the year 2012.

Making significant entitlement changes will significantly benefit the economy, and will forestall the need for more drastic tax and spending decisions in future years. . . .

The money ceilings and floors, together with congressional philosophy, set down within House Concurrent Resolution 84 portrayed Congress's leanings and mood in 1997. The warnings about how entitlements would soon eat up most of the federal budget unless they were reduced indicated that the lawmakers realized they would have to choose between guns and butter in the future.

Lawmakers who favored guns over butter would have to mobilize quickly if they were to obtain more money for the Pentagon than the resolution allowed in the five-year period fiscal 1998 through 2002. Yet, to assault House Concurrent Resolution 84 frontally might amount to committing political suicide. After all, it was considered the holy grail by the majority of the Congress and presumably millions of American voters. Smashing this grail might look to voters like attacking mom, apple pie, and the American flag. Congressional defense hawks in 1997 and early 1998 looked for a way to rob this legislative holy grail of its powers without smashing it. Going around the grail by passing emergency appropriations bills that were not covered by the caps appeared to be the best tactic to a growing number of lawmakers as the second session of the 105th Congress got under way in 1998.

Spurning the Holy Grail

CHAIRMAN FLOYD SPENCE of the House National Security Committee was frustrated and angry in early 1998 as he prepared to hold hearings on the defense authorization bill that would set ceilings on how much the military services could spend on their far-ranging activities—everything from training soldiers to buying new airplanes—in fiscal year 1999, running from October 1, 1998, through September 30, 1999.

One military officer after another had come to Spence's office for private chats on the defense budget. They all had warned the sympathetic chairman that they could not keep their outfits ready to fight on a total defense budget of $250 billion a year plus inflation. The 1997 budget agreement set the ceiling for fiscal 1999 at $270.8 billion.

Spence told me he had asked his military visitors pointedly, "Why keep telling me? Tell the secretary of defense. Tell the president. You're part of the problem by not speaking out." Spence saw getting military officers to lobby Defense Secretary William Cohen for more money as one tactic in his fight to persuade Congress to appropriate more defense dollars and the Clinton administration to accept them.

Ever since Cohen took office in January 1997 he had been denying that there were any serious readiness problems within the Army, Navy, Air Force, or Marine Corps—certainly not in their front-line units. Spence felt Cohen's staff was keeping him in the dark about the perilous state of readiness. He wondered who was blocking all the e-mails from troops in the field about their readiness problems, such as shortages of spare parts. Congressional offices received a steady flow of such alarms. How did Cohen let himself become so isolated? Spence wondered.

Spence himself sounded the alarm about readiness every chance he got as part of his campaign to get more dollars for the armed forces. He complained that he and his committee were caught between a rock (the "holy grail" 1997 budget balancing agreement) and a hard place (the need for more defense dollars). The distressed chairman told his House colleagues in a floor speech on May 19, 1998, that his committee was recommending an underfunded defense budget to them but had no choice.

"Caught between an international geopolitical environment that requires an expansive United States national security strategy and a domestic political environment bounded by declining defense budgets locked in place by the Balanced Budget Act," Spence said, "the committee is left to figure out how best to manage risk. And there should be no illusions about the level of risk associated with the problems that our military confronts in carrying out its mission.

The Joint Chiefs of Staff recently assessed it as moderate to high. Thus, our actions in this [fiscal 1999 authorization] bill are intended to protect as best we can those programs that will help lower the risks to our national security interests by improving readiness, enhancing quality of life, and increasing the pace of which the rapidly aging equipment is modernized.

Despite the nation's extensive national security requirements and the administration's heavy use of the military all over the world, the fiscal 1999 defense budget continues for the fourteenth consecutive year a pattern of real decline in defense spending.

The president's budget request represents a 1.1 percent decline from current defense spending levels and is $54 billion short of even keeping pace with record low inflation over the next five years. The spending levels authorized in this bill are almost 40 percent lower than those of little more than a decade ago, and, in fact, represent the lowest level of inflation-adjusted defense spending since before the Korean War.

Unfortunately, it is not hard to appreciate why the unofficial motto of today's military is "doing more with less." Force structure and resources continue to decline while missions continue to increase.

Since 1987 active duty personnel have been cut by more than 800,000.

Since 1990 the Army has been reduced from eighteen to ten divisions.

Since 1988 the Navy has reduced its ships from 565 down to 346.

Since 1990 the Air Force has reduced its fighter wings from twenty-four down to twelve.

And since 1988 the United States military has closed more than nine hundred bases and facilities around the world and ninety-seven bases and facilities here at home.

At the same time our military is shrinking, operations around the world are increasing:

Between 1960 and 1991 the Army conducted ten operational events. In just the last seven years, they have conducted twenty-six such operational events.

In the seven-year period from 1982 to 1989, the Marine Corps participated in fifteen contingency operations. However, since 1989 and the fall of the Berlin Wall, they have participated in sixty-two such contingency operations.

Similarly, high operation national tempos are also impacting the Navy and the Air Force.

The threats and challenges America confronts around the world today and the resulting pressures they have placed on a still shrinking United States military have been underestimated by the administration and by many in Congress.

At this critical point in history, the mismatch between the nation's military strategy and the resources required to implement it grows larger every day. Consequently, a wide range of qualify of life, readiness, and modernization shortfalls have developed. If left unresolved, these shortfalls threaten the viability of today's All-Volunteer Force, risk a return to the hollow military of the late 1970s, and jeopardize America's ability to effectively protect and promote its national interests around the world.

Spence stressed that "these are not just my own personal conclusions.

They reflect a consensus view held by the Committee on National Security's senior leadership on both sides of the aisle." He noted that senior Democrats and Republicans had written President Bill Clinton on April 22, 1998, urging him to increase his defense budget.

Rep. Ike Skelton, ranking Democrat on the committee, reminded his colleagues that "we are operating under the restrictions of the Balanced Budget Act of 1997. The totals on defense were agreed to by both executive and legislative branches last summer. As a result, the overall total for the defense budget today, $270 billion in budget authority, which we handle in our committee, is as much a reflection of congressional priorities as it is of executive priorities. . . .

"Because of the changed economic conditions in which we find ourselves," Skelton said in reference to the booming U.S. economy and budget surpluses of early 1998, "I believe we should place an increase of defense spending on the national agenda. I believe that we can increase defense spending without having to reduce domestic spending; that we can increase defense spending and also reduce the national debt; that we can increase defense spending and still save Social Security. But we will also have to arrive at a new national consensus to do so."

An Emerging Strategy

While publicly firing away on several fronts, Spence engaged in a political version of guerrilla warfare behind the closed doors of Capitol offices. He told me that he went to House Speaker Newt Gingrich, Georgia Republican, in the summer of 1998 to seek his help in lifting the caps holding down defense funding. "I told the Speaker that I and a bunch of others would not support this year's budget resolution unless it provided more money for defense" than specified in the 1997 agreement.

"The Speaker said, 'Don't do that. Defense needs more money, but people don't know it. Use all forums to get that message out.'"

In the Senate, Majority Leader Trent Lott of Mississippi also was looking for ways to lift the caps for defense without appearing as if Congress was eating its own child, the 1997 budget-balancing legislation. Lott wrote to Clinton suggesting the need to raise the caps on defense spending. Clinton rejected the suggestion, serving notice he was not going to risk being blamed for breaking the bipartisan budget agreement.

Rebuffed by Clinton, Republican congressional leaders discussed other ways to obtain more money for defense in calendar 1998 without making a high-visibility, direct assault on the budget caps. Ted Stevens of Alaska, chairman of the Senate Appropriations Committee, favored an emergency appropriation. His House counterpart, Chairman Bob Livingston of Louisiana, told me that a wing of his party "took a dim view" of such legislative end runs. Livingston at the time had ambitions to become Speaker of the House and did not want to risk losing support of House conservatives.

The "best bet" for raising the caps on defense, Gingrich told Spence in mid-1998, was to jam extra money into a continuing resolution at the tail end of the congressional session. Such a measure is passed when Congress has failed to appropriate money to keep government departments in business for the new fiscal year. The resolution empowers the department to spend money until the appropriation is voted. Although the spending is usually limited to the previous year's level, Congress could authorize it to be higher—one way to end run the caps and give extra money to the Pentagon.

House Budget Committee Chairman John Kasich played into the hands of those trying to bust through the previously agreed upon money ceilings he had worked hard to impose. He did this by pushing through the House in 1998 a new budget resolution, despite colleagues' warnings that the Senate would not pass it. The Senate indeed did not act on the House-passed budget legislation, leaving the 1997 agreement as the only one embraced by both chambers. The majority of the Senate felt Kasich's proposed tax and spending cuts were excessive. For the first time since the House and Senate Budget committees were established in 1974, Congress in 1998 failed to pass any budget resolution at all.

Obey's Explanation

Rep. David R. Obey of Wisconsin, ranking Democrat on the House Appropriations Committee, gave me this frank, and admittedly partisan, explanation for the failure of Kasich's plan:

"What Kasich essentially did was overreach by saying, 'I'm going to
find a way to finance a tax cut no matter what the realities are, and then
Bob Livingston is going to be left to pick up the pieces.' What Kasich didn't
count on was that the Senate itself would view that as so irresponsible that
they wouldn't move on it." Kasich and his allies "put their party's political
needs for a tax cut ahead of everything else. Not that he was the driving
force behind it, but he acquiesced" to the requests of right-wing Republicans. "He's running for president. He recognizes that if you don't satisfy
the right wing you don't have the money to run for president. So they put
the need for a tax cut above everything else. The Heritage Foundation [a
conservative think tank] and all the rest. They don't give a damn about a
balanced budget. They care about tax cuts for rich people." (Kasich declined to be interviewed to give his side of the story.)

Spotlighting the Joint Chiefs

Chairmen Stevens of the Senate Appropriations Committee and Pete
Domenici of the Senate Budget Committee decided that the best way to
obtain more money for the Pentagon without making a frontal assault on
the caps was through an emergency appropriation at the end of the 1998
congressional session. They began crafting a catchall emergency appropriations bill with the help of House and Senate leaders and executives
within President Clinton's Office of Management and Budget. To help
make the case for the emergency defense appropriation and perhaps embarrass the Democratic administration as well, the Republican majority
of the Senate Armed Services Committee scheduled an open, televised
hearing for September 29, 1998, where the Joint Chiefs of Staff would be
pushed into telling the nation that Clinton's defense budget was too

small. The Chiefs' politically damaging testimony would be broadcast just before the November 2 election when all the House seats and one third of the Senate's would be up for grabs.

In a parallel effort to make the case for more money for defense, Sen. John McCain, a Vietnam War hero and prospective Republican presidential candidate in 2000, asked the commanders of the four armed services to document their military readiness in written reports to be sent directly to him. Their replies, released to the press, documented that the Chiefs wanted more money than Clinton's fiscal 1999 defense budget provided. Clinton and Democrats in Congress were faced with the choice of arguing against the nation's top military leaders or admitting that Spence and others had been right in claiming the American military's fighting edge was being lost for lack of money.

6

Heating Up the Iron

"THE COMMITTEE WILL COME to order," Chairman Strom Thurmond of the Senate Armed Services Committee declared at 9:02 A.M. on September 29, 1998, in a giant-sized hearing room in the Hart Senate Office Building. The ninety-five-year-old South Carolina Republican squinted at the four bemedaled generals and one admiral sitting side by side at the same witness table where Secretary William Cohen had sat only a few months earlier. Cohen in February had assured the senators that President Clinton's new defense budget had enough money in it to keep the armed forces ready to fight—an assurance that was about to be challenged by the very same military commanders who had echoed the assurance eight months earlier.

Continuing his opening remarks, Thurmond said that "Today, the Armed Services Committee meets to receive testimony from the Joint Chiefs of Staff on the status of the U.S. armed forces and their ability to successfully execute the national military strategy.

A number of reports have recently surfaced that indicate our military capabilities are beginning to suffer as a result of increased deployments, decreased modernization, declining pay and benefits, and insufficient funds to train the personnel, maintain the equipment, operate the facilities, and repair the infrastructure.

While these reports were once declared to be simply anecdotal evidence of readiness problems at the tactical level, they're now capturing the attention of our senior military leaders, especially Gen. David Bramlett, a former commanding general of U.S. Forces Command. The picture he paints regarding the training and Army readiness is startling and should serve as a wake-up call for the administration and members of Congress.

The Army is not alone in experiencing readiness degradation. The committee has heard testimony from other services outlining the decreased mission capable rates of equipment, decreased retention and recruitment, and the increased workload being placed upon our men and women in uniform.

The deterioration of our military capability is particularly disturbing given growing instability around the world. Asia is in the midst of economic turmoil, creating great regional instability. Russia's own economic problems have led to the increased power of hard-line nationalists. North Korea's recent launch of a three-stage missile demonstrates a strategic threat emerging much earlier than anticipated.

We are forced to retain significant U.S. military personnel in Bosnia because of continuing problems in that country while the situation in Kosovo continues to deteriorate, threatening to also pull us and our NATO allies into that troubled region.

Despite the economic sanctions of the past eight years, Saddam Hussein [of Iraq] remains a threat to U.S. interests in the Persian Gulf. There is also the global danger posed by terrorism, drug trafficking, and other transnational threats.

I believe, and have stated repeatedly, that the Clinton administration cut our forces too deeply, beginning in 1993. The additional funds that the Republican Congress provided for military modernization and readiness sustainment was siphoned off, in large part, to pay for Bosnia and other peacekeeping efforts. Several of us in the Congress, while supporting a balanced budget agreement, expressed concern that the funds provided for defense were insufficient considering the demands of our overly ambitious foreign policy.

In Defense of Clinton

Thurmond's remarks amounted to the Republican brief for providing more money for the Pentagon than the 1997 budget agreement allowed.

It fell to Sen. Carl Levin of Michigan, as the ranking Democrat on the Armed Services Committee, to take the partisan sting out of Thurmond's remarks and defend President Clinton while the television cameras whirred.

After noting that the Joint Chiefs had met with Clinton two weeks earlier at Fort McNair to discuss their readiness problems and had been assured that the administration would address them, Levin sought to make the Republican-controlled Congress share the blame for any shortfalls. He said:

> Congress and this committee also have some responsibilities in this process. After all, the level of defense spending for the last two years has been set at levels that were agreed to by both the Congress and the president. I think we have to acknowledge our own responsibility—that Congress has left undone some things that we should have done to support the readiness and modernization of our armed forces. And we've done some things that should not have been done.
>
> In our undone category is our continuing failure to allow the Department of Defense to close more bases. For the last two years Secretary Cohen and the Joint Chiefs have pleaded with Congress to give them the authority to close unneeded bases in this country to reduce overhead and cut wasteful infrastructure spending. Unfortunately, even this committee has not given the Department of Defense this authority.
>
> Just as important as how much money we give to the Department of Defense to spend is how we tell them to spend it. I went back and looked at how Congress has adjusted the defense budget in the last four years. Of the $23 billion that Congress added to the defense budget from 1995 through 1998, the vast majority, 85 percent, was added to procurement, research and development, and military construction. Only 10 percent of the money went to the personnel and operations and maintenance accounts [which] have the most immediate and direct impact on day-to-day readiness and quality of life of our military forces.
>
> Eighty-five percent of the congressional add-ons went to one-third of budget. . . . There's just too many examples where we added money for programs that the services did not request and told us that they did not need. The fiscal 1999 authorization act increases the budget request for procurement by almost $800 million and includes funding for planes and ships which are not even in the future years defense program. And it

reduces operations and maintenance funding by almost $350 million below the fiscal 1999 budget request. And that's what the Chiefs asked us not to do.

The deputy secretary of defense, John Hamre, noted in a letter to me today that of the approximately $3.1 billion in procurement and research and development programs added to the budget request in the fiscal 1999 Department of Defense authorization bill, $2.1 billion, or two-thirds, was not on the list of recommendations that we received from the Chiefs earlier this year.

In a word Levin did not use, the senators spent billions on "pork," projects the Pentagon did not want but that would benefit the home areas of politicians sponsoring the unwanted add-ons.

Thurmond then invited each of the military leaders at the witness table to make a statement. It might appear that the four generals and the admiral were revolting against civilian authority by criticizing the defense budget their commander in chief, President Clinton, had sent to Congress earlier in the year. But the real politics differed from this perception. Clinton had urged the Chiefs in their private meeting at Fort McNair to make their best case for more money. His message was that if Congress decided to lift or end run the caps on defense spending in 1998, so be it. It would not be Clinton who broke through the caps but the Republican majority in Congress. The Chiefs, too, had decided to play smart politics. They compared notes before the Senate hearing to make sure they did not contradict each other. They agreed to be unanimous in telling the senators that liberalizing the military retirement system was their number-one priority. They could explain away their seeming inconsistency by declaring that ever-changing and unforeseen circumstances make it impossible to predict their services' future money needs with precision.

"Our readiness is fraying and the long-term health of the total force is in jeopardy," Gen. Henry H. Shelton, [who had succeeded General Shalikashvili as chairman of the Joint Chiefs of Staff], told the committee. ["Total force" is Pentagonese for collectively describing the Army, Navy, Air Force, and Marine Corps.] "The U.S. military has been busier than we anticipated it would be just eighteen months ago when we completed the

Quadrennial Defense Review. . . . The good news of the nation's continuing strong economy has been bad news for our recruiting and retention as we have struggled to attract bright young people and to keep them from opting for higher paying jobs in the private sector after completing their enlistments."

Shelton urged the senators to "first" return to the old retirement system, which paid a soldier 50 percent of his base pay after twenty years of service. Congress in 1986 reduced the benefit to 40 percent in hopes of encouraging military people to stay in uniform longer. They would receive 75 percent of their base pay under that system if they served thirty years.

Gen. Dennis J. Reimer, Army chief of staff, told the committee that "If we don't do something" to address readiness and procurement problems, we run the risk of returning to the hollow Army or else run the risk of not being able to execute the national military strategy."

Adm. Jay L. Johnson, chief of naval operations, said that "With readiness as a top priority and a flat top line [on the budget], the Navy bill payers have been modernization, infrastructure, and procurement. . . . My number-one short-term concern is taking care of our people: pay, retirement, op tempo (operational tempo), and stability at home. My number-one long-term concern is enough ships to recapitalize the force we know we need, and that's at least three hundred ships. We can't sustain that Navy with the budget that we have. Our sailors are counting on us to do something now, and once again I ask for your support."

Gen. Michael E. Ryan, Air Force chief of staff, noted that although "we have the most potent Air Force in the world, . . . readiness is slipping. I'm truly concerned about the downturn in readiness, not only of the equipment but the loss of our people. If we do not reverse these trends through substantial and sustained funding of our forces, our concern that's expressed today, I believe, will rapidly turn into a readiness crisis."

The Marine Corps commandant, Gen. Charles Krulak, told the committee that "The problem is a lack of adequate funding for modernization and for the overall force."

Joint Chiefs' "Wish List": $17.5 Billion More

Chairman Thurmond asked each service chief to state his "personal opinion" on how much money above the 1997 budget caps they needed to maintain readiness and modernize their forces by buying new weapons. Their answers: Reimer, an extra $5 billion a year; Johnson, $6 billion; Ryan, $4 billion to $5 billion, not including the cost of higher pay and improved retirement; Krulak, $1.5 billion. All told, the Chiefs were asking for an extra $17.5 billion a year. That requested addition would serve as a marker for lawmakers trying to get around the caps in the 1997 budget agreement.

Not one senator on the committee suggested that the Chiefs give up a cold war weapon—such as the Army M-1 tank, the Navy $2 billion attack submarine, or the Air Force $187 million F-22 fighter—to free money to address readiness and personnel problems. Instead, the senators' negative comments zeroed in on the failure of the Chiefs to seek more money earlier instead of continuing to support the fiscal 1999 defense budget President Clinton had submitted to Congress in February 1998.

"I must say that this is almost an Orwellian experience for me," Sen. John McCain told General Shelton, "to have you here today as opposed to your appearance last February when you came before this committee and gave a dramatically different view of the readiness and requirements that the military needs to maintain our capabilities.

"General Shelton, in February you said, 'While we are undeniably busier and more fully committed than in the past, the U.S. military remains fully capable of executing national military strategy with an acceptable level of risk. I can assure the Congress that we are not returning to the 1970s. We are fundamentally healthy and will continue to report our readiness status to the Congress and the American people with candor and accuracy.'

"General Shelton, did you think that Saddam Hussein was going to join the Boy Scouts? Did you think we were going to leave Bosnia within a year, as Secretary Cohen testified before this committee that we would? Did you think that the bribe we paid to (North) Korea back in 1994 would last forever? [McCain was referring to the U.S. offer to supply civilianized rather than militarized nuclear reactors to North Korea if it would stop making nuclear weapons material.] Did you come over in February and ask for a change in the retirement system?"

Shelton replied: "The statement that I made then [in February 1998] about where we stand on readiness, I stand by today. In terms of overall, fundamentally we're healthy. But there are some troubling trends right now, trends that are going in the wrong direction."

McCain: "You stand by this statement: 'The U.S. military remains fully capable of executing the national military strategy with an acceptable risk?'"

Shelton: "With an acceptable risk—the risk having gone up, there hasn't been a significant change in that, but we are headed in the wrong direction in terms of risk."

McCain: "The fact is, that you and [the Chiefs], with the exception of the Marine Corps, were not candid with this member."

Sen. Robert C. Smith, New Hampshire Republican, complained similarly to Shelton and the service chiefs, declaring: "We're not getting direct answers until today. Does anybody have any idea of what it's like politically" to press for things the generals and admirals do not request? "How can you increase an inadequate budget that you tell us is adequate" and "sell it to the American people? That's the problem."

The Chiefs, by testifying that they could not keep their forces ready to fight under the money ceilings established in the 1997 budget agreement, had heated up the iron for those trying to bend the caps. The American military had just said it needed emergency appropriations. What politician would dare to oppose in election year 1998 a bill containing the emergency money? The appeal of holding onto the Holy Grail of fiscal discipline was fading fast.

Rep. Jack R. Murtha of Pennsylvania, ranking Democrat on the House Appropriations Subcommittee on National Security, saw a way to capitalize on the Chiefs' statement that reforming the military retirement system was their number-one priority. Murtha would seize the moment by jamming the reform into the emergency appropriations bill being written behind closed doors of the House and the Senate. The wily old marine set out to take this hill for the boys in uniform, score some points for his Democratic Party, and give fits to the Republicans who ran Congress.

Realpolitik Behind the Scenes

"JOHN, THIS IS an expensive proposition, but this is a frigging problem here," Representative Jack Murtha told Deputy Defense Secretary John Hamre in a parade ground voice with almost enough volume to reach from the Rayburn House Office Building to the Pentagon without benefit of the telephone wire connecting the two old friends.

Murtha's proposition was to scrap the military retirement program called Redux, which the Joint Chiefs of Staff had complained about a few days earlier at the September 29, 1998, Senate hearing. Instead of keeping Redux, Murtha told Hamre, the government should go back to the old system where the soldier received 50 percent of his base pay after serving twenty years, not Redux's 40 percent.

Neither Hamre nor anyone else in the Clinton administration dared ignore Murtha's demands. The Pennsylvanian could make or break an administration project by granting or holding back money for it from his powerful position of ranking Democrat on the House Appropriations Subcommittee on National Security.

The Retention Problem

Murtha reminded Hamre that thousands of experienced soldiers, sailors, airmen, and marines were quitting the All Volunteer Force (which replaced the draft in 1973) long before they reached the normal exit point of twenty years' active duty service. Recruiters in 1998 were having trouble finding fresh volunteers to fill the ranks. Murtha saw the whole All Volunteer Force in peril. He told me the nation might have to go back to the draft to provide enough soldiers for the twenty-first century military. He was determined to do what he could in these closing days of the 105th Congress to save the All Volunteer Force.

The quickest fix, Murtha had concluded from his conversations in August 1998 with officers and sailors aboard the aircraft carrier USS *Abraham Lincoln,* would be to restore the 50 percent retirement benefit before Christmas 1998. Officers and experienced sailors who knew how to run a $5 billion carrier like the *Lincoln* had complained to Murtha that the nation broke faith with them by lowering their retirement benefit from 50 percent to 40. "Why should he get 50 percent and me 40 percent when we're doing the same work?" one sailor asked Murtha and Greg Dahlberg, a staffer from the House Appropriations National Security Subcommittee, who had flown out to the Persian Gulf with Murtha to board the *Lincoln.* Some of the men on the carrier would come under the old 50 percent retirement system and others would get Redux's 40 percent.

Sitting at his Pentagon desk, Hamre spoke quietly into the phone as he responded to Murtha's booming voice. "Well, you know there are a lot of problems here," Hamre told Murtha. Hamre's deputies had calculated that raising retirement pay at the twenty-year mark from 40 percent to 50 percent would cost $15 billion for the period fiscal 2000 through 2005, an amount sure to horrify the bean counters in the White House who had not yet been clued in on Murtha's assault on Redux.

Undeterred by the caution he detected at the other end of the line, Murtha continued to press his case with Hamre. Chairman Henry Shelton of the Joint Chiefs of Staff believes that Redux is at the heart of the military's revolving-door problem, Murtha said, so what the hell is holding you and the White House back?

Hamre realized he could not slow down the hard-charging Murtha over the phone. He suggested a meeting, offering to come to Murtha's office. Who goes to whose office is a status symbol in political Washington. Hamre was deferring to Murtha. But Murtha offered to drive to the Pentagon the following Saturday morning (October 10, 1998) to lay out his battle plan.

Murtha talked up among fellow Democrats the advantages of killing Redux before the November 1998 midterm election that would in effect be a national referendum on the Democratic Clinton administration and the Republican Congress. The president's party usually loses House seats at midterm. The move to kill Redux would ease the military's recruitment and retention crunch while undercutting the Republican campaign to hold Clinton and his party responsible for the readiness problems the Joint Chiefs of Staff had just finished complaining about in the September 29 Senate hearing. Also, in his gut Murtha believed that going back to the 50 percent retirement benefit was the right thing to do; that the country owed it to the troops.

Hamre and his Pentagon deputies had an agenda, too. They wanted to improve retirement but also increase pay for the midlevel military ranks. The high-tech All Volunteer Force could not stay viable if it lost too many experienced people who manned sophisticated weapons and communications. But Hamre told Murtha that officials at the White House Office of Management and Budget doubted that better retirement would encourage more people to stay in uniform.

"Their view," Hamre told Murtha, "is that there is very little evidence that retention is being affected" by retiring at 40 percent rather than 50 percent pay. "They're taking a very hard-edged, analytical view of this problem. 'Are they leaving? No. Are they bitching? Yes, but they always bitch.' We keep saying this is a big deal, but there is very strong opposition at the White House staff level."

"Well damn it, John," Murtha boomed. "Tell those OMB bean counters to get their asses out to the field and talk to the troops before they make up their minds."

At the eleventh hour of the 105th Congress, when the crafting of the emergency supplemental appropriations bill was a touch-and-go process,

Hamre and Co. did not want to make a frontal assault on the White House to replace Redux as part of the bill. But if Murtha junked Redux on his own, be our guest. That was Hamre's thinking when Murtha settled into the chair in Hamre's conference room on the third floor of the Pentagon on October 10. Sitting in on Hamre's meeting with Murtha were Rudy de Leon, under secretary of defense for personnel and readiness; Sandy Stuart, assistant secretary of defense for legislative affairs; and a military aide.

I was not there to witness this episode, but Hamre later reconstructed it for me. It was a prime example of *realpolitik*, which *Webster's Collegiate Dictionary* defines as "politics based on practical and material factors, rather than on theoretical or ethical objectives." Murtha's campaign was a case history of the art of the possible as it is actually practiced in Washington; of how things get done; of how passion can move a bureaucracy off its fixed position, for better or worse.

"Our goal," said Hamre in reconstructing the October 10 meeting, "was to say, 'Mr. Murtha, we want to change Redux. But we don't want to do the full plan you've got. We think there's a better way to do what you're trying to do. We'd like to take two thirds of the money, and, instead of putting it on the retirement, we'd like to put it on the pay tables. We'd like to raise the pay of the midlevel military people, both officers and enlisted [whom the services need most].'"

"We were very worried about just going back to where we were" in the retirement system, Hamre told me. "We frankly thought we wouldn't get the payoff simply by repealing Redux. We thought there would be maximum benefit for the department" if there were a combination of 50 percent retirement at twenty years and raising the pay of senior noncommissioned officers (NCOs).

"Our NCOs are significantly underpaid," Hamre continued in describing the behind-the-scenes fight on the Murtha initiative. "The E-1s through E-4s [private, E-2 private, private first class, and corporal, often called specialist four] are really not badly underpaid compared to the private sector. But when you get to be an E-5, E-6, or E-7 [sergeant, staff sergeant, sergeant first class] the gap between military and civilian pay starts to widen.

"All the analytic data suggests that you get a much stronger return on your investment if you can pay people better in the near term. That will do more to hold on to people than just improving retirement."

Hamre proposed to Murtha that $5 billion be earmarked to restore the 50 percent benefit and $9 billion go to raise pay in the middle enlisted grades. The retirees would get 50 percent of their active duty pay but receive less in cost-of-living allowances under the Hamre plan. The savings from reducing the cost-of-living allowance from the full civilian price index to 1 percent less than that, the same as retired government civilians receive, would go into the pay raises.

"I like it," Murtha replied after hearing Hamre's alternative proposal. "We'll do it."

But "doing it" when the opposite party controlled the House and Senate and when President Clinton's own budget office was cool to the idea, if not outright opposed, would require Murtha to employ all the lobbying skills he had learned in his twenty-six years in Congress. Hamre, although very much on Murtha's side, would have to help from behind the lines of this battle rather than get out in front of the White House.

Complicating Factors

"We were in a very awkward spot," Hamre told me, "because in all candor the White House wasn't anxious for us to up the ante" by adding more money to the emergency supplemental appropriations bill. Hamre, the former Senate staffer, and White House operatives figured that for every dollar added to defense in the emergency supplemental the Republican conservatives would demand that a dollar be cut from Clinton's prized domestic programs, such as education.

"Fortunately Mr. Murtha was taking the lead on this thing," Hamre said. "We were able to leapfrog the politics of OMB on Redux." Hamre believed White House bean counters in OMB would have tried to derail Murtha's drive if they had known about it. They did not want to add money to Clinton's budget at this late date. So Murtha went over the heads of the OMB people and dealt with Clinton's top deputies instead.

Hamre and Co. had to get involved at the edges of Murtha's battles, however, because Chairman Bob Livingston of the House Appropriations Committee, a courtly Louisiana Republican given to sudden bursts of temper, had decreed that nothing would go into the House version of the supplemental unless the White House requested it, or at least signaled that a proposed addition would not trigger a presidential veto.

Murtha jumped into the fray with both boots, further discomfiting Republicans who were in a series of internecine fights with one set of conservatives pushing for tax cuts and another set insisting on adding billions to the Clinton defense budget before the November 1998 election. Further turmoil was caused by the usual struggle for pork, typified by Senate Majority Leader Trent Lott's championing shipbuilding money for the Ingalls yard in his state and House Speaker Newt Gingrich's insisting on making the Air Force buy more Lockheed C-130J transports, made in his home state of Georgia, than it wanted.

There was also a bidding contest under way between Chairman Ted Stevens of the Senate Appropriations Committee and Gingrich in the fall of 1998 as they built the giant emergency supplemental appropriations bill, which provided additional money not only for the Pentagon but also for scores of other government departments. The supplemental bill was growing fast as a big Christmas tree of money for almost every interest group in Congress, deterring representatives and senators from opposing it for fear of losing what their home folks would get off the tree. Stevens insisted on inserting as much money in the emergency measure for missile defense as Gingrich added for U.S. intelligence gathering. "They got into this kind of silent auction," said Hamre, who watched with dismay as $1 billion went into the supplemental for missile defense, more than the Pentagon could spend effectively, and a like amount for intelligence. Neither add-on would improve military readiness even though that supposedly was what the defense money fight in the closing days of the 105th Congress was all about.

"The White House was beside itself with joy," one top administration official told me, because under the Stevens-Gingrich dollar-for-dollar agreement, the more each Republican leader added to the supplemental for defense, the more Democrat Clinton could add for his domestic programs under the "what's-good-for-the-goose-is-good-for-the-gander" modus operandi of the fevered, last-minute budget negotiations. The result was the realpolitik of the Pentagon budget in the preadjournment rush of late 1998. "The Republicans never homed in" on these nondefense additions "because they were so busy doing this little bidding war among themselves," said the administration insider. "If they had said, 'You want $300 million for climate change? Let's go public with that and see if you have any support.' The White House would have lost."

By the time Murtha made his assault on the emergency supplemental appropriations bill to add money for reform of military retirement, the bill had become part of a $221 billion Christmas tree taking 919 pages to print. Many members of Congress freely admitted that they did not have time to read the monster before voting on it.

Murtha ran into resistance from the authorizers, members of the House and Senate armed services committees who recommend dollar ceilings for weapons and other Pentagon projects. They lost much of their power when the House and Senate Budget committees were formed in 1974 to set ceilings on spending by the Pentagon and other government departments. The authorizers were fighting in 1998 to hold on to what little authorizing power they had left, with John W. Warner of Virginia and Carl Levin of Michigan leading the way in the Senate. Warner and Levin, ranking Republican and Democrat, respectively, on the Armed Services Committee, shot at the Murtha proposal, arguing that it was too important and complicated to be slam-dunked into the emergency appropriations bill. Murtha fired back from his powerful post as ranking Democrat on the House Appropriations Subcommittee on National Security, declaring that "we're not going to put anything into the supplemental for national missile defense until we take care of the troops." Missile defense was at the top of the Republican add-on list.

Murtha wheeled and dealed to get the White House on his side, telling Erskine Bowles, Clinton's chief of staff and field marshal for the emergency appropriations bill, that his office should put the Redux initiative on its list of add-ons. Bowles bucked Murtha's plea to a deputy, Jack Lew, deputy director of the OMB. Lew heard Murtha out and then called Hamre for a fuller explanation because, as Murtha put it, "Redux is a complicated son of a bitch." Despite the explanations from Murtha and Hamre, and even though General Shelton had told the Senate that fixing the retirement system was his top priority when it came to improving the military's readiness, Lew and his colleagues "didn't get the urgency of it," Murtha said.

Murtha said that he went to Rep. David R. Obey, ranking Democrat on the House Appropriations Committee, who in turn sought advice from Greg Dahlberg, the subcommittee staffer who winnowed wheat from chaff for the lawmakers so they could make an informed judgment on such costly and involved proposals. "I'm for it," Obey told Murtha.

Obey was a key ally because the Democrats had entrusted the Wisconsinite to be their chief negotiator for the complicated and politically explosive emergency supplemental. Shortly after Murtha had enlisted his support, Obey met with Bowles and Lew in the office of Senate Minority Leader Thomas A. Daschle, South Dakota Democrat.

"You ought to grab this thing and do it," Obey said he told Bowles and Lew of Murtha's Redux plan, "because it would be good substantively and politically. I want to offer it to the Republicans" for insertion in the catchall emergency appropriations bill. "We'll win either way. If they accept it, we'll win substantively. If don't accept it, we'll win politically."

The congressional appeals court for Obey's offering such an insert to the bill consisted of the Big Four: the chairmen, Livingston and Stevens, and the ranking Democrats, Obey and Robert C. Byrd, West Virginia, respectively, on the House and Senate Appropriations committees. If the Big Four could not resolve a given issue, it was bucked up to Speaker Gingrich, Senate Majority Leader Lott, and the White House—the equivalent of a congressional supreme court for such budget exercises.

"I offered Stevens the package" at a Big Four meeting, Obey told me in reconstructing the presentation of the Murtha initiative. "He was obviously very uncomfortable about it. He obviously didn't want to be on record a opposing the damn thing. Stevens and Livingston were concerned about the costs. They said, 'Let's see it.' Obey said he had found a way to cut the price in half by reducing the cost-of-living allowances. At that point, Obey quoted Stevens as saying: " 'Well, the authorizers are against it.'

"I got to tell you," Obey said to me, "that there were five hundred items in the damn bill that the authorizers were against. So I pushed it to an official act on their part. They [Stevens and Livingston speaking for the Republicans in Congress] said, no; they weren't going to take it."

Later, in a Democratic strategy meeting on the emergency budget appropriation in the office of House Minority Leader Richard Gephardt, Missouri Democrat, Obey said he told Bowles and Lew that "they ought to lay the issue back on the table" by formally requesting that the Redux redo be included in the bill.

The White House Offer

Shortly after that—on Sunday, October 11, 1998, at 12:45 P.M.—Obey and other top budget negotiators met with Clinton at the White House. After a brief discussion with the president, Obey said he and the others closeted themselves with Bowles and John D. Podesta, White House deputy chief of staff.

"I walked them through it," Obey said of his briefing on the Redux package. "We agreed that they ought to go back and put it on the table again" for inclusion in the catch-all bill. "They did, but in kind of a confused fashion."

All this time Murtha kept charging along his own path toward the objective. "Stevens turned it down," Murtha said, "because Warner was against it. Then Erskine offered it to Trent Lott and to Gingrich. They turned it down the first time.

"I called Jimmy Dyer," the Republicans' staff director for the full House Appropriations Committee, who would advise Stevens on what to do about Murtha's Redux initiative.

"I said, 'Jimmy, what the hell happened here? They [the White House] offered it' [the overhaul of Redux].

"'They weren't really strong,'" Dyer said of the White House offer regarding Redux.

"I said, 'Jeez, what do you mean strong? It's hard enough to get the frigging White House to agree. What are you talking about strong? They offered the damn thing.'"

"Jim said, 'Well, have them offer it again.'"

The White House did so, Murtha said, but this second request failed to persuade Stevens, the Senate's top appropriator, to go against the wishes of two of the Senate's top authorizers, Warner and Levin. Gingrich and Lott were not willing to use their power to get Murtha's addition into the final version of the $221 billion omnibus appropriations bill.

Obey said the Big Four bucked the Redux proposal up to Gingrich, Lott, and Bowles. Gingrich refused to insert it in the bill, stopping Murtha, Obey, and their allies in their tracks.

"I thought we had it," said Murtha. "I couldn't believe they turned the son-of-a-bitch down. I did my work. I convinced the White House. Livingston was for it. [Chairman C. W. "Bill"] Young [of the House Appropriations National Security Subcommittee] was for it. Floyd Spence was for it. Ike Skelton was for it. All these guys were for it."

Chairman Shelton of the Joint Chiefs, who had persuaded the commanders of all four armed services to list fixing retirement as their number-one priority during their high visibility appearance before the Senate Armed Committee on September 29, telephoned Murtha to thank him for his effort. Both old soldiers vowed to keep pressing on toward the objective.

Days after Murtha's legislative charge was thrown back, Obey said White House aide Podesta visited him in his office in the Rayburn House Office Building. "I asked him why in hell they hadn't insisted on this item. When I walked him through it again, he said, 'Oh hell, that's the first time I really understood it. It's a winner either way.' He committed to putting it in the White House budget" to be sent to Congress in 1999.

I asked Obey why Gingrich, who had assailed Clinton for allowing military readiness to decline, opposed the Murtha retirement fix that the Joint Chiefs of Staff sought. "I think the Republicans simply wanted to delay it for a year and try to do it on their own in 1999," the House Democrats' top budget negotiator on the emergency appropriations bill replied. He said Gingrich's top priority during the negotiations was getting an extra billion for U.S. intelligence agencies while Livingston pressed for accelerating a homeland missile defense. "Their position was, 'Let's get what we want now and then come back and revisit this next year,'" Obey told me. "They also wanted to deny this [Redux substitute] to Clinton" for fear it would blunt their charge that he was responsible for the military's readiness problems.

The seesaw battle over Redux drew in most of the power centers of the federal government. But the public got only glimpses of the contest where $15 billion of its tax dollars were at stake. Most of the nation's press neglect to zero in on such complicated but important behind-the-scenes battles. Congress managed to hide its wheeling and dealing on the supplemental by shortcutting the standard legislative process, which would have included hearings where pros and cons could be aired. Instead, Congress wrote a law costing the taxpayers $221 billion mostly in the dark.

Livingston Blames, and Explains, the Process

"That shouldn't happen," House Appropriations chairman Bob Livingston told me. "Frankly, I lay principal blame on the budget process." Since 1974 when the House and Senate Budget committees entered the process by setting ceilings on spending for every government department, he said, "we've spent months and months on determining what the budget should be, and then a few weeks ignoring it. These mindless and rigid guidelines, the caps" on how much government departments can spend in a given fiscal year, "don't mean much if they're unrealistic and you've got to bust them at the end" of the congressional session. "If you're in a war, it makes no sense to say you're going to live within the caps no matter what the caps are.

"You've got this rigidity built into this ridiculous budget process," Livingston continued. "Clearly, we need to save money" and abiding by the caps set by the Budget committees is one way to do it. "But when the process broke down" in 1998 because the House and Senate could not write a mutually acceptable budget resolution setting caps, "and you dithered, dickered, and just fiddled around so you didn't start the appropriations until late July, the Republican majority virtually handed Clinton the keys to the Treasury because they gave him a crisis. All he had to do was sit back and say, 'I want X amount of extra dollars for my priorities'" in the emergency supplemental appropriation "or else we're closing the government down. When it puts it in that frame, our guys [the Republicans] get all nervous because we already did that in 1995. We got blamed for it even though he didn't sign the [appropriations] bills. So they're [the Republicans] are hysterical and will do anything to keep from shutting the government down, which means they're giving him the opportunity to extract tribute of tens of billions of dollars more than they wanted."

An orderly process of providing money for the Pentagon and other government departments, Livingston said, "would simply include setting a target; saying that's our target, it's not going to be mindless, and get that part of the process out of the way early in the year" so the Appropriations committees could begin their work early in the congressional session instead of waiting until the last minute to make the big funding decisions. The chairman said Congress either has to acknowledge that the caps may be lifted for emergencies or "you've got to be prepared to say early, up front, what you're going to cut" to stay within the caps after appropriating money for unexpected wars or natural disasters such as hurricanes and floods. "Whenever they get into these wars," Livingston said of executive branch leaders, "they never, ever say, 'OK, we'll cut this in return for that.'"

Livingston said he found it ironic that Congress reformed its budget process in 1974, creating the Budget committees and empowering them to establish money ceilings, "and the astronomical deficits this country ran were all subsequent" to that attempt to impose fiscal discipline on the U.S. government. "We literally never really had more than a $3 billion to $4 billion deficit until after 1974, and then it went to the hundreds of billions of dollars. I think that was directly attributable to an inoperable, foolish budget process." Although Livingston did not mention it, President Ronald Reagan's big defense buildup, accompanied by "supply-side economics" tax cuts, also helped to widen the federal government's gap between income and outgo.

"The military doesn't get hurt, the taxpayers get hurt, and the process" of determining such questions as how much is enough for defense "gets hurt" by Congress's budget system, Livingston said.

The reason the military did not get hurt in Congress's last minute grab-bag emergency appropriation of 1998, Livingston added, "was that there were a lot of things the military wanted and should have gotten and was prevented from getting by the administration, which has been overly restrictive on the Defense Department over the last several years, that Congress knew it had to pay for eventually." The military got the money through "the back door" with the emergency supplemental. "Was it thoughtful and orderly? No. Was there waste built into that process? Of course. Absolutely."

Had the appropriations process "begun in a more orderly fashion without all this charade of maintaining the caps at first and then busting them later" with the emergency supplemental, "you wouldn't have had that waste," the House Appropriations chairman contended.

I asked Livingston at this point to pretend he was explaining to an Army major sitting in a war college classroom why Congress handles dollars for defense and other government activities in such a sloppy, wasteful way.

"Well, major," Livingston began, "you have the advantage of a bifurcated government. It's the worst of all possible systems except there aren't any better. If one person made all the decisions it would be much more orderly but much more stupid and perhaps much more dangerous. So you have to accept the good with the bad. And as much as I might decry some of the foolishness in the process, the fact is that I take great pride in having participated in it for twenty-two years and trying to make it work. Could we make it work a lot better? Of course we could. But it's not a matter of throwing up your hands in despair and running away and saying let's chuck the system for something else. There isn't anything better. You can tweak the system. Unfortunately there are not enough people in Congress who truly understand how the budget process works and how to restrain the appropriations process in an orderly manner. It's a difficult process. It takes a lot of thought. There's no easy answer. It takes a lot of schmoozing, a lot of communication between people who have philosophical and managerial differences of opinion. But it can be done better than it is.

"For the military, Congress is a reactionary force," Livingston continued in his mock explanation to the mythical major. "When we see something going wrong, we can fix it. Unfortunately, we often wait until the last minute. We're crisis oriented. For example, right now you have a tremendous fall off in enlistments" into the armed services and in retaining those already in uniform. At some point Congress will accelerate its efforts to solve those problems by appropriating more money for housing and retirement pay for military people, Livingston predicted. "The machinery grinds slowly, but the biggest problems do get addressed sooner or later. Does the delay cause military people to become disenchanted and leave the service? We already know a lot of them have. So Congress has to be inventive and figure out how to fix" the exodus problem.

"We're going to have another problem" in the future "because this administration has not seen fit to replenish its declining reserves of tanks, planes, and ships. That tells me that probably within the next two to five years we're going to be on a crash program to build new ships. It's simply a matter of Congress's suddenly saying, 'OK. We've got to face up to it.' The pressure has got to mount. And it will mount. And it will be addressed in terms of national security. You can question whether it will mount quickly enough to meet contingencies."

Obey, Livingston's political rival and personal friend, not only believes the process for providing dollars for defense is "an abomination" but also has strong convictions about how to improve it. He expressed to his House colleagues his sorrow about voting for the emergency appropriations. The bill, he told them, "represents an absolute, total institutional failure. We should not be here in this position, but we are, and we have to make some hard choices, given the only choices before us. That is why I will reluctantly urge a yes vote on this proposal."

The Upshot

Members of the House and Senate voted overwhelmingly for the omnibus appropriations bill and President Clinton signed it into law. Upon close examination, it turned out that the Defense Department received only $7.8 billion of the $21 billion in supplemental funds inserted into the giant measure. And only about $4.0 billion of that $7.8 billion went for operation and maintenance, the fund that contains money for spare parts, training, and other readiness needs of the military.

Shortly before Christmas 1998 the Clinton administration took the unusual step of unveiling part of the president's fiscal 2000 defense budget before it went to Congress. The new budget, administration officials disclosed, called for scrapping Redux, restoring the 50 percent retirement benefit, and raising military pay. The disclosure was apparently designed to preempt the Republicans on that issue and reassure the troops that their concerns were being addressed by President Clinton. "I've got the money," Defense Secretary William Cohen told the troops over the Christmas season in referring to increases in the budget to go to Congress in 1999.

Was Congress's 1998 end run of the 1997 caps the beginning of another Reagan-style spending binge on missile defense and other military programs, or was it a one-time spastic reaction to readiness problems spotlighted in an election year? What did the abominable process—to use Dave Obey's word—of hammering together the emergency supplemental say about the inside politics of providing America's guns and soldiers? For answers I went to Obey, a thoughtful lawmaker who had been a participant and observer in that scene since 1969 and did not mind shouting out when he saw a king with no clothes. He does so in the next chapter.

8

Is There a Better Way?

DAVID R. OBEY of Wausau, Wisconsin, walks and talks like a farmer who would keep you laughing with wisecracks and put-downs as he showed you around the barn and the lower forty of his place. There would be a mortar of wisdom between the wisecracks, however. You would expect him to say in his twangy, broken voice, "The damn gov'ment," at least once every five minutes. But you sure as hell would not expect this man to be part of the gov'ment. Not until he let you get deeper inside him, anyway.

In the House, Obey was considered irascible and highly partisan by friend and foe alike. But no one could rightly accuse Dave Obey of being shallow. He thought deeply about the nation's problems and how to solve them, including how to provide the best defense without bankrupting the nation in the process.

Obey since being elected to the House in 1969 had seen the best and worst of the inside politics of providing America's guns and soldiers. Chosen to chair the powerful House Appropriations Committee in 1994 when the Democrats were the majority party, Obey participated in the government's top budget negotiations. Because the Republicans won back control of the House in 1994, Obey held the chairmanship for only one year. But he remained a power as ranking Democrat on the committee and most likely would regain the chairmanship if the Democrats regained control of the House before Obey decided to retire.

In the primarily dairy state of Wisconsin, Obey is not dependent on the defense industry to win reelection. His views about the process of providing for America's defense, and how it could be improved, are those of a relatively free politician.

Son of a factory worker, Dave Obey has been part of government since 1962 when, at the age of twenty-four, he was elected to the Wisconsin state legislature. In 1969 he wrested a House seat from the Republicans when he was elected to fill the seat of Melvin R. Laird, who had resigned from Congress to become President Richard Nixon's secretary of defense.

Obey had been in the House one year short of three decades when we talked about the "abomination" of the emergency appropriations bill. He had both a love for and despair of Congress because, like an undependable farm, it sometimes redeemed his hard work. Other times it left him with nothing to show for his labors. Yet, the Wisconsinite could never bring himself to give up on the place, for, by God, next year there might, just might, be a bumper crop of legislative accomplishment.

The witty, shrewd, compassionate, and explosive Obey sometimes compared debating on the House floor with standing in a bacon bin out West where farmers keep live pigs stacked up in one pen atop another: "Inside, the shit really flies," he said of both places. This was certainly true of the defense debates over the years. Despite all the speeches members of Congress made in 1995, 1996, and 1997 about the need to upgrade the readiness of the armed forces, Obey said, little of the $17 billion Congress added to the president's defense budget went into readiness accounts. He decried the fact that only $2.5 billion of the $17 billion in add-ons went into the operation and maintenance account, which pays for training troops and operating tanks, ships, and aircraft.

Congress "No Help"

"If you stretched the definition" of what accounts make the armed forces more ready to fight, "at most a total of $5 billion was for readiness. When you look at the internal mix" of where congressional add-ons go, "the Pentagon is getting no help from the Hill" in its efforts to upgrade readiness and restructure forces.

"If you look at the people in Congress who have the power levers," continued Obey, "the Pentagon is getting no help from them to help refashion its response to the new century. The Pentagon has begged for additional base closings and they say no."

The veteran lawmaker also lambasted Congress for continuing to appropriate money for the B-2 bomber after the Joint Chiefs of Staff testified they did not want it. He similarly assailed his colleagues for rejecting the General Accounting Office's recommendation to withhold production money for the Air Force F-22 fighter until it was more fully flight tested.

In 1997, Obey continued, "[House Speaker Newt] Gingrich attacked the White House for having an intelligence budget that was too low, and then he agreed to cut it some more in order to fund, among other things, [Senate Majority Leader Trent] Lott's [DDG-21] destroyer" to be built in the Ingalls shipyard at Pascagoula in Lott's state of Mississippi, and "Gingrich's C-130J" transport planes to be built in his home area of Marietta, Georgia.

Besides such lobbying by leaders of Congress, its committees entrusted to oversee the Pentagon budgets act like "a pork machine," Obey contended. Members of those committees concentrate on saving or creating defense jobs for their constituents back home, instead of considering the needs of the nation as a whole.

"I think the way we review many parts of the budget has become dysfunctional," he said. The way Congress reviews the Pentagon "has certainly become dysfunctional. Congress instead of being the watchdog is the dog that has to be watched. I think there is a reason for that, philosophical and geographical.

"Philosophically, the Republicans have taken over Congress [by win-ning the majority of the seats in the House and Senate in 1994, 1996, and 1998], and they are much more conservative than Democrats. So they are naturally inclined to cut domestic programs to fund defense.

"But there is also a huge, regional imbalance in terms of power and the way it plays out with the defense budget. If you look at the major players, it's harder than hell to find any [of those players] outside of Texas, Florida, Louisiana, Mississippi, South Carolina, and Virginia. This GAO report states that over 40 percent of military procurement goes to four states."

Obey as he spoke patted a blue-covered paper report issued in August 1998 by the General Accounting Office, the investigatory arm of Congress. Entitled, "DEFENSE SPENDING: Trends and Geographical Distribution of Prime Contract Awards and Compensation," the twenty-seven-page re-port states that "four states—California, Virginia, Texas and Florida—accounted for $81 billion, or about 40 percent, of Department of Defense prime contract awards and Department of Defense compensation. In 1988 the same four states accounted for 39 percent of the total and, again in 1992, they accounted for 39 percent of the total." The five states that in-creased their shares of defense prime contracts the most between 1988 and 1997, GAO discovered from examining Pentagon records, were, in descending order of increase, Georgia, home state of Speaker Gingrich; Virginia, home of John Warner, the senior Republican on the Senate Armed Services Committee, who became its chairman in 1999; Florida, home of Chairman Bill Young of the House Appropriations National Se-curity Subcommittee in 1998 and the full committee in 1999; Kentucky, home of both Senate Minority Whip Wendell H. Ford and Rep. Ron Lewis, a Republican on the National Security Committee; and Hawaii, home of Sen. Daniel K. Inouye, a senior Democrat on the Senate Appropriations Committee.

Knowledge Is Power

If an aircraft factory or shipyard is in a representative's or senator's back-yard, Obey said, he or she will learn more about aircraft and ships than his or her congressional colleagues. The lawmaker will employ that expertise to win arguments during closed-door debates on how much money should go to what accounts in the annual defense budget. The net result, Obey said, is that the lawmakers who know the most about defense programs from direct exposure to them "have the least incentive to actually change the way the budget is shaped." To do so would cost jobs and generate political heat from workers and contractors.

As a result, Obey continued, the civilian leaders have to buck not only the stand-pat military services as they try to change the Pentagon, but also their champions in Congress. "Congress is the major impediment to change at this point. It will add money to the Pentagon budget, but primarily to keep the [Lockheed Martin] C-130 [transport plane] going, the F-22 [fighter], the B-2 bomber." The Pentagon budget "has become the new public works bill."

Because there is no enemy aircraft matching the fighter planes the United States already has flying, such as the Lockheed F-16 and McDonnell Douglas F-15E fighter bombers, Obey reasoned, a logical person would not rush into building a new Air Force fighter like the F-22, which costs $187 million a plane. He termed it "outrageous" for the Air Force to assert that "the reason we have to build the F-22 in the first place is because we sold so many goddam F-16s around the world that we have to keep a qualitative edge over them. Goddamighty! So then we say, 'OK. We'll put a limit on your ability to sell the F-16s abroad.' And then they say, 'You can't do that because it costs jobs.'"

Livingston's Amiable Dissent

Chairman Bob Livingston of the House Appropriations Committee has always been a hawkish lawmaker and has done what he could to help the Avondale shipyard in his home area. He thought Obey had overstated the problem of lawmakers' distorting the defense budget and wasting taxpayer dollars to create jobs back home.

"You're always going to have parochial interests," Livingston told me in a separate interview. "You're always going to have people who have interests back home that they want to protect. That's human nature. You're not going to turn the Congress into a bunch of nuns.

"I think the process" of defending the nation "did get too heavily bureaucratized, with the best of intentions perhaps," through congressional reforms. The reformers tried "to rein in the abuses and indiscretions of the procurement officers in the Pentagon" but in doing so compounded paperwork, complicated requirements, and added too much oversight. "You had people watching the watchers."

Is the process of providing national defense "an efficient, greased, well-working system?" Livingston asked rhetorically. "No. We spend too much on bureaucracy. The real purchasers, the war fighters, are probably the last ones to be consulted in selecting the weapons. But even they cannot anticipate what's going to work and what's not. It is a political process. I do not think that by taking the process" of buying weapons and raising armies "out of the hands of the Congress, which I don't think would ever be done, you're necessarily going to improve the process. It's just a matter of whose subjective decision is ultimately going to carry the day.

"I think oftentimes that members of Congress create great benefit to the system because they sit back somewhat apart from the machinations between bureaucracy and administration and the military man who wants virtually all the bells and whistles. The members of Congress select with a rather impartial view those things that work.

"I can remember during the Afghan war that the military did not have the better answers. Guys like [Rep.] Charlie Wilson [Texas Democrat] stepped up and said" to the Afghanis fighting the invading Soviets, "'Do you need Stingers? [heat-seeking antiaircraft missiles to knock down Soviet planes and helicopters]. 'We're going to get you Stingers. Do you need antimine detonation cords? We're going to give you those.' Frankly, if it hadn't been for Charlie Wilson the Russians might still be in Afghanistan."

It took Representative Jack Murtha and other members of Congress, not the Pentagon, to get comfortable and durable boots for American troops, Livingston added.

"Impediments to Discipline"

I asked Obey how he would restrain the politicking on the defense budget to get more bang for the taxpayer's buck. I reminded him that the House and Senate Budget committees had been established in 1974 to discipline the process; that they seemed to have been successful in setting money ceilings in 1997, only to have those widely hailed ceilings exceeded in 1998 through what Obey called the "abominable" passage of the emergency appropriations bill.

"I think they are an impediment to discipline," Obey said of the Budget committees. He was not at all inhibited by my tape recorder spinning on his desk in his congressional office. "That may seem weird," he acknowledged. "But in my view, all that ever happens when you pass a budget resolution is that you pass an institutional press release which says you're going to hit certain targets.

"I voted against the Clinton budget deal in 1997 because I thought it was a goddam public lie on the part of the White House and the congressional leadership because we were promising in those out years to hit spending levels that anybody who knew the pieces knew they would not reach. So now, what have you got? You've got them looking for ways to reinvent bookkeeping," such as pressuring the Congressional Budget Office to rejigger its arithmetic and simply not count certain spending, euphemistically called "directed scoring."

"No matter which party runs" the operation of setting money ceilings for the Pentagon and other government departments within a budget resolution, "this place puts so much goddam energy into passing the budget resolution, which has no force of law, that the congressional leadership has exhausted its ability to get people in line" to do anything else that is real about disciplining the government's budgeting.

"Yet when you match micro with macro," the comparison of money needed for individual programs with money allowed for them in the budget resolutions, "it shows your macro stuff was just B. S. The Budget Committee should be called the B.S. Committee. Not because it purposely lies, but because it promises things that the institution [of Congress] will not produce."

Livingston agreed with Obey here, declaring that the House and Senate Budget committees eat up legislative time that could be used more profitably by the House and Senate Appropriations committees.

Also dysfunctional, Obey contended, are the House National Security and Senate Armed Services authorizing committees, which are supposed to assess the Pentagon's policies, determine how much money should go to what weapon, and how many people the armed services should keep on active duty in the year under review. "The problem with them," Obey, an appropriator, said, "is that they are spending so much time trying to line item [assess every research and procurement project in the vast Pentagon budget] that they don't spend nearly enough time on the thinking part of their job. They are competing with appropriations in trying to be bookkeepers and power brokers on pork. Instead of looking at every weapons system in terms of where it is going to be used conceptually, they look at it in terms of where it's made. So all they do is provide an additional finger on the cash register to ring up sales. But they don't do nearly enough long-term thinking.

"I don't think it's any accident that Les Aspin [the Wisconsin Democratic representative who left the chairmanship of the then House Armed Services Committee in 1993 to become President Clinton's first defense secretary, only to be fired from the post] was not defined as a great success as a defense secretary. He was about the only guy who did any thinking about the shape of the Pentagon. And it was because he came from a state where he didn't have any vested interests." Georgia Democrat Sam Nunn, former chairman of the Senate Armed Services Committee, was thoughtful like Aspin but "was sort of captive" of the big defense contractors, such as Lockheed Martin in his home state of Georgia, Obey said.

I asked Obey if the House National Security and Senate Armed Services authorizing committees were worse in 1998 than they were early in the cold war when two venerable Georgia Democrats, Rep. Carl Vinson and Sen. Richard B. Russell, ran those committees in a dictatorial manner.

"It was a different time," Obey replied. "Even though they were pushing pork, everybody agreed on what kind of stuff we needed" to counter the threat of the Warsaw Pact threatening Western Europe. "We had an enemy; we thought we knew what the threat was even though the Central

Intelligence Agency grossly overestimated the strength of the Soviet economy. So it was more, 'Well, we know what we need. It's just an argument over where it is going to be produced.' But today, with the collapse of the Soviet Union and the changing nature of technology, you've got an entirely different set of threats. It's not that the pork barreling is any worse than before. It's just that it has worse consequences because we need to be moving to prepare against a different set of threats. And we're not doing it very significantly," partly because of Congress's resisting change. "And so you're not getting very much of a bang for your buck."

Although Obey did not exempt fellow members of the Appropriations committees from his broadside attack against congressional review of the Pentagon, he said that "at least intellectually some of them understand the problems" being generated by continuing to prepare for the previous war. However, most of them "come off at the same place" because of the pressure to satisfy the demands from their colleagues to throw defense business to their states.

"If I were czar, I wouldn't have a budget resolution because it's an institutional press release that lies. I would merge the House Appropriations Committee and the House Ways and Means Committee. [Ways and Means writes the tax legislation that raises money for the government.] I would take away from the merged committee those issues which were not directly related to taxation or budget and turn them over to committees like Commerce and Agriculture.

"One of the main reasons we have been having so much difficulty in staying near balance on the budget is because the committee that has the responsibility for spending—the Appropriations Committee—isn't the same committee that has the responsibility for the taxing" needed to raise the money to be spent. Instead of linking spending and taxing, Obey lamented, Congress in establishing House and Senate Budget committees "set up this Rube Goldberg budget operation which pretends that a bunch of people without institutional power can force the institution to do something by having a bunch of accounting rules. It hasn't worked. If you look at how much the deficits have exceeded the estimates, they did it by much less before we had the Budget Act than we have since.

"Right now all that happens politically is that you produce a budget resolution, and then the press only asks one question: Does it get to the targets" of zero deficit budgets? "And the public isn't paying enough attention to know if it gets there for real or on the sly. And the press, by and large, doesn't write that, either," to help the public make a judgment. "So you don't get any real" accountability. "You pretend that you put out a budget that meets the goal, no matter whether it's the White House or the Congress that does it. Once you play that 'Let's Pretend' game out front, then the heat's off" because neither the press nor anyone else looks under the numbers which promise a balanced budget. It then falls to the chairmen of the Appropriations committees "to struggle with realities."

During that struggle, Obey said, the Budget committees have no power to enforce what is in their resolutions. "They've got some rules and regs, but no political power. Kasich [John Kasich, chairman of the House Budget Committee] doesn't scare anybody. He doesn't have anything to take away or to give people. That's why I say for budget purposes I would merge Appropriations and Ways and Means and have them become the Budget Committee because what they agreed to would be deliverable. You'd start out with a lot more honest statement of what your goals are, you'd have a hell of a lot more chance of meeting them, and we'd all be a hell of a lot less discredited than we are right now."

Here Livingston distanced himself from part of Obey's suggested reforms, declaring: "David has pushed for a revision of the budget process" in many ways, "much of which I agree with. If you want to find a superfluous committee, just look at the Budget Committee. I think it's a waste of time. They're supposed to set targets. Instead they try to do everything for everybody."

As for merging Appropriations and Ways and Means and eliminating the House Armed Services Committee, which authorizes but does not appropriate money for the Pentagon, Livingston said, "I'm not convinced a bifurcated process is inoperable. I think authorizers are needed to do in-depth investigations of particular problems in the military. The appropriators come at these problems from a different perspective so there is a certain degree of check and balance there."

Under Obey's suggested reform, Livingston said, "if Ways and Means folks tell us how much money is available, then the appropriators can just spend it. But when you get any one group, it gets so vested with authority and power that there are fewer checks. Then the system does tend to go awry. Livingston opposed the idea of merging the House Appropriations and Ways and Means committees into what Obey would call the budget committee. Some congressional committee chairmen "are going to be great and some are going to be terrible," Livingston acknowledged. But he said the system of government that raises, pays, arms, and deploys military forces "will survive that. We just have to not opt for the simple solutions. So many quick, easy fixes are suggested in Congress to fix the budget process. The solutions have to be worked down with common sense and open dialogue, and America will get there."

Elaborating why he is more critical of the budgeting process than his good friend Bob Livingston, Obey said, "I feel very frustrated by the fact that the system as now constituted is not delivering what it needs to deliver. There is virtually no congressional oversight," a situation aggravated in 1998 by the obsession in Congress and elsewhere with President Clinton's personal conduct with one-time White House intern Monica Lewinsky. "There's political oversight; there's gotcha oversight on politics, but on policy there is far too little thoughtful oversight on policy going on in this place." Obey wanted one kind of oversight, where committees would examine the policies of the executive branch in depth to learn and debate their effects on all the citizens, not just those in a given congressional district, and on the world beyond Washington.

"The authorizing committees are either trying to investigate or be involved in the appropriating process," Obey said. "They are not exercising their oversight responsibility. They aren't long-scoping these issues by and large. You've got a bunch of committee chairs who are so busy playing the short-term political game that they aren't thinking about the long-range problems. You've got people talking about how we ought to have two-year appropriations. Hell, we haven't been able to get one-year appropriations through this place.

"What you really need are multiple-year authorizations so the authorizing committees when they are not bringing bills to the floor are looking at how these damn programs are actually working and looking at what the long-term needs are. And nowhere is that more important in defense where you have the big bucks. [Under a multiple-year authorization for a new airplane, for example, the money would be approved for a four-year period in one bill, rather than authorized every year for four years.]

Another reason the American military was not restructured for the twenty-first century after the cold war ended in 1989, Obey maintained, was that Clinton was unwilling to take on military leaders and order change. A number of lawmakers believe Clinton was intimidated by his own lack of military service and efforts to avoid being drafted for the Vietnam War. "I half-kiddingly said this is the last time I will support any presidential nominee who does not have two Congressional Medals of Honor, six Silver Stars, and fourteen Purple Hearts. If they don't have medals, presidents are at a disadvantage every time they try to speak out on defense because the Establishment eats them for lunch."

Chairman Livingston once again agreed with his political rival. "I don't think we have had any real long-range planning for many years" on how the American military should be structured and what it should and should not do in the world," Livingston said. But, unlike Obey, he blamed "the president and some members of Congress" for intimidating the military. Obey's objection was just the opposite, that President Clinton deferred to the generals and admirals rather than command them. Livingston maintained that military leaders during the Clinton years have not had the freedom "to do what they thought was right." They were hamstrung "by a lot of politicizing and social agendas and stuff that transcend common sense."

To develop and impose long range plans that make sense militarily, Livingston said, "you need a strong president who understands the military and is prepared to back it up. Bill Clinton has no credibility when it comes to dealing with this military establishment because he really doesn't understand it."

Asked how even a president with credibility in the military's eyes could get Congress to go along with restructuring the armed forces to meet the post–cold war threats, Livingston, the veteran lawmaker, replied: "I don't think you get evolutionary reform just by putting together a single package. I think it's incremental, especially with this system; this Congress; any

Congress. The president is going to have to make his proposals and sell them by force of his moral authority as commander in chief of the armed forces. That's not happening right now."

Besides expressing his dismay over the lack of proper congressional oversight of the Pentagon and its programs, Obey told me in a voice heavy with regret that the U.S. government failed to exploit the "very rare opportunity" between the end of the cold war and the emergence of another major threat to reflect on where the military should be going in the new century and start it moving in that direction.

"There is not a military force on the planet that will be our military equal in my lifetime," said Obey, who was sixty years old when we talked in the late fall of 1998. "So that ought to give you the opportunity to deal with your domestic problems and to retool for the day when you might have a competing power.

"If you asked average Americans as they sat around the kitchen table in the morning, 'What is the biggest threat?' It sure isn't a threat that you would have to respond to by buying a bunch of new tanks or a bunch of new fighter planes a decade before they're needed. It's better quality schools, more drug treatment slots, covering the gaps in health insurance. And you're not going to have the money to address those needs if you don't change the way you're doing things domestically and in defense."

If you built the schools the nation needs and cleaned up rivers and addressed other vital civilian needs, "you'd have plenty of jobs in this country without using the defense budget as a jobs bill."

Does this powerful appropriator see a guns-versus-butter fight or a train wreck around the bend?

"I suspect if you had a recession," Obey answered, "you still would have the same squeeze-out mentality" in regard to military weaponry because of where the congressional overseers of the defense budget come from. "They come from areas where it is their number-one political requirement to preserve the status quo in the military. So as long as this place is run lock, stock, and barrel by one region of the country that is most economically dependent upon the old style of defense, I don't see this Congress being part of the solution" to the problem of making the right choices when it comes to guns versus butter.

Butter is not winning, Obey said. "Pork is winning. That highway bill [in 1997] went through like you know what through a goose because the Public Works Committee has taken a big lesson from the defense committee. Pork pushes.

"People on the defense committee know damn well that we're missing opportunities to really change our focus to the threats that we face, such as cyber wars, terrorism. They know we need to shift there. But because of what they're getting out of it in the old pipelines, they can't resist staying with them.

"On the highway bill, everyone knew it was outrageously out of balance. But here is a case where you had so much pork, it drew all other considerations off. There were over 1,260 projects in that bill. That's more than you had in all the forty-two-year history of the highway bill. In defense, at least they have to have a prime contractor," which subcontracts most of its work to companies in other states. "But with highways, they don't have to worry about the prime contractors" spreading money all across the country instead of in a single congressional district or state. The favor of highway money extended to a politician is undiluted.

Doubts About Missile Defense

I asked Obey if a new "Star Wars" missile defense—a network of radars and antimissile missiles—could turn out to be the Pentagon's highway program in the sense that it would draw off billions of dollars from weapons and manpower needed to fight the likeliest wars and spend them on the unlikeliest one—a nuclear missile exchange. Once again, Obey displayed the skepticism of a midwesterner who has seen the government try to do too much too soon on missile defense, wasting billions of taxpayer dollars in the process.

"Not enough people are asking what's the absorptive capacity of the missile defense program; how fast can you absorb it. It's just like medical research. It's like the old cancer war that we had when Mary Lasker [a wealthy benefactor for health causes] convinced Nixon and [President

John F.] Kennedy to fight each other over who was most against cancer. They looked at it as a simple engineering problem: if you can get to the moon, why can't you cure cancer? So the cancer budget went from $289 million to over $1 billion. For the first half of the war on cancer, half the money was wasted. Now it's doing much better. You've got the same problem here with missile defense."

Why is the case for a missile defense stronger in the twenty-first century than it was in the twentieth century when the United States decided to forego deploying a missile defense even though the Soviet Union had thousands of nuclear warheads aimed at us? "I don't think it is," Obey replied. "But the argument they [Star Wars advocates] will make is that Russia was never going to use them, but some of these terrorist countries are more likely to behave irrationally. The argument is persuasive enough to people to resurrect this stuff. Let's grant their premise. There is no evidence to indicate that you can afford to put an additional dime in that program right now because it has not progressed far enough technically to produce" a missile defense that could use additional money productively. "For those systems to work, everything has to work the first time and it will never have been tested in battlefield conditions.

"Conservatives scream about liberals looking for eternal security by seeking a leakproof antimissile umbrella. My God, they're doing the same thing on this. I'd be for it if I thought by pouring more money in it you could accelerate the development of it. But I don't think it can.

"I'm a hell of a lot more scared of loose nukes in the Soviet Union than I am of facing a nuclear weapon by some terrorist country. If it should launch just one nuclear missile against the United States, its leaders know their country will be incinerated. The most effective missile defense would be to eliminate every damn missile that you can in Russia, and that would mean greatly expanding what we're doing with their conversion program" of junking old nuclear weapons. "And anything we can do to help their military regain their sense of dignity before it turns into a fascist type of right-wing resentment" would help make the United States and other nations more secure.

Unresolved Problems

Changing the subject to how much was too much when it came to spending money to entice young men and women to voluntarily fill billets in the All Volunteer Force, Obey said, "I was one of the last holdouts for a volunteer Army because I thought it would make it easier to fight wars that we should not get into. But I think we've crossed that. Short of being in a combat-around-the-corner situation, I don't think you would have a prayer of reinstituting even a partial revival of the draft [which was suspended in 1973 at the end of major U.S. participation in the Vietnam War]. For better or worse, we've got a volunteer Army. And with the economy going as well as it is going right now, it's going to be damn hard to get the quality recruits that you need almost no matter what you pay."

What do you see Congress doing in the future when it comes to choosing between defense and nondefense programs? More of the same, the veteran lawmaker replied. Pork and more pork in the defense budget. "Every time you question the expenditure of a dollar for a questionable defense program," said Obey of his own experience in the post–cold war years, "you're somehow antidefense. Hell, I'm not antidefense, for God's sake. I'm for us having a defense that will help us fight the real problems: chemical and biological; weapons proliferation. You've got people running for the hills, buying ammunition, and storing up water because of the Y2K problem" [of not having computers programmed to adjust to the number 2000 when that year arrived]. But you've got a hell of a lot more serious problems on the military side" that nobody is taking seriously. For example, he said, "Name me a society that is more vulnerable to having its information systems attacked than we are." The fact that defense problems like this can be virtually ignored, Obey concluded, is just one more indication that our budget system is broken and badly in need of repair.

The Turnaround

BECAUSE DEFENSE SECRETARY Cohen was just under six feet tall and Chairman Shelton of the Joint Chiefs of Staff was six feet five, they looked like a basketball center and forward as they walked together through the halls of the Pentagon and Congress. And the analogy held in the way they played the Washington political game in mid-1998. Cohen was the crowd-pleasing shooter; Shelton, the steady, silent playmaker who kept getting the ball to the shooter.

A defense secretary needs the chairman of the Joint Chiefs on his side if he is to have any hope of Congress's approving the president's defense budget or any other major military endeavor, such as troops to Bosnia or deployment of a national missile defense. The chairman, in turn, to deliver for the secretary must win the minds of the Joint Chiefs: the Army chief of staff, chief of naval operations, Air Force chief of staff, and Marine Corps commandant. Otherwise critics in Congress and elsewhere would exploit the splits and direct defense money into their pet projects, ruining the Pentagon's overall game plan.

Shelton's predecessor as chairman, Gen. John Shalikashvili, had delivered for Cohen in 1997 by persuading the Chiefs to support the Quadrennial Defense Review report even though it called for less money than they wanted. Cohen by mid-1998 had persuaded himself, largely from talking to troops in the field, that there were indeed shortages of spare parts and other serious readiness problems, just as his critics had charged all through 1997 and into 1998. He concluded that the four military services all needed more money than President Clinton's budget provided. He feared the All Volunteer Force, which replaced the draft in 1973, might break for lack of enough money to attract and keep young men and women.

Pointing to the conference room adjoining his third-floor Pentagon office, Cohen told me that he met with the Joint Chiefs on July 2, 1998, and said to them, "'What I'm picking up and what you're telling me now is that we can't carry out the missions with the readiness that is required, given the budget we've got. So now we have to start building a case for more.'" Besides Shelton and the Chiefs, attendees at this crucial turnaround meeting included Deputy Defense Secretary John Hamre; Air Force Gen. Joseph W. Ralston, vice chairman of the Joint Chiefs; William J. Lynn, who had taken over Hamre's former post of comptroller; Pentagon spokesman Kenneth Bacon; and Marine Lt. Gen. James L. Jones, Cohen's principal military assistant.

"I knew I was going to have to make a case, which is what I have always tried to do going back to my law school and law practice days," Cohen told me. "You've got to make a case. You've got to put the facts out. You've really got to master them. And then you've got to persuade."

Cohen's speech was music to the ears of Shelton and the Chiefs. They had been robbing Peter to pay Paul to buy essentials, such as fuel, ammunition, and food. There seemed to be no letup in the "911 calls" asking the armed services to deploy to one global hot spot after another. What they called *Pers Tempo,* for personnel tempo, connoted the speed with which soldiers were yanked from one spot to another. *Ops Tempo,* for operational tempo, was a measure of how hard they worked once they arrived on scene. The combination of tempos was wearing out both people and equipment. Nor was all well with the rear areas. Shelton before he was sworn in as chairman on October 1, 1997, had been hearing at his old job of commander of the United States Special Operations Command headquartered at Tampa, Florida, that many of the military's best and brightest were quitting because they perceived that retirement and other benefits were no longer worth waiting for. His own son, Jeff, then a first lieutenant, was among those considering quitting the Army because of that perception. "That got my attention," Shelton told me.

So Cohen did not have to say much to win over Shelton and the Chiefs. But the defense secretary knew it would be tougher to win over the mind of President Clinton, whose advisers at the Office of Management and Budget had warned against taking any action that would derail the drive to balance the federal budget by 2002. Clinton had concluded on his own that raising the money ceilings put on the Defense Department in 1997 under a bipartisan agreement would damage him and his party politically. He had refused the invitation from Senate Majority Leader Trent Lott to be the first to recommend breaking the agreement and raising the caps. Lott and the rest of the Republican leadership in Congress recoiled from breaking the caps for fear this would enable Democrats to portray them as the budget busters. This "after you, Alfonse" dueling gridlocked the defense budget game in the summer of 1998 when Cohen and Shelton decided to drive through the opposition and score.

Political gridlock imposes a form of suspended animation on the process for providing and distributing defense dollars. Congressional committee chairmen cannot tell how the ultimate defense budget will affect nondefense programs. How much will chairmen have to cut education benefits, for example, to offset increases in defense so the whole federal budget will stay under the caps? If the caps were to be raised, those chairmen could move ahead on their money bills knowing they would not have to impose offsetting cuts. Gridlock keeps Pentagon procurement chiefs from signing contracts with manufacturers for fear Congress will not vote the money needed to fulfill them. The inability to tell whether the defense budget will move up or down creates ripples of uncertainty all through the political-military-industrial complex. Secretaries of defense for decades have pleaded vainly with Congress to stabilize the process by appropriating a chunk of money for an airplane, for example, that the Pentagon could dole out over five or six years. But Congress to control defense dollars prefers to appropriate the money a year at a time for most Pentagon programs.

Cohen, as he surveyed the opposition down court, saw that even if he won over the president and got the total for defense increased, the extra money would fall short of the $148 billion additional the Chiefs had told Congress they needed for the new six-year budget plan running from fiscal 2000 through 2005. Cohen and Shelton would have to persuade the Chiefs to settle for less. Otherwise there would be a split between the president and the Chiefs that would polarize the politics of defense into a wasteful and bitter free for all.

Pay and Retirement Problems

Even before Cohen's crucial July 2, 1998, meeting, Shelton's qualms about readiness had impelled him to ask Brig. Gen. Pat Adams, the Joint Chiefs' director for manpower and personnel, to take an in-depth look at the retirement and pay problems his son and others had told him about back in Tampa. "Tell me what has changed in the retirement system that has created this kind of problem," Shelton told Adams. Shelton needed more than soldiers' horror stories to make his case to the Chiefs and his civilian bosses. Adams came through with what Shelton termed a "magnificent" briefing paper entitled "Houston, We Have a Problem." Adams's paper detailed what had happened to retirement and pay over the years and laid out possible remedies, ranging from jumping military pay by 13 percent all at once to giving small raises over a long period of time.

Before Shelton had briefed Cohen and other top civilians on "Houston, We Have a Problem," the independent *Army Times, Navy Times,* and *Air Force Times* newspapers published Adams's findings, provoking a flap inside the Pentagon. Washington policy makers hate to have what they are working on behind the scenes made public before they have it in final form. They want to brief their superiors in private. Once the contents of "Houston, We Have a Problem" were published, Cohen might scold Shelton for not telling him about them before he read them in the newspaper. "I wanted to get it up to the Sec Def (secretary of defense) and his staff and say we've got a problem and we need to look at this and see where we want to go from here" before the briefing paper became public,

Shelton told me. "We wanted a chance to work it inside the system; to go up to OSD (Office of the Secretary of Defense) and say we've got to fix this and get buy-in over at the White House" rather than make an end run to Congress. Shelton went to Cohen to assure him he planned no end run. The flap generated by the *Times* papers died down. In official Washington, a new flap always comes along to replace the old one. Shelton and Adams in the summer of 1998 went ahead and briefed "Houston, We Have a Problem" to Cohen's top deputies, including Deputy Secretary Hamre, Pentagon Comptroller Lynn, and Rudy de Leon, under secretary for personnel and readiness. They reacted coolly, according to Pentagon insiders. The civilian defense executives saw the need for extra money, but at the same time did not believe it could be obtained without colliding head on with Clinton and his already beleaguered White House budget balancers.

Cohen reacted differently, however. Shelton's briefing of "Houston, We Have a Problem" galvanized the defense secretary, especially after Shelton told him: "We cannot keep going downhill. We have to start working on this problem now or it's going to bite us big time in the future." Participants in that top-level briefing said that Cohen listened intently to Shelton and Adams and then declared to his deputies: "We have to go forward with this thing. Get on the program." As one flag officer put it, Cohen's message came through to the civilian hierarchy as "move out and draw fire." Pentagon civilians saluted and moved out to wring extra money out of the White House for defense.

While Shelton the playmaker moved methodically around the military and civilian bureaucracies, Cohen the shooter streaked toward the White House to score. "I decided that not only did we need to build a case" for extra money, Cohen told me, we had to bypass the usual preparing, presenting, revising, and re-presenting of paper after paper within the Pentagon bureaucracy before taking one to the president. "I decided that I had to go to the top rather than go through the system," Cohen said.

In preparation for his face-to-face meetings with Clinton, Cohen went to the field to gather evidence. "I went to Moody Air Force Base [ten miles northeast of Valdosta, Georgia], Fort Drum [fifteen miles northeast of Watertown, New York] and Norfolk [Virginia] naval base" in 1998. "I'd ask,

'OK. Let's talk about readiness. What's the problem?' I became satisfied that we needed to get a better handle on it because it was not just anecdotal. We were starting to see some real shortages."

Letters to Clinton

Cohen told me that from the time he took office at the Pentagon he had been sending biweekly letters to the president about what he saw going on in the field of national security. As evidence piled up during his visits to the field in the summer of 1998, Cohen said, "I started adding to my letters my concerns about readiness, recruitment, retirement, pay, and other problems. I would tell him what I was doing and what I heard at Moody, Drum, and Norfolk; what I was picking up in the field. I told him that I was persuaded that we were going to have to have increases" in the defense budget above those projected earlier in 1998.

The president himself, Cohen told me, was picking up the same kind of vibes from military people when he went out on aircraft carriers or onto military bases. "When the president goes out and sees the troops," Cohen said, "he is extremely impressed with what he sees out there. Reports he receives about helicopter collisions and airplane crashes also make him sensitive to the need for the best equipment."

Cohen in the summer of 1998 also discussed the military's money problems face to face with Vice President Al Gore. "I told him that there were some serious issues we had to address. We're not going to be able to do it with the existing [budget] restraints. I wanted the very top levels to know what I was doing; that it was not any kind of end run."

Besides his warnings in the letters sent directly to President Clinton and in periodic chats with Gore, Cohen said that in July, August, and September of 1998 in odd moments he would say to either or both of them: " 'I'm telling you right from the very beginning that we're going to have to do more,' " for the military to keep the All Volunteer Force from eroding. " 'I will work within the system with the Chiefs and the CINCs [commanders in chiefs of specific areas of the world] to develop this.' " The response from both Clinton and Gore, Cohen said, was: "'You make the case, and we'll basically support it.'"

The campaigns of Shelton and Cohen were to converge at Fort McNair in Washington, D. C., on September 15, 1998, when Shelton, the Chiefs, and the CINCs would meet with Clinton behind the closed doors of the National Defense University. In advance of that meeting Cohen said he told the Chiefs and CINCs:

"'Look. I want you to lay it out for the president. This is our chance to make our case directly to the person who is going to make the ultimate decision on this.'"

The military leaders took Cohen at his word. They subjected Clinton to friendly verbal fire, complaining that he was asking the armed forces to do too much with too little. History buffs might recall that the site of this barrage of words directed at the president was named after Army Gen. Lesley J. McNair, who was killed in 1944 in Normandy, France, by his own side's bombs.

Participants in the flag officers' summit meeting with Clinton at McNair said the president asked incisive questions and thanked the military for always coming through for the nation in splendid fashion. He promised to address the problems the generals and admirals had laid out. The participants told me afterward that their commander in chief urged them to "lay it out" similarly for the senators and "tell it exactly like it is" when they testified before the Senate Armed Services Committee on September 29, 1998.

One day after the military's summit meeting with Clinton at McNair, Clinton wrote Cohen a highly significant letter about it. The president's letter, Cohen told me, went like this: "'In view of what I've heard, I want you to work with OMB and this administration to see what you can develop in the way of a budget proposal that will address these needs.'" The president was willing to raise the top line of his heretofore ironclad, inviolate defense budget. Cohen and Shelton were winning the war for the president's mind and defense dollars—the war that really mattered to them at the close of the twentieth century.

The turnaround on the defense budget gained momentum from the

September 29 Senate Armed Services Committee hearing, despite the roasting Shelton and the Chiefs received for not speaking out earlier on their unmet needs. However, the turnaround could not be completed until Clinton solidified his promises into actual new numbers in his defense budget plan for fiscal 2000 through 2005.

White House Meeting

Toward this end, Cohen arranged for Shelton and the Chiefs to meet with Clinton in the Cabinet Room of the White House on December 7, 1998— Pearl Harbor Day. "I wanted the Chiefs to have another opportunity to present the case to the president," Cohen told me. "I started off telling the president that this was a historic day and gave an overview of the dimensions of the problem. Then the chairman spoke and then every service Chief spoke directly to the president."

Shelton told Clinton that the military units that would be deployed first in an emergency were still in a high state of readiness but that this was not true for their backups. He said the shortfalls in recruiting and retention testified to the troops' unhappiness with their pay and retirement benefits. Cohen did the summing up, telling the president that the Chiefs needed $148 billion more than was projected for fiscal 2000 through 2005 but could meet their most pressing needs with an additional $112 billion.

Participants at the White House meeting said Clinton responded this way: "I understand. I've looked at this. One of the problems we'll have with the caps is a timing problem of how fast we can do this and still stay within the caps. But I'm committed to getting it done. You all stick with me. We're going to find a way to make it happen." Then Clinton looked over to Deputy Budget Chief Lew, who was sitting on Shelton's left, and said, "Jack, we've got work to do."

Although Clinton during his 1992 election campaign was widely assailed for avoiding the draft, several military leaders who talked to him one-on-one told me that they came away awed by his intellect, warmed by his interest, and assured by his promised support of their needs. Shelton, for example, told me this:

"I think the military has been listened to by President Clinton. He has been very supportive. He has a great appreciation for what we do. You can tell both he and Mrs. Clinton are very touched when they are around military personnel. And he can get to the heart of a problem quicker than anyone I have ever seen." Shelton recalled that when he commanded the U.S. military operation in Haiti in 1994 he spoke to the president by phone. Even though Clinton had not been briefed on Shelton's concerns, "he asked me about three or four questions, and they were central to the tough issues that I was dealing with."

The wife of another four-star general told me that at a festive White House party Mrs. Clinton turned to her and said of the military: " 'You're the only group in town who hasn't dumped on us.' "

Cohen Slam-dunks One

After the Pearl Harbor Day meeting at the White House, Cohen and the Chiefs met in the defense secretary's conference room office at the Pentagon. "I went around the table and asked, 'What did you think?' " Cohen recalled. "They basically said it was a good meeting but there was no real final commitment. I said there can't be until we finish this with OMB." Cohen said he believed he and the Chiefs had won over the president but that there was always a chance OMB would talk him out of big increases for defense. Cohen took another run toward the basket to nail down the promised increases.

"I went out to Sandy Berger's house on a Sunday morning and met with him, Jack Lew [who had moved up to the directorship of OMB] and Dr. Hamre," Cohen said. [Samuel R. "Sandy" Berger was the president's chief national security adviser.] "Lew asked how do we deal with this issue" of defense's receiving a bigger money increase than the total increases for all the other government departments. Berger favored more money for defense, Cohen recalled, but White House budget chiefs fretted over how to insert extra money for defense in the fiscal 2000 budget at the last-minute without generating criticism that the Pentagon was receiving special treatment. The OMB chiefs, Cohen recalled, warned that other cabinet members and members of Congress would ask, "What about education? What about environment? What about all these other programs" that the president has committed himself to advancing?

In response to those objections, Cohen said he told Berger and Lew: "Well, we agree. But the president also made a commitment to me in his letter saying we've got to have additional funding. So how do we work this out?"

The Joint Chiefs, meanwhile, in the sanctity of their Tank at the Pentagon, fretted over endorsing a budget that provided significantly less of an increase than they had told Congress they needed, $112 billion versus $148 billion, or $36 billion less. "They didn't want to give Congress the chance to say, 'You guys are politicians in uniform,' " said one flag officer involved in the deliberations. On the other hand, the Chiefs knew that both Clinton and Congress believed that balancing the federal budget would strengthen the nation as much as buying more guns. So, with assists from playmaker Shelton, the Chiefs persuaded themselves that settling for the promised $112 billion addition was their most prudent course. The Chiefs were promised that all the troops would receive a raise; pay scales would be revised to reward experience; the former retirement system that allowed a soldier to retire at half pay after twenty years would be restored—all actions that Representative Murtha had unsuccessfully fought for in the closing days of the 105th Congress. The money for these personnel benefits would be contained in the president's regular fiscal 2000 budget as well as in a separate emergency funding bill.

All told, Clinton in his regular budget requested $280.5 billion for fiscal 2000 running from October 1, 1999, through September 30, 2000. That total included money for the Energy Department to build warheads and is lodged in the federal budget's account designated as 050. When the higher Clinton defense budget was unveiled in early 1999, chairmen of congressional committees grudgingly acknowledged that the president was going upward with defense dollars but complained of unrealistic projections.

$288.8 Billion Approved

"There is some good news," Chairman Spence said February 2, 1999, as he opened the House Armed Services Committee [it reverted to its old name at the start of the 106th Congress] review of Clinton's new defense budget. "The budget does call for an $84 billion top line increase over the next six years. Of course, the president has indicated that $80 billion of this increase is expressly predicated on Social Security reform as well as on renegotiation of the Balanced Budget Act. With fairly significant strings like this attached, it is difficult to judge just how serious the president is about addressing even the limited share of the Chiefs' unfunded requirements this budget professes to do."

Addressing Cohen, seated at the witness table beside Shelton, Spence said, "Mr. Secretary, you deserve a lot of the credit within the executive branch for getting the administration to at least recognize the seriousness of readiness problems."

Spence told Cohen that "likewise you deserve much of the credit for convincing the administration to at least begin confronting defense shortfalls and the need for increased spending. The bottom line, however, is that this budget falls well short of adequately addressing the services' unfunded requirements.

"This budget does not represent a $12 billion increase in fiscal year double zero or a $112 billion increase over six years. Instead, it proposes a $4 billion increase next fiscal year, and I would note that $2.9 billion of this $4 billion is perhaps suspect, and an $84 billion increase over the six-year plan. The difference is about $28 billion worth of assumed savings and reductions from within the budget. Even if valid, these assumed savings in no way represent increased top line spending. And as I just indicated, the degree to which the president is serious about the $84 billion increase remains an open question in my mind."

Despite his qualms about Clinton's budget and his conviction the armed services needed much more money than it contained, Spence felt obligated to obey the orders of House Republican leaders to report a defense bill that stayed under the money ceilings imposed in 1997. The House

Armed Services Committee subsequently approved and sent to the House floor for an up-or-down vote a fiscal 2000 defense budget authorizing the Treasury Department to deposit $288.8 billion in the Pentagon's bank account, or $8.3 billion more than Clinton had requested.

"With the Joint Chiefs speaking more openly over the past year about these significant risks and problems and shortfalls," Spence told his House colleagues in a floor speech on June 9, 1999, "the administration seems to be turning the corner on the issue of America's national defense needs." The committee, in turn, the chairman continued, added as much as it could to Clinton's defense without busting through the 1997 money ceilings. By authorizing the additional $8.3 billion, Spence said, "we are only managing the growing risks to our national security, not eliminating them."

Rep. Ike Skelton of Missouri, ranking Democrat on Armed Services and thus the representative expected to defend the Democratic president against Republican attacks, followed Spence's floor speech with one of his own. Skelton declared: "This is an excellent bill; the best defense bill that we have had in this chamber since the early 1980s. It deserves support from every member in this House."

A dissenting, minority view came from another Democrat, Rep. Barbara Lee of California. Although she knew she was greatly outnumbered in the fight over defense dollars, Lee stood before her House colleagues and said: "I believe that this budget is counterproductive to our domestic requirements and goes far beyond our national security needs. Today national defense consumes 48 percent of our discretionary budget. [The part of the federal budget Congress controls as distinguished from nondiscretionary accounts, such as Social Security benefits, that Congress is contractually obligated to pay.] American cities receive only twenty-five cents for every $1 that the Pentagon collects. That twenty-five cents must be spread thin to protect our environment, feed and house families, educate our children, provide health care for the elderly, and to fund other essential programs. . . . We must stop giving the Pentagon more money than it asks for or that it requires. I urge a no vote on this costly bill."

The House approved the $288.8 billion defense authorization bill by a vote of 365 to 58. The Senate passed a similar version of the House authorization bill by a vote of 92 to 3. These lopsided votes dramatized some of the central issues in the fight over defense dollars at the close of the twentieth century, such as how much was enough for the armed services; how the money should be distributed among guns or between guns and soldiers, and whether military spending could go up while federal taxes went down without unbalancing the whole federal budget.

New "Iron Triangle"

A senior Pentagon executive mused to me that a new "Iron Triangle" had been formed in the closing years of the century. One side of the new triangle was discretionary spending, including dollars for defense; the second was nondiscretionary spending such as Social Security; and the third side was tax cuts. The old Iron Triangle consisted of the Pentagon and its multibillion-dollar programs, the defense industry that vied for the money, and Congress, which decided how much defense money would be appropriated and where it would go.

Obey's Warning

Rep. David Obey of Wisconsin, ranking Democrat on the House Appropriations Committee, took note of the looming conflicts between the three sides of the new Iron Triangle. "No promise in either public or private life is worth much if the promiser doesn't have the means to deliver," Obey said while the committee was marking up the fiscal 2000 defense appropriations bill on July 16, 1999. "The current public claim that budget surpluses over the next ten to fifteen years will be enough to permit politicians to offer up large tax cuts is just such a false promise.

"A huge percentage of the predicted surpluses that are being sprinkled around Washington like fairy dust come from the assumption that the Congress, the president, and the country will agree to deep cuts of nearly 20 percent in real terms [meaning subtracting the increase due to inflation] in everything we do at the federal level to meet our education, health, environmental cleanup, transportation research, and law enforcement needs.

"The real story is that without a 20 percent cut in those investments the huge tax cuts would take this country back to another round of deficit spending. With the expected growth of our population and our economy, the cuts in those investments, and services are even deeper. . . .

"The prediction that we will have $996 billion in budget surpluses over the course of the next ten years is dependent on a huge cut in the annual level of all discretionary spending," the spending Congress can control for both defense and domestic programs. "Virtually no one believes that the Congress is likely to enact defense cuts of that magnitude. In fact, this defense appropriations bill that is before us today is 2 percent above the president's request and 5 percent above the 1999 levels in real dollar terms. If the Congress backs down on those increases and restrains itself from spending above the Clinton projected plans for defense over the next decade, nondefense discretionary programs will have to be cut by 23 percent. If not, the cuts will have to be about 38 percent. . . .

"And we must face the fact," the blunt talking and forward thinking Obey continued, "that the United States will be a different country ten years from now than it is today. That will require funding for some [nondefense] programs to rise above inflation in order to keep existing levels of service." Obey then ticked off examples of what he saw as the fuel for a guns-versus-butter fight within the first decade of the twenty-first century:

- "The overall [U.S.] population will increase by more than twenty million.
- "High school enrollment will increase by more than 10 percent.
- "The number of people enrolled in higher education will grow by more than a million.
- "The economy will be about 24 percent bigger after adjusting for inflation.
- "The number of products shipped will be much greater, as will exports and imports going through American ports.
- "There will be nearly 50 percent more commercial airline flights and about 60 percent more airline passengers.
- "The number of vehicles on the highways may increase by as much as 40 million.

- "The annual number of visitors to our national parks will increase by more than 50 million."
- Illegal immigration and public demands that U.S. authorities control it are "certain to grow."

Obey told his House colleagues, committee staffers, and members of the public sitting in the crowded hearing room on the third floor of the Rayburn House Office Building that those pressures would be among those "that will produce stronger, not weaker, demands for public service." In other words, the public will demand more butter, not less.

If Obey's reading of the nation's crystal ball was correct, the "Can You Top This?" game that Congress and the president played over defense spending in the 105th Congress and first year of the 106th (1999) may be played again early in the twenty-first century—this time over domestic spending.

Although Obey's warning provoked little comment among his colleagues in the hearing room, their action on the Air Force F-22 fighter plane spoke louder than words about their convictions that the Pentagon cannot have all the money it needs for everything; that choices must be made, and if the executive branch will not make them, the legislative will. The House lawmakers chose soldiers over guns in refusing to appropriate the requested $1.8 billion to start producing the air superiority fighter. Obey's warning that they would soon have to choose between guns and butter was not so urgent in their view as obtaining money for the near-term needs of the troops.

"The Air Force has not demonstrated that it can control F-22 costs," the committee said in its report recommending denial of the money earmarked for producing the first six aircraft. Because of skyrocketing costs, the committee lamented, each of the Lockheed Martin F-22s slated for production would cost $300 million compared with $55 million for the F-15.

"The Air Force's acquisition strategy requires the purchase of over $13 billion worth of aircraft before completion of basic operational testing," the committee said in its report on the fiscal 2000 defense appropriations bill.

The unit cost of these initial aircraft increased 40 percent over the last two years, and any problems found during the next four years of testing will simply add to these costs.

Current threat projections for 2010 indicate that the United States will have a 5 to 1 numerical advantage of advanced fighters against our most challenging adversaries without the F-22. Against what could be considered the most likely medium term adversaries used in Air Force scenarios, the United States enjoys a numeric advantage of 26 of our advanced fighters for every one belonging to our adversaries.

California Republican Jerry Lewis, chairman of the House Defense Appropriations Subcommittee, which initiated the cut in F-22 production money, told me that he and fellow members were trying to help the Air Force, not hurt it. He said "we are not here to rubber stamp" their programs but rather to make sure Air Force leaders do not let one program bankrupt the rest of the service.

The House later went along with the recommended F-22 cut, but the Senate had not yet acted on it when this book went to press. The fighter's immediate future was therefore in doubt, but its rising costs threatened to price it out of existence eventually. "A patriotic decision," Obey said of the committee action on the fighter. "One of the most important decisions of the past decade. The Air Force leadership has lost its sense of proportion."

The fact that a prodefense congressional subcommittee would, for the first time in the memory of veteran congressional staffers, derail a major aircraft program like the F-22 indicated that even hawkish lawmakers are willing to economize on defense when the case is compelling. Such an attitude should lessen congressional resistance to closing excess military bases to save billions of dollars. But, as the next chapter explains, Clinton so politicized base closings that Congress is unlikely to approve any additional ones until after he leaves office.

Shooting the Messenger:
A Case History

FOR DECADES CONGRESS has been looking for ways to take polarizing politics out of closing excess military bases. No business owner, no city council member, no mayor, no governor, no member of Congress wants to see the dollars and jobs connected to a military base in his or her home area suddenly disappear. Yet it wastes millions of tax dollars every year to keep on the heat and lights and maintain the roads and water works of bases that the U.S. military no longer needs.

President John F. Kennedy shortly after taking office in 1961 unleashed his aggressive secretary of defense, Robert S. McNamara, to close surplus military bases. More than sixty major military bases were closed under procedures that many lawmakers attacked as partisan. Republicans in Congress complained, for example, that the process favored the Democrats because a disproportionate number of bases closed were in areas represented by Republican lawmakers.

An angry Congress passed a succession of laws in the 1970s to restrict the freedom of the executive branch to close bases. The most severe one, passed in 1977, required the executive branch to notify Congress about any base the Pentagon wanted to close or downsize. Before any base could be closed or shrunk, the executive would have to follow procedures so cumbersome that the base-closing drive often was derailed.

After the Reagan defense buildup of the early 1980s peaked and began to decline, the armed services found themselves in a money crunch. Civilian and military leaders saw closing and shrinking bases as a way to ease this crunch. The executive and legislative branches found enough common ground to agree in 1988 on procedures for closing and shrinking bases. Those efforts were accelerated by the ending of the cold war, the drive to balance the federal budget, and cries from the armed services that they needed more money to stay ready to fight.

In 1990 Congress passed and President George Bush signed into law PL 101-510, the most ambitious effort since World War II to close or shrink bases with a minimum of political interference or bias. The Defense Base Closure and Realignment Act became nicknamed BRAC for both the act and the commission it created to recommend bases to close or downsize. The act called for three rounds of closures purposely timed to be in the nonelection years of 1991, 1993, and 1995.

The military services under BRAC submit to the secretary of defense their candidate bases for closing or reduction. The secretary culls through the list and submits his choices to the independent and ostensibly nonpolitical BRAC commission for review. Although the president nominates and sends to the Senate for confirmation the eight members of the BRAC, two of the nominees are chosen or endorsed by the House Speaker, two by the Senate majority leader, one by the House minority leader, and one by the Senate minority leader. This leaves the president with two unfettered choices of his own. The president also chooses the chairman.

The commission reviews the defense secretary's list of proposed base closures and realignments for four months. It can add or delete bases from the list and otherwise revise the secretary's recommendations. On July 1 of the year the commission is in business, it submits its list to the president. He can accept or reject all of the bases on the commission's hit list. He cannot revise it. He has until July 15 to make his up-or-down decision. If the president accepts the list, it goes to Congress. The lawmakers, like the president, can accept or reject the whole list. They cannot tinker with it. If they do nothing about the list for forty-five days, the commission's recommendations become law.

High Stakes

In 1995 President Bill Clinton was already campaigning for his reelection in 1996. California with forty-seven electoral votes, the most of any of the fifty states, and Texas with twenty-nine, third highest, were considered crucial to the election of Clinton or his Republican opponent, Senate Majority Leader Bob Dole of Kansas. In the 1992 presidential election, Clinton had beaten President Bush in California by a margin of 46 percent to 33 percent and had lost Texas to him 37 percent to 41 percent. It was widely reported in early 1995 that the BRAC had recommended closing the giant McClellan Air Force Base in Sacramento, California, and Kelly Air Force Base in San Antonio, Texas. Thousands of jobs and votes hung on the decisions made about those two bases.

Would Clinton go along with closing McClellan and Kelly to save money and preserve the BRAC process, or would he reject the whole list in the interest of getting reelected? This question became hot in the spring of 1995 as the president's July 15, 1995, deadline for accepting or rejecting the BRAC recommendations neared.

Clinton raised hopes of Californians on April 7, 1995, by declaring during a visit to McClellan that "the recommendation from the secretary of defense [to BRAC, which was not required to follow the secretary's recommendations] for McClellan is that the air base should stay open because of the very important mission you are pursuing. But you know that California has been very hard hit by base closings in the aftermath of the cold war's end.

> I took the position, which I hereby reaffirm today, that when the United States asked the people of California and the people of the United States all across this country to host our bases, to host our military families, to play a role in winning the cold war—if we have to downsize the military, we have an affirmative obligation to help the communities and the people

rebuild their lives and to have prosperity and strength in the future. That is part of building economic opportunity. That's why I fought so hard to have conversion funds to help people move from a defense-based to a civilian-based economy.

Shortly after that speech in Sacramento, Californians learned that the commission had rejected the defense secretary's advice about McClellan and had recommended that it be closed. This put Clinton on the defensive, generating a drive within his administration to find a way to save the jobs at McClellan without taking the unpopular step of rejecting the commission's entire base-closure list.

Trying for a middle-ground solution, President Clinton on July 13, 1995, sent the BRAC hit list to the Senate even though both McClellan and Kelly were on it. But he gave himself some political cover and touched off political explosions by adding this caveat in his letter of transmittal:

> In a July 8, 1995, letter to Deputy Secretary of Defense [John] White, Chairman [Alan J.] Dixon [of BRAC] confirmed that the commission's recommendations permit the Department of Defense to privatize the work loads of the McClellan and Kelly facilities in place or elsewhere in their respective communities. The ability of the Defense Department to do this mitigates the economic impact of those communities while helping the Air Force avoid the disruption in readiness that would result from relocation as well as preserve the important defense work forces there.
>
> As I transmit this report to the Congress, I want to emphasize that the commission's agreement that the Secretary enjoys full authority and discretion to transfer work loads from these two installations to the private sector, in place, locally or otherwise, is an integral part of the report. Should the Congress approve this package [of commission base-closing recommendations] but then subsequently take action in other legislation to restrict privatization options at McClellan or Kelly, I would regard that action as a breach of Public Law 101-510 in the same manner as if the Congress were to attempt to reverse by legislation any other material direction of this or any other BRAC [Base Realignment and Closure].

Furor over Privatization

Clinton's conditional approval infuriated three sets of politicians: those who had taken political heat by going along with previous base-closing recommendations in their home areas, those who had bases lusting for the work done at McClellan and Kelly, and those who had bases on the new hit list but were not getting special privatization-in-place attention from Clinton. Mayors, city council members, governors, and members of Congress in one or more those categories cried foul. They complained that Clinton was trying to be half-pregnant on McClellan and Kelly. He was approving a report to close McClellan and downsize Kelly but trying at the same time to keep them in full swing by getting private contractors to take over the government work, using the same labor force and facilities at the same place. Critics howled that Clinton's privatization-in-place scheme not only was political favoritism but also a violation of federal law. McClellan, Kelly, and all the other bases on the list should be treated the same by the federal government, including the president, the critics said.

"Mr. President," a reporter asked Clinton in the White House Rose Garden on July 13, 1995, "how do you answer the charge that the White House has injected politics into the base-closing process?"

"First of all," Clinton replied. "It is absolutely false. Let's look at the facts here. Where is the politics? This Base Closing Commission made far more changes in the Pentagon plan than any of the three previous Base Closing Commissions. Far more. They've been under a lot of political pressure. I understand that. I don't disagree with all the changes they made.

"They acknowledge, secondly, under the law they are supposed to take into account economic impact. Based on their report, which I have read and I urge all of you to read it if you haven't before you make any judgments about where there was political influence. They took twenty-three bases or realignments off the list [recommended to the commission by the Pentagon] and put nine more on, three of which happen to be in California. . . . The biggest job loss by far [would be] in San Antonio at Kelly Air Force Base." Clinton noted that the commission rejected the Pentagon's recommendation to downsize Air Force repair depots at McClellan, Kelly, and three other places rather than close those at McClellan and Kelly outright.

"But let's look at the facts on this politics," Clinton urged the reporters standing in the Rose Garden. "This is about economics. In the report itself they acknowledge that at Kelly Air Force Base 60 percent of the employees are Hispanic; 45 percent of the Hispanics employed in the entire area work there; that it will have a devastating impact. And they [the commission] were willing to shut down about sixteen thousand jobs when there was another alternative [of downsizing all five repair depots rather than closing those at McClellan and Kelly].

"In California," Clinton continued, "here are the facts. The law requires economic impact to be taken into account. When this Base Closing commission process started, California had 13 percent of the population; 15 percent of the people in the military; 20 percent of the defense budget. In the first three [rounds of] base closings, they sustained 52 percent of the direct job losses. We're not talking about indirect jobs. We're not talking about speculation, 52 percent.

"In this [fourth round recommendation to the commission] the Pentagon hit them [Californians] pretty hard" by recommending closing "Long Beach, a big facility. This Base Closing commission, not satisfied with that, made a decision that they had to add back a lot of other jobs. So they decided to take almost all the jobs they took out of one place, San Antonio, and by closing three California bases, taking the California job loss in this round to almost 50 percent.

"Now you tell me that my concern over that economic situation when their [California's] unemployment rate is 8.5 percent [and] they have borne over 50 percent of the burden of the job loss is political. [That] my concern in San Antonio where one decision could virtually wipe out the Hispanic middle class is political when there was another alternative that the Pentagon said was better for national security.

"I am tired of these arguments about politics," Clinton said. "My political concern is the political economy of America and what happens to the people in these communities. . . . Are they being treated fairly?

"Now, I do not disagree with every recommendation the Base Closing commission made, but this is an outrage! And there has been a calculated, deliberate attempt to turn this into a political thing and to obscure the real economic impact of their recommendations in San Antonio and California, which were made solely so they could put back a lot of other things."

"What is the reason they did that?" a reporter asked.

"I don't know," Clinton responded. "I'm not imputing motives to them. I'm just saying it's very interesting to me that there has been almost no analysis of anything. This whole thing became, 'Well, this is a big political story about California.' This is an economic story, and it's a national security story. And there has been no analysis of what [facilities] got put back and why, and what got taken off and why.

"And I have been doing my best to deal with what is in the national interest," Clinton continued. "There are two considerations here. We have to reduce our base capacity for the size of the military force we have. That is a national security interest, and this is my first and most important duty. But, secondly, under the law economic impact was supposed to be taken into account. And as nearly as I can determine it wasn't anywhere, never in the [commission's] determinations with the possible exception of the Red River Depot, based on my reading of the report.

"Now the question is, is there a way to accept these recommendations? Because even though they're not as good as what the Pentagon recommended and they do a lot more economic harm for very little extra security gain, is there a way to accept them and minimize the economic loss in the areas where I think it is plainly excessive? And that is what we have been working on. But I just want you to know that I deeply resent the suggestion that this is somehow a political deal."

The Case for Closing Bases

The commission, as was its right, had amended the hit list of 146 bases submitted to it by the Pentagon. The commission had recommended to Clinton that he close or shrink 123 of the bases and nine others that were not on the list. "The commission estimates that the closure or realignment of these 132 military installations will require one-time, upfront costs of $3.6 billion and will result in annual savings of $1.6 billion once implemented," said the independent body's report of July 1, 1995. "Over the next 20 years, the total savings will be approximately $19.3 billion."

In explaining its controversial recommendations on McClellan and Kelly, BRAC wrote that "significant excess capacity and infrastructure in the Air Force depot system requires closure of McClellan Air Force Base. The Air Force recommendation to downsize all five Air Logistic Center depots through mothballing excess space would reduce the amount of space utilized by the depot, but would not eliminate infrastructure and overhead costs. Downsizing would result in elimination of depot direct labor personnel, but not overhead personnel. The commission found that closure of McClellan AFB permits significantly improved utilization of the remaining depots and reduces DoD operating costs." The commission estimated that closing McClellan would save the taxpayers $159.7 million a year.

As for Kelly, the same report said: "The commission found that closure of the San Antonio Air Logistic Center and related activities, including the distribution depot and information processing megacenter, permits significantly improved utilization of the remaining depots and reduces DoD operating costs.

"The level of Hispanic employment at Kelly AFB was recognized by the commission. The commission took steps to minimize the negative economic impact on the community by cantoning [establishing small units of] a significant portion of the Kelly AFB activities.

"The commission staff presented data indicating large annual savings could be realized by consolidating engine maintenance activities at Tinker Air Force Base, Oklahoma. Both Kelly and Tinker are operating at less than 50 percent of their engine maintenance capacity." The commission said the downsizing of Kelly would save $178.5 million a year.

The closing and downsizing of Air Force logistic centers at McClellan and Kelly, which repaired military aircraft under multibillion-dollar maintenance contracts, would enable three other Air Force logistic centers to bid for the work formerly done at McClellan and Kelly. The three were Hill Air Force Base, twelve miles southwest of Ogden City, Utah; Warner

Robins Air Force Base, sixteen miles south of Macon, Georgia; and Tinker Air Force Base, nine miles southeast of Oklahoma City. Politicians from Utah, Georgia, and Oklahoma mobilized to get the work. Billions of dollars and thousands of jobs were at stake.

Representatives and senators with military bases, shipyards, or laboratories on their home ground found it mutually productive to band together in what is called a *Depot Caucus*. There is one in the House and another in the Senate. The unity increases their political clout on common interest questions such as divvying up by law the percentage of aircraft repairs and ship overhaul that government and private facilities can do.

The president's announced intention to privatize the work at McClellan and Kelly infuriated lawmakers, especially those whose home area bases stood to gain from the recommended closings. James V. Hansen, a Republican House member from Utah, was at the forefront of the congressional critics, contending that Clinton's privatization scheme was not only political but immoral and illegal as well.

Preserving the Process

A countervailing political force in Congress, however, was the realization that rejecting the whole BRAC hit list to spite Clinton would destroy the painfully crafted base-closing process and lose the billions in potential savings.

Republican Floyd Spence of South Carolina, chairman of the House Armed Services Committee (then called the National Security Committee), used his considerable influence to try to preserve the process. He urged his colleagues not to vote down the whole BRAC closure list. "The Department of Defense is counting on the savings resulting from base closure and realignment to fund currently underfunded modernization [buying new weapons] and infrastructure improvements late this decade and into the next century," Spence said on the House floor September 8, 1995.

"According to the commission, implementation of their recommendations would result in one-time costs of approximately $3.6 billion," Spence said. "However, the commission expects $1.6 billion in annual savings and net present value savings of $19.3 billion over the next twenty years to result from the 1995 base-closure recommendations.

"There is no question that presidential politics were paramount in the White House's very public and tortured consideration of the commission's recommendations. Fortunately, common sense prevailed over politics and the administration backed down and allowed the process to proceed. However, I remain concerned about recent comments made by senior administration officials implying that the White House will find a way to assist a select few installations in politically sensitive states by 'privatizing in place.' Some have gone so far as guarantee employment to workers at installations scheduled to be closed—a guarantee that everyone knows will be nearly impossible to honor."

Noting that his committee had voted 43 to 10 against a resolution [House Joint Resolution 102] to reject the BRAC commission's recommendations, Spence urged the full House to reject the resolution in the floor vote as well.

Hansen, in supporting Spence's plea, told his House colleagues, "I know BRAC is painful. The First District [of Utah, Hansen's district] has lost a base in each round of BRAC and will lose Defense Depot Ogden if this list is accepted. While I may not agree with every decision, I believe the BRAC process is fair and must remain independent.

"Now, after the game has been fairly played, the president wants to go back and change the rules. Under Public Law 101-510, the president had two choices: either send the list back to the commission with recommended changes or accept the list in total. The president instead decided to play outside the law and forward the list to Congress with two substantial changes.

"The president's unprecedented direction to the Pentagon to privatize in place the majority of jobs at the McClellan and Kelly Air logistic centers is nothing more than an attempt to circumvent the independent BRAC process for the political expediency of satisfying northern California.

"The administration has continued to play fast and loose with the law. On a recent visit to McClellan White House Chief of Staff Leon Panetta issued the following threat:

"'If there is any action in Congress or by any other depots to try to inhibit the privatization effort, the president has made it clear that we will consider that a breach of process, and he will order that McClellan be kept open.'

"I find that kind of blatant disregard for the law offensive and contemptuous of the law and of Congress. I want to be very clear. I do not consider the president's letter directing privatization in place to be part of the BRAC recommendations we will approve here today.

"I also want to point out that any plan to do so would clearly violate five sections of Title 10, U.S. Code. The president simply cannot ignore current law to solve his own political problems. Our country has found, several times in our history, that no one is above the law.

"It appears the president has once again come up with a lose-lose-lose compromise by worrying about political repercussions instead of leading the nation. This plan to privatize inefficient excess capacity and guarantee jobs is bad for the Department of Defense because it does not address the fundamental excess capacity questions in the depot system and will only result in higher maintenance costs and substantially lower savings.

"It is bad for the country because it undermines the integrity of a process designed to be free from this kind of political tampering. And it is bad for many of the workers at McClellan and Kelly who will now lose the option to follow their federal job to another Department of Defense depot.

"This recommendation [to privatize McClellan and Kelly] ignores the BRAC commission findings that 'the closure of McClellan AFB and the San Antonio Air Logistics Center permits significantly improved utilization of the remaining depots and reduces Department of Defense operating costs.' The closure was deemed a necessity given the significant amount of excess depot capacity and limited defense resources."

Republican J. C. Watts, whose Oklahoma district included Tinker Air Force Base, which stood to gain work from the closing of aircraft repair facilities at McClellan and Kelly, told the House that "the president's decision to accept the BRAC list with a privatize-in-place option" at McClellan and Kelly "is a play that wasn't in the playbook or within the rules of the game. He has taken an apolitical process and turned it into a zero sum game. If this Congress allows the Department of Defense to privatize in place, we will never achieve the savings that were clearly identified by the

BRAC's recommendation nor will the BRAC process retain the credibility it has worked so hard to achieve.

"But that fight is for another day. Today we have the question of rejecting the BRAC list. This question has but one answer. No.

"BRAC is a proven process, and to dismantle that process by disapproving the list would, in the words of Chairman Alan Dixon [former senator and BRAC chairman], 'destroy the BRAC process forever and fail to save an estimated $19 billion.' This is simply not an acceptable course of action."

Hansen, Watts, and 341 other representatives on September 8, 1995, voted down the joint resolution to reject the commission's entire list of base closings. Seventy-five House members voted to reject the BRAC list. The base closing process survived.

After voting in 1995 to support the base-closing system, Hansen and Watts were at the forefront of those closely watching the White House for any other sign that Clinton was not following the rules on base closings.

Clinton won California in the 1996 election, garnering 51 percent of the vote compared with Dole's 38. The president lost Texas to Dole, 44 percent to 49 percent. But even after the 1996 elections a number of lawmakers, especially those with military bases in their home areas, worried about Clinton's end-running the commission's recommendations for McClellan and Kelly. In 1997 they sought to rein in Clinton by inserting into the National Defense Authorization Act for fiscal 1998 (PL 105-85) language stating that contracts for work to be done at McClellan, Kelly, or any other base on the commission's 1995 hit list could be signed only after a competition was held. A military base or a private contractor or a team of both could bid. The law stipulated that "any offerer, whether public or private, may offer to perform the workload at any location or locations selected by the offerer. . . . No offerer may be given any preferential consideration for, or in any way be limited to, performing the workload in-place or at any other single location."

In other words, the writers of that law decreed to President Clinton, in effect, "You cannot dictate who will do aircraft maintenance nor where. The contractor, or team of contractors, who wins the Air Force competition can perform the work wherever it chooses. Your privatization-in-place scheme for McClellan will work only if the winning contractor chooses to do his work there and hires the base's work force."

The Peters Memo

Stepping into this boiling political cauldron in 1997 was a Washington lawyer named F. Whitten Peters. His credentials were impeccable, including a doctorate from Harvard Law School and enough skill in the office and courtroom to command a $300,000-plus yearly salary with the high-powered Washington law firm of Williams and Connolly. He had left private law practice in 1995 to become a top lawyer for the biggest public corporation in the world, the Department of Defense, with the title of principal deputy general counsel. Peters on November 13, 1997, became the under secretary and acting secretary of the Air Force. Clinton had not filled the Air Force secretaryship since Sheila Widnall resigned on October 31, 1997.

Although Peters's legal skills were not in question, his political skills were largely untested when he was thrust into the front lines of the battle over base closings. His seemingly impossible political mission would be to cool the passions of the Hansens of the 105th Congress who still seethed over Clinton's privatization-in-place ploy. He was supposed to do this at the same time he made good on Clinton's promise to ease the pain of closing or downsizing McClellan and Kelly.

Peters had been around the Pentagon and Congress long enough to realize that his new job called for him to be "chief javelin catcher" for Air Force base closings. And he knew a lot of those javelins would be coming at him from Capitol Hill. But his experience had not prepared him for the wave of javelins coming at him from within the administration, including some from inside the Pentagon itself. Friends said the main hurlers for the Clinton administration were Sheila C. Cheston, the Air Force general counsel who reportedly had hoped to become under secretary of the Air Force herself, and Dorothy Robyn, special assistant to Clinton for economic policy with an office in the White House. Cheston and Robyn kept demanding that Peters use his position vigorously to make good on Clinton's promises regarding McClellan and Kelly, according to Air Force insiders. "You've got to help them," was the constant refrain, they said.

In December 1997, for example, Peters approved sending about $11 million in Air Force funds to repair hazardous conditions at Kelly, including replacing old wiring. At the time, a re-use authority in San Antonio was in the process of taking over the base from the Air Force for conversion to a civilian facility. Such improvements would make the base more attractive to private contractors who might establish aircraft repair centers at Kelly after San Antonio took it over. The private contractors, if they could be enticed to establish themselves at Kelly, would bring back some of the lost defense jobs there.

When Robyn heard about the assistance going to Kelly, Air Force officials said, she pressed Peters to extend the same kind of help to McClellan to facilitate the privatization in place, which Clinton had promised. Peters refused because he did not have the same safety problems at McClellan, his aides said.

Peters found himself in a three-front political war on base closings composed of administration officials, members of Congress and their staffers, and contractors, many of whom made big campaign contributions. The three fronts were linked by old ties and constant communication. Representatives, senators, and congressional staff directors take pride in placing their colleagues in the executive branch and expect payback in the form of intelligence and other favors. Those placed communicate with their placers without going through channels. It is all in the family. Robyn was a former technology specialist with the Joint Economic Committee of Congress and John D. Podesta, deputy White House chief of staff in 1997, was formerly a lawyer on the Senate Judiciary Committee and chief counsel on the Senate Agriculture Committee.

Cheston, Robyn, Podesta, and others in the family concerned about coming through for Clinton at McClellan were worried in April 1998 that the giant Lockheed Martin aerospace corporation might not bid to perform aircraft maintenance at McClellan, and no other qualified private bidder seemed interested. The trade press had run stories that Lockheed Martin, if it won the Air Force maintenance contract for KC-135 tankers, might do the work at its own plant in Greenville, South Carolina, rather than at McClellan. This prospect alarmed Clinton aides who saw Lockheed's hiring a work force at McClellan as the way to redeem Clinton's preelection promises.

Podesta asked Deputy Defense Secretary Hamre to meet with him to discuss McClellan's prospects. Hamre could not make the suggested meeting time and told Phebe Novakovic, his special assistant, to represent him at the White House meeting with Podesta and Robyn. Peters was to go along.

On April 23, 1998, Peters met at the White House with Podesta, Robyn, Novakovic, and Robert G. Bell, a Clinton adviser at the National Security Council who previously had worked on the Senate Armed Services Committee staff with Hamre. Peters would later describe the meeting to the House National Security Committee this way:

"The meeting was called because, as I understand from talking to Ms. Robyn, there was concern that she had, based on some discussion she may have had in California, about whether or not Lockheed was serious about bidding to be the private sector bidder for this workload" at McClellan. "There is no other private sector bidder at this point, so this would be essential to have a private sector bidder in order to have a true competition" as Congress demanded in enacting the National Defense Authorization Act in 1997.

"The purpose of the meeting was to allow me to give them a briefing on where I thought the matter stood. At the conclusion of that briefing, there was concern expressed, I think, first by Ms. Robyn, that they did not believe that Lockheed would bid. Ms. Novakovic at that point offered to have Dr. Hamre have such discussions" [with Lockheed's chief executive officer Vance Coffman during an already scheduled meeting].

"The point of the meeting was to encourage Lockheed to make a serious bid. That was because we needed to have two competitors to have a competition. And they were the only competitor left who was interested in doing the work. And as part of that process, the message was to be, basically, 'Look. We want you to be serious here. We want you to bid. And, in particular, you know, get your ducks in a row. Get your agreement signed with Sacramento [setting forth the cost of using the former Air Force facilities at the base the city was taking over].' I believe the White House folks understood that Lockheed doing the work at Sacramento was really the only option that realistically was available" [for saving workers' jobs at McClellan by contracting with a private firm to take over the Air Force's aircraft work].

Peters was asked to write a memo summarizing the White House meeting for Hamre. He had been around Washington long enough to know that putting anything on paper about such a hot politic subject was a bad idea. It might leak out. Anything controversial appearing on official stationery could be exploited by those with contrary views. Pentagon insiders said that officials in Hamre's office insisted on having a memo. So Peters wrote it at his Cleveland Park home on April 26, 1998—a Sunday— on Air Force stationery. His memo started out like this:

MEMORANDUM FOR THE DEPUTY SECRETARY OF DEFENSE

FROM: ACTING SECRETARY OF THE AIR FORCE, F. Whitten Peters

SUBJECT: Meeting with Lockheed Martin—Sacramento Depot Contract

John Podesta has asked that you mention the Sacramento depot competition to Vance Coffman during your meeting(s) with him during the coming week. The point he would like you to make are to encourage Lockheed Martin (1) to bid to win the work and (2) to perform the work at Sacramento. . . .

The Leak and Repercussions

I happened to be sitting at the press table covering the House National Security Military Personnel Subcommittee for the *Washington Post* Legi-Slate News Service on April 30, 1998, when Representative Hansen held up a copy of the Peters memo for all to see. The leaking of the memo confirmed Peters's worst fears. Hansen said angrily to the people in the packed hearing room that it represented "another way" the Clinton administration was trying "to circumvent the law" on base closings.

Other members of the subcommittee seemed shocked. California Republican Duncan Hunter said that "this memo brings the administration down to a new low of credibility."

Another Republican member of the National Security Committee who expressed anger was Saxby Chambliss, whose Georgia district included Warner Robins Air Force Base, which hoped to get some of the McClellan aircraft repair work. Chambliss said "this smoking gun proves the White House has compromised the integrity of the base-closure process. With this new evidence, as far as I'm concerned, any attempts for additional rounds of base closure with this administration are dead on arrival. This memo strikes at the heart of what we've been saying all along, which is the president has politicized the BRAC issue to such an extent I simply cannot trust him to implement the BRAC commission's recommendations. As long as President Clinton sits in the Oval Office, BRAC legislation will be dead."

Representative Hansen wrote to Committee Chairman Spence demanding an investigation into the Clinton administration's "continuing efforts to evade the BRAC law and keep jobs in California. The collusion between the White House, the Deputy Secretary of Defense and the Secretary of the Air Force—who is the ultimate source selection authority for this competition—to favor one contractor and one location is outrageous, unethical and potentially illegal."

Hamre and Peters rushed to Capitol Hill to try to repair the political damage the Peters memo had inflicted. But it was too late. Too many angry lawmakers already had vowed publicly that they would not act on any more base-closing recommendations until Clinton was out of office.

Two years later, Defense Secretary William Cohen requested two more rounds of closures, one in 2001 and another in 2005. "There is never a good year" for closing surplus military bases, Cohen told the House Armed Services Committee on February 2, 1999, in explaining why he was requesting Congress to approve the new rounds of closures. "We picked 2001 to try to get it beyond the presidential campaign and 2005 in a nonelection year," Cohen said.

Cohen's plea that "two additional rounds of BRAC in the next decade will save the department more than $20 billion between 2008 and 2015 and $3 billion every year thereafter" had been derailed by Peters's April 1998 memo. Peters had been summoned to testify before the House National Security Committee on June 4 of that year to explain his memo and the White House politicking it seemed to represent.

"That memo appears to be the most recent and the most public evidence of what many see as a consistent problem and pattern of behavior on the part of the administration to skew the competition for depot workload in the aftermath of the 1995 Base Realignment and Closure commission's recommendations to reduce overhead and infrastructure among Air Force depots by closing McClellan and Kelly Air logistics centers," Chairman Spence said in opening the February 1999 hearing.

"The root cause of the on-going three-year depot controversy can be traced directly to the administration's decision to circumvent the 1995 BRAC findings by directing privatization in place at the two Air Force depots recommended by the commission for closure.

"I cannot ever remember such a direct White House involvement in any day-to-day defense issue, let alone one as esoteric as depot maintenance. If not for political reasons, how else can you explain such intense White House interest in such an arcane defense issue? Everyone should realize that the impact of this three-year controversy has had implications that reach far beyond depot maintenance issues or the prospect for future base closings. This controversy continues to erode the critically important trust that must exist, at some level, between the Congress and the administration if the federal government is going to effectively address the wide range of security issues that confronts us on a routine basis."

"Mr. Chairman, here we go again," complained Representative Hansen. "I guess I could give you the dates that I have heard Secretary [William] Perry, Secretary Cohen, [Deputy Defense Secretary John] White, [Air Force Secretary Sheila] Widnall, Mr. [Jacques S.] Gansler [under secretary of defense for acquisition and technology], and others talk about fair and open competition. And yet, sometimes we find out things that are going on in the funny building across the river there.

"It's been almost three years since the president promised to find a way around the BRAC law and keep nearly nine thousand jobs in Sacramento, California. This was an election year scheme that has already cost the Air Force over $1 billion in wasted savings and higher-than-necessary maintenance costs. The commander of the Air Combat Command told me that depot maintenance is his number-one readiness problem and is caused by the delay in closing the excess capacity.

"I thought we had put an end to this last year with the language we worked out in the Depot Caucus, but my optimism was misplaced. Despite hollow attempts to hide behind words like competition, the clear and single-minded goal of the administration remains one thing: to guarantee 8,700 jobs in California and 16,000 jobs in Texas.

"It's kind of refreshing, to have members from the California delegation come up to me and say, 'Maybe we've told the White House the wrong thing. Maybe they should learn that rather than keep these jobs up to the end of that time [the year 2000 when McClellan was scheduled to close], when everybody knows they're going to lose them anyway, that we do it now.'" The gradual closing of McClellan and Kelly, Hansen said, was "kind of like saying you cut off a dog's tail an inch at a time so it doesn't hurt so bad. And that's basically what we're doing in California and Texas."

Hansen told his fellow committee members and the three witnesses in the hearing room that he had gathered "a mountain of information" which documented that the Clinton administration had exerted "an unprecedented level of influence" over the base-closing process. He read several excerpts from his paper mountain, including these:

"Former secretary Widnall signed an MOU [memorandum of understanding] with Sacramento which states, in part, 'the Air Force will use its best efforts to give privatization every permissible opportunity to succeed.'

"Former deputy secretary of defense John White says, 'We have very clear instructions from the president to make this work.'

"John Hamre states, 'The Air Force cannot conduct a meaningful competition without a strong private sector partner for Sacramento.'

"In response to a congressional inquiry," Gen. George T. Babbitt, commander of the Air Force Materiel Command at Wright-Patterson Air Force Base at Dayton, Ohio, "confirms, 'the president stated the employment goals for Kelly and McClellan were to maintain employment levels at 16,000 for Kelly and 8,700 for McClellan. The president publicly articulated these employment goals for Kelly and McClellan. We are not aware of any justification for the administration's employment goal.'

"How do you like that last one?" Hansen asked his House colleagues. "We are not aware of any justification for this. Air Force documents uncovered in the last few months clearly state the number-one planning fact remains meeting the employment goals, and assumes the private sector wins the remaining competed workloads [at McClellan and Kelly] and performs the work in place. That sure doesn't sound like competition to me, Mr. Chairman. It sounds to me like the definition of competition will only be met if the work remains in Sacramento or McClellan."

Hansen called on the committee to disqualify the Air Force from selecting the contractors who would take over aircraft maintenance at bases like McClellan and Kelly on the commission's closure list. "This committee must move to restore the integrity of the BRAC process," he said.

Representative Watts told Peters that his memo on the White House meeting with Podesta and Robyn "presents prima facie evidence that the Air Force is not interested in obeying the law. And Mr. Peters your memo signifies that you are interested in circumventing the law, in my opinion —both last year's defense bill [containing the competition requirements for contracting for work done at bases slated for closure] and the 1995 BRAC law.

"And in several meetings with you in previous months you consistently promised the Depot Caucus you would work with the Congress to allow free and fair competitions for depot workload. In light of this memo and all that has happened over the last two to three years, how are we to have any confidence in the system or in the process as we go forward?"

Pentagon procurement chief Gansler replied that Peters would not participate in selecting contractors to do work at McClellan and Kelly and that he himself had "the ultimate responsibility for assuring" that the competition be "fair and open." Also, three non–Air Force overseers would monitor the Air Force competition to make sure it was fair. Gansler said that he personally had had "no contact with or any discussions with anybody at the White House or elsewhere in the executive branch" with regard to the McClellan and Kelly contracts. He said the combination of oversight by the General Accounting Office, three outside advisers, and himself would ensure a fair competition.

Darleen A. Druyun, principal deputy secretary of the Air Force for acquisition and management, told the committee that she would be running the competition day by day. "I am personally deeply committed to making the competition" fair and objective. "I take very seriously the fact that I am a steward of the taxpayer. I am also not a shrinking violet. If I don't like something, I don't sit there and keep my mouth shut. I do something about it. I can assure you that the integrity of the process will be pristine. And the documentation supporting my decision will also be impeccable."

Democratic representative Ciro D. Rodriguez of San Antonio, whose Twenty-eighth District was home to many employees of Kelly Air Force Base, said he found it "ironic" that House members representing bases still open were fighting off private contractors who hoped to get work from the bases being closed. "I know we would love to privatize welfare," Rodriguez said. "We would like to privatize housing. We would like to privatize prisons. But when it comes to national defense, there seems to be a contradiction. That goal that's being mentioned of sixteen thousand jobs at San Antonio is only a goal. I haven't seen one job yet." He said Kelly lost out to another public bidder, Warner Robins Air Force Base in Georgia, for the job of maintaining Air Force C-5 transport planes. Kelly was ahead of schedule in closing most of its facilities by the year 2001 as recommended by the commission. "If anyone should be upset, it's me because I haven't seen one of those sixteen thousand people" get a job from privatization in place.

Chambliss, whose district included the Warner Robins base, told Peters, "I have an opinion of you that is very high. Based on the discussion we've had, I think you're honest. You're straightforward. And you appear to me to be trying to do the right thing.

"Because of your honesty, you put down on paper the substance of a meeting that took place where unquestionably you must have had horrific pressure put on you by this administration and by the number-three person at the White House whose title is assistant to the president and deputy chief of staff for policy and political affairs, Mr. Podesta.

"There's no question but that politics has played a significant role in the failure to close Kelly and McClellan. I think, if it were up to you, you would have moved forward to do what the law required you to do. But undoubtedly you were blocked by this administration. And you were required to put politics into the mix again.

"Frankly, I'm disappointed that you became mired in that same political process that this White House just can't get away from. And the people who are really going to suffer the most by it are the people of the United States Air Force. But we've got to continue to try to get to the bottom of this and move this forward. And again I think you're the type of individual that probably can help that cause.

"We've lost a number of Air Force officers over the last several years solely because of the policies that have been put out there and espoused by Dr. White and by Dr. Gansler," Chambliss asserted without documenting the charge. "I'm absolutely convinced of that. We've lost some good people because you are moving the Air Force in the wrong direction on a very significant issue. But based upon the law that's now in effect, you're not going to be able to do that."

Chairman Spence closed the hearing with these words:

"This is just part of the whole politicalization of our Department of Defense by the White House. I've got a list of fifteen or twenty things that I can add to this list that show how the Department of Defense has been politicized. Even our intelligence agency has been politicized, all in carrying out the wishes and philosophies of the White House. It's nothing unusual with you. All people appointed by the administration have owed their allegiance to the administration. But you have to understand that we owe our allegiance to the people of this country, the taxpayers. We don't have allegiance to the administration. That's why we're concerned [about the base-closing process]. And we're trying to do our job. Appreciate your help. Thank you."

Epilogue

Peters himself did not give up on repairing the damage his memo had inflicted. He kept going from one congressional office to another until he had accomplished a remarkable turnaround. He converted his former critics into supporters of himself and, perhaps, the base-closing process once Clinton left office. Hansen and twenty-nine other lawmakers became so impressed with Peters's sincerity that they pleaded with Clinton to make him Air Force secretary rather than just acting secretary. Their September 18, 1998, letter to Clinton said:

"Our United States Air Force has been without a Secretary for over one year. The lack of leadership at a time of so many challenges is unacceptable. All of our military services face serious challenges which are impacting everything from recruitment to readiness, retention to retirement. The Air Force is no exception. Solutions must start with dedicated leadership.

"Fortunately, since last March the Air Force has had this leadership from its Deputy Secretary, F. Whitten Peters. Mr. Peters' hard work, forthrightness and dedication to the men and women in the Air Force has, in a short time, and under decidedly trying circumstances, established a high level of trust and respect among leaders here in Congress and within the Pentagon. Perhaps more importantly, he is well liked and trusted by airmen and their families throughout the Air Force.

"Mr. President, our Air Force needs a leader. In Acting Secretary Peters they already have a good one. We respectfully request you nominate him quickly to serve as Secretary of the Air Force. We are confident he would receive quick confirmation in the Senate and could take office prior to our adjournment."

Administration leaders brushed off the plea. The fact that it was Podesta who said the upsetting words and that Peters just wrote them down as ordered did not impress Clinton, Cohen, Podesta, or other administration officials. They insisted on shooting the messenger. They balked at giving Peters the top job.

Hansen complained to me: "They'd rather put someone in there who knows as much about the Air Force as a Holstein cow. Did you ever try to talk to a Holstein cow?"

In what some would consider poetic justice and others power politics, the Air Force on October 9, 1998, announced that McClellan's highly lucrative work of conducting depot-level maintenance on Air Force A-10 antitank aircraft and KC-135 flying tankers would be done by the team of the Air Force's Ogden Air Logistics Center and Boeing Aerospace Corp. The A-10 work would be performed at Hill Air Force Base in Hansen's district, not McClellan, which was slated to be closed by 2001, and the KC-135 maintenance work would be done at Kelly in Texas, which Clinton lost to Dole in 1996. Lockheed Martin did indeed bid for the work at McClellan in California, as Podesta and Co. had hoped, but it lost to Hansen's constituent facility in Utah.

On February 12, 1999, however, Lockheed Martin was on the team that won a fifteen-year, $10.2 billion Air Force engine repair contract. The company was teamed with Oklahoma's Tinker Air Force Base. Oklahoma Republican James M. Inhofe, a Senate Armed Services Committee member who had assailed Clinton's attempts to privatize McClellan, said the award to a military base in his state "affirms" that the base-closing process had returned to the intended fairness.

But political memories are long. When Clinton renewed his pleas in 1999 for Congress to approve another round of base closings, Republican representative Curt Weldon of Pennsylvania told him: "I don't think you're going to get it [the approval]. And you know why as well as I do. Not because of you; [but] because the commander in chief interjected himself in two situations that offended Democrats and Republicans alike."

The base closing process stopped, but Peters kept going on being the top civilian in the Air Force. Clinton nominated Daryl L. Jones, a black Air Force reserve captain and Florida Democratic politician, to be Air Force secretary. The Senate Armed Services Committee in July 1998 recommended against his confirmation after hearing fellow Air Force officers testify that Jones was unfit for the office. Jones withdrew. The White House, still shooting at the messenger, passed over Peters again and in early 1999 chose Charles B. Curtis, a Washington lawyer and former Boston University Law School colleague of Defense Secretary Cohen, to be Air Force secretary. But Curtis, who served as deputy secretary of the Energy Department from 1995 to 1997, withdrew in the face of the congressional flap over alleged spying at the department's nuclear laboratories. Only then did Clinton nominate the man-in-waiting since November 13, 1997—F. Whitten Peters. The Senate quickly confirmed him on July 30, 1999. Shaking off his White House wounds, Peters stood straight and tall to be sworn in as Air Force secretary on August 2, 1999.

Peering into the Future

To HELP GET INSIDE the fight for defense dollars, I sat down in early 1999 with the two most powerful, day-in and day-out warriors in that fight— Defense Secretary William Cohen and Joint Chiefs chairman Henry Shelton. In separate interviews, both men told what military threats to the United States they foresaw and expressed their hopes and fears for the future. In counterpoint, Franklin "Chuck" Spinney, the Pentagon's most persistent and outspoken internal critic, told me why he believes the U.S. military is deteriorating because of decisions its civilian bosses made since the Vietnam War.

Secretary of Defense Cohen

A demanding clock has been ticking in the ear of Bill Cohen as long as he can remember. It summons him to be up and doing at four in the morning and to keep moving until eleven at night.

The twentieth secretary of defense told me he did not hate this dictatorial clock in his head even though it made him act like a young man in a hurry—despite his not-so-young fifty-eight years, his age when we talked in February 1999.

"I've always had sort of a Gothic preoccupation with time," he said. "Even as a young man I was always concerned about time. Could I do enough to really say at the end of the line that I really put the maximum effort into everything I had done?

"I take a look at life," continued the lawyer-politician-poet-novelist and CEO of the biggest corporation in the world, "and say there's not much time for any of us. You're only here for a brief moment. In any cosmic sense it's a flick of an eyelash."

Such an attitude, along with smarts and energy, makes for an overachiever. In 1969, while the Vietnam War he missed was still raging, the twenty-nine-year-old Cohen was assistant county attorney for Penobscot County, Maine; a member of the Bangor city council; a business teacher at the University of Maine, and a practicing lawyer. "It didn't leave much time for sleep," he acknowledged. "I'd average about three-and-a-half to four hours a night."

While Cohen was serving as mayor of his native Bangor in 1971-1972, Republican Party leaders urged him to run for Congress. He did and won a House seat. He was named to the Judiciary Committee just as it was mobilizing to impeach President Richard Nixon. Cohen was elected to the Senate in 1978 and was appointed to the Senate Armed Services Committee, where he came to know John Hamre, then a committee staffer.

"As the years went by," he said of his twenty-four years' service in the House and Senate, "there seemed to be more focus on trivial matters as opposed to big issues. You could find yourself in the Senate at eight, nine, ten, or eleven o'clock at night debating some issue that had no relevance to you. I just found that I was sitting around. I felt time leaking through my fingers." So he obeyed that internal clock and left the Senate in 1997 with no plan to stay in government.

He was going to work with Georgia Democrat Sam Nunn, who was leaving the Senate at the same time. "I had been negotiating with a law firm for a part-time commitment," Cohen said. "I was going to spend a lot of time in the Asia-Pacific region and Europe as well. I was finishing up another book I was writing. I was planning a much different life."

Then President Clinton called Cohen and asked him to be his secretary of defense with the mission of building a bipartisan consensus for a strong and steady national defense. "It was one of those offers I really couldn't reject."

Even though as a senator he had served ten years on the Select Committee on Intelligence and eighteen years on the Armed Services Committee, the veteran lawmaker said he had no idea what his life was going to be like as the top executive of the Department of Defense. He found a bureaucracy eager to commit his every moment, scheduling everything from talks with heads of state to making multibillion-dollar decisions on complicated weapons, and from keeping peace among the generals and admirals to signing orders that could send the sons and daughters of America to their deaths in some remote hellhole on the other side of the globe.

But, and this was the bottom line, Bill Cohen, the man with the ever-ticking biological clock, loved being more efficiently busy than he had ever been. Also, the issues he wrestled with really mattered to him. They often were matters of life and death for the planet.

"The absolute management of time was something I didn't fully appreciate," Cohen told me. "I didn't appreciate the hydraulic pressure that is involved—which I like. I like having meetings starting on time and finishing on time. In the Senate you can say we're going to begin work at ten and you never really know when it will begin and when it will end."

In fact, Cohen liked his Pentagon work so much that that he found himself running zestfully up the River Entrance steps of the Pentagon before seven every weekday morning so he could start feeling that pressure. Wading into his work and feeling the pressure on his brain appealed to Cohen, much as wading into a fast stream and feeling pressure on his boots appealed to a trout fisherman.

First order of business in the typical Cohen day at the Pentagon is a brief meeting with his personal staff; a briefing by a CIA officer on what the world had been doing while Cohen slept; a gathering of the Top Four (Cohen, Deputy Defense Secretary Hamre, and the chairman and vice chairman of the Joint Chiefs of Staff, Gen. Henry Shelton and Air Force Gen. Joseph W. Ralston, respectively). This is followed by a larger Daily

Coordination Meeting, or DCM, where the day's activities are discussed by the civilian secretaries of the Army, Navy, and Air Force and top deputies within Cohen's directorate—including manpower, public affairs, and congressional liaison chiefs.

"Everything is laid out and it all happens according to a fixed time frame," Cohen said of his workday. "I really like that." Another difference from Congress, he said, is that as secretary of defense "You make a decision and it's carried out." In a legislative body, "you've got to get a majority. You can have a great idea, but you have to spend hours going around to each and every senator. You work with him or her and then task your staff to work with his or her staff to make sure you've dealt with all their concerns. You have to build a majority consensus on all the big issues you're working on. Here I can say, 'OK. I've listened to the pros and cons. This is what we're going to do.' And it happens.

"You have to be really careful" what you say to subordinates. "Because just by implying something, [you'll be ordering it and] they'll carry it out, and it will be done by tomorrow morning, and it may not be something you wanted done. So there's a real difference here."

Cohen also said he could not speak publicly as freely as the defense secretary as he had as a senator because the world hangs on every word. If one word is wrong, or wrongly interpreted, troublesome headlines can result, requiring the government to take time out to fight a public relations battle.

The biggest psychic income of the job, which pays $148,000 a year in bankable income, is talking with the troops up close and doing things for them, Cohen said. His wife, Janet Langhart, a former television personality, feels the same way. "She wants to hear their concerns and looks upon them as her children, as I do. We come back truly enthused, enlivened. It has been a life-enhancing experience for us because every time we're with them we're sky high. They feel the same way when we're with them. And I didn't see that as a senator, being just one of a hundred. We were kind of looking and inspecting" rather than interacting with the soldiers, sailors, airmen, and marines.

The downside of feeling so connected with service people comes when one of them is hurt or killed. "Knowing you are sending somebody into harm's way is not one of the better parts of the job," Cohen said in understatement. "But as I tell the troops, one of the reasons I really need to meet them is that I want to put a face with all those deployment orders I sign. When I see how young and vibrant and energetic and idealistic they are, then I have that in my mind when I'm signing those deployment orders."

I asked this man with twenty-four years in Congress and two years as secretary of defense—a job in which he received top-secret briefings every day on dangers all around the world—what worried him most as he looked at threats to the United States in the twenty-first century. He said his first worry was that the All Volunteer Force would become disconnected from the mainstream of American society. He did not believe an out-of-sight, out-of-mind military—a separate French Foreign Legion of sorts—was a healthy development for a democracy.

"My fear is that the country no longer sees on a day-to-day basis what their military is doing, how good they are, the roles they are playing in world affairs, and shaping things in ways that that are favorable to us." The American people "don't see that, they're not reminded of that until there is a Saddam Hussein [the Iraqi dictator whose invasion of Kuwait sparked the Persian Gulf War]. They don't see the great humanitarian effort. They don't see what's involved on a day-to-day basis. And so there is a real concern on my part and Janet's when we're out there to reconnect" the military and civilian societies.

Downsizing the U.S. military and making it more efficient "is a two-edged sword," he said. The smaller the military becomes, "the less visibility you have in the lives of the American community the less support there is for defense spending. People don't see us involved in their affairs. You don't have participation in the Rotary, the Lions, and the other service clubs on a regular basis. And the consequence is that when they don't see that, the domestic pressure is to cut money out of defense and spend it for social programs.

"When a community really understands what the military is doing and how that interacts with them on a social basis, as well as a military point of view, then you have a much better case to make," Cohen told me. "They see the planes take off. They know they have a [Air National] Guard participating in an operation that weekend. So the smaller the force, the less visibility of it. It presents a problem for the long term. That's why we keep talking about reconnecting. How do we get America to look at this? How do we get the press to focus on these issues in a different way?"

Cohen's worries about two separate societies, military and civilian, impelled him in 1999 to lecture the Illinois House of Representatives about the needs of the U.S. military; to sponsor with his wife a "Pentagon Pops" concert in Washington's Constitution Hall to salute the military musically; to meet with executives of the Microsoft Corp. in their headquarters in Redmond, Washington, to explain how military men and women were out on the point protecting them, enabling American industry to prosper.

Looking outside the United States at threats he considered the most menacing, Cohen said terrorists or rogue nations capable of chemical or germ warfare are "perhaps the biggest worry for me, and I think for all of us. How do you defend against somebody who has a biological agent?

"Let's suppose he releases it in a plane that leaves Buenos Aires, stops off in Los Angeles. The plane goes on to Montreal. Then over to London or Paris or Munich or wherever. Suddenly you've got all the people on board that plane who become infected with these microbes who get off the plane that get on other planes and spread it even farther, and you don't even know anything about it until three or four days later when the symptoms set in and people start dying. You have no way of knowing where it originated, who set it off, who to respond against. How do you deal with it?

"It is going to require us as a society to change the way we look at this," Cohen told me. "It's going to require us to think about privacy. How much are we willing to give up? How much are we willing to give up in the way of our civil liberties in terms of the demand to protect us?

"You saw the flurry of questions being raised just by having a CINC [commander in chief of a geographical area, such as the Pacific region] for homeland defense: 'Wait a minute. You're going to have the military involved in providing protection for Americans at home? Isn't this a matter of police, fire, and the Federal Emergency and Management Agency and the Environmental Protection Agency and county government and state government?' Suddenly you've got the specter of the military being somehow involved in providing for the American people who are raising these concerns. I'm glad they are.

"If you say how do we deal with this threat that is real and is quite terrifying, you [might] say we have to have better intelligence. What does that mean? How do you have better intelligence? It means you have to have greater technological capability. It means you have to be more watchful. It means you have to start looking at specific groups. Does that get into profiling people? How much are you willing to have the government really follow these groups and what procedures will you allow the government to trace? Must you have encryption devices that can't be penetrated? You now have terrorist groups operating inside the United States but they have encoded communications systems that can't be broken. And you say, 'Well we don't want you to break them.'"

Another problem gnawing at Cohen as he tried to prepare the nation for the new threats of the beginning century was "technology proliferation." He lamented that "it just takes somebody sitting with a laptop with access to the Internet to start picking up technology that before would be unheard of. So it is the proliferation of high technology that can put our system down. The so-called cyber terrorism is something that all of us have to be concerned about."

The Galaxy IV satellite failure, which cut pager service for 45 million customers, halted pay-at-the-pump service at 5,400 gasoline stations, and caused communications problems in hospitals and other emergency facilities in January 1999, was very much on Cohen's mind as he talked about cyber terrorism. "You had panic that started to set in just with one satellite that happened to be tilted the wrong way for a few hours," he said. "So the ability of external forces to actually shut down key components of your society—that's a real threat that I worry about. We're taking measures to combat that.

"Those are all issues we have to face up to, and they're coming at us far more rapidly than we were contemplating. So those are the kinds of things we have to start dealing with in addition to dealing with a North Korea that is still posing a threat, a Saddam Hussein or a Libya or Iran. All of those threats still remain, but now you've got this other element, asymmetric warfare. That's when [potential enemies] look at your Achilles Heel and say, 'Here is a society that is so interlinked with all this wonderful technology, but it is only as good as its weakest link. We think we've found a way to penetrate their air control system, shut down their power grid. We can penetrate into some of the Pentagon's classified systems.'"

Potential enemies, Cohen continued, "now have teams dedicated to this as opposed to a couple of teenagers who were simply hacking around to see how good they were. All of that is going to cause us to look at ourselves and how we can function as a free and open society in a world in which you've got enemies which are not identifiable or traceable but who can cause massive consequences to you."

Cohen as a senator was at the forefront of those lawmakers championing arms control agreements that would lessen the chance of the two big nuclear scorpions in the bottle, the United States and Soviet Union, striking each other. He went along with the cold war strategy of relying on an overwhelming offense of nuclear weapons in underground silos and in submarines prowling the depths to deter the Soviets from pushing the button. The United States tried deploying a thin missile defense in the 1970s and pursued a Star Wars missile-proof umbrella in the 1980s but gave up on both as not practical.

But in the late 1990s a new drive—this one lead by Congress to deploy some kind of missile defense—seemed unstoppable. The action-reaction phenomenon of the cold war era could turn a light defense into a heavy defense as the offenses of potential enemies continuously improved. I asked Cohen, the one-time arms controller, whether he believed in his heart that the United States should deploy a missile defense in the new century.

"Given the nature of technology that is being spread around the globe," Cohen answered, "I don't see how we can avoid it. For me the question is: Is it there yet? Will it be there by next year? We're going to see the threat increase. We cannot protect against an all-out Russian assault as such, and that's where our deterrent comes into play. But if you have a North Korea that has nothing to lose, and in a moment of madness unleashes one of the Taeopo Dong 2's or 3's, should they have them, with a chemical or biological warhead, you need some kind of missile defense to stop it.

"You say, 'Wait a minute. The Chiefs are concerned about a suitcase bomb filled with bio or chemical. Or a tourist puts it out [unsuspectingly brings in a terrorist suitcase bomb]. They say that's a more likely threat that we face.' And it is.

"How do you protect against that? What about the anthrax shots for the general public. How do you manage this with the first responders [local police, firemen, doctors, nurses] who can't even identify what the biological agent was? They're may be several calls coming in: 'Well its anthrax. Well no, it's something else.' It could be any number of things. Well, how do you identify it? Those kinds of threats are the most dangerous right now because we aren't prepared to deal with them. It's going to take us some time to organize, to train, to have supplies on hand to deal with it. All of that is very imposing.

"From an ICBM [intercontinental ballistic missile] threat," Cohen continued, "you have a strong deterrent. That's not going to go away. Any country that would think of letting loose an ICBM on the United States will be vanquished in the process. There may be some countries who say we have nothing left to lose. You may have a situation where Saddam Hussein says don't even think about your containment policy because you never know that in a moment I might unleash one [a biological or chemical missile] in downtown New York or Washington or Detroit or wherever it might be. You say, not a credible threat. Could be with this guy. So you want to have something that would give you protection against that kind of a threat. And that's something that I've always supported.

"Now, is the NMD [national missile defense] technology going to be there in the year 2000?" [when President Clinton was scheduled to decide whether to deploy a system or order further flight tests]? "I don't know. I think we're still in the infant stages of trying to put this together. I think we will see technology develop rapidly once we get the first systems in place and make us much more capable."

Cohen rejected arguments that the Russians would refuse to reduce their nuclear arsenal and perhaps would sell some of it to other countries if the United States broke away from the antiballistic-missile (ABM) treaty and started erecting a protective missile umbrella over the fifty states. The ABM treaty of 1972, as amended later, limits the United States and the Soviet Union to building a thin missile defense at one site. The idea was to ensure that neither side could stop an all-out missile attack by the other. Therefore, it was reasoned, neither superpower would attack the other because it could not stop the retaliatory blow.

Misleading the Russians about U.S. intentions is "something we ought to avoid," Cohen said. "I am convinced we can persuade them that this is not directed against them by saying, 'You are as vulnerable to us as we are to you. We need to amend this treaty so it allows us to have the protection against that rogue state or accidental launch.' I think we can persuade them of this if we deal with them on a very direct basis. But the president needs this one year of time. That's why I think this confrontation coming up [over breaking or abandoning the ABM treaty] is unnecessary. I think it's wise to say give us this next year while we're testing [missile systems] also to negotiate with the Russians; persuade them that this is the right thing for us to do and the right thing for them to agree to without saying we're deploying whether you like it or not."

If the United States took the like-it-or-not approach, Cohen reasoned, "you take away the opportunity to work it out with them. I think we can. I think we will."

I asked Cohen whether the United States could negotiate arms control agreements with North Korea and other threatening nations that would obviate the need for the United States, Japan, and other nations to deploy missile defenses. Answered the secretary of defense with so many fires to watch as he peered into the twenty-first century:

"I'm the eternal optimist in saying anything is possible. Who would have said five years ago that you could have agreement in Ireland? Who would have thought you would have [Israeli prime minister Yitzhak] Rabin negotiating an agreement with [Palestinian leader Yasir] Arafat? Anything is possible, but I think what we have make sure we have a very strong deterrent coupled with strong diplomacy. We've got much of the world going our way."

Joint Chiefs Chairman Shelton

The Goldwater-Nichols Department of Defense Reorganization Act of 1986, the law Henry Shelton has to live by as the top-ranked soldier in the United States, makes his job sound like Mission Impossible. And it often is.

The chairman under that law does not command any combat forces himself. He may draft their orders and transmit them to the field, but he is not the official originating or issuing authority. The orders go from the president to the secretary of defense to the theater commanders, or CINCs (commanders in chief).

Yet, it is the chairman—even though he is not in the official chain of command for combat operations—who often takes the point to explain what the American military is doing in the world and why. Former chairman Colin L. Powell did this in Desert Storm in 1991. Chairman William J. Crowe went on international television in 1988 to try to explain why the warship USS *Vincennes* mistakenly shot down an Iranian civilian airliner, killing everyone aboard.

Also, the Goldwater-Nichols Act requires the chairman to be the chief military adviser to the president and to be the link between him and the chiefs of the Army, Navy, Air Force, and Marine Corps. Specifically, the law states that the chairman "is the principal military adviser to the President, the National Security Council and the Secretary of Defense."

The chairman also is responsible for crafting plans for wars that are happening and might happen. He must look into the future and make sure the armed forces will have the ships and planes they need to fight a war on the other side of the world. And he is supposed to warn his civilian bosses when he senses that U.S. military forces are losing their edge to fight.

To enable him to assess the readiness of the American military, the law makes the chairman responsible for "establishing and maintaining, after consultation with the commanders of the unified and specified combatant commands, a uniform system of evaluating the preparedness of each such command to carry out missions assigned to the command."

To help him do this and a thousand other chores, the chairman is allowed to have a staff numbering as many as 1,627 people. The staff of the Joint Chiefs of Staff numbered 1,487 in 1999.

Much of the chairman's time for doing these and other duties is eaten up by appearances at hundreds of congressional hearings and meetings every year and by travel to discuss a myriad of topics with foreign leaders and the chairman's military counterparts all over the world.

As we have seen in tracing his work in raising the defense budget,

Shelton in his first year on the job proved to be a gifted coordinator despite his limited Washington experience and strong preference for duty in the field. It is no small feat to coordinate the congressional testimony of three generals and one admiral who make up the Chiefs of Staff, all of whom have large egos and variegated constituencies, and to deal successfully with a Congress of hidden agendas. Shelton did that on the divisive issues of military readiness and the defense budget in 1998 and in early 1999.

But the biggest challenge to Shelton or any chairman is not spelled out for him in the Goldwater-Nichols Act. It is to structure the right kind of Army, Navy, Air Force, and Marine Corps and ensure they buy the right kind of weapons for the next war, not the previous one, with the troops and money available. To do this requires the chairman to look into the misty future and discern, as best he can, the threats U.S. forces are most likely to face.

It was this last job I asked Shelton to talk about in February 1999 when he was defending before Congress President Clinton's new six-year plan for the American military while, at the same time, trying to discover what would be threatening the nation early in the twenty-first century.

Shelton told me that his "foremost concern" was the "asymmetric" threat —Pentagonese for an enemy's finding the chinks in U.S. armor and attacking them. Cyber warfare, an enemy's attacking the U.S. computerized network and disabling it, is in this category. Cyber attacks could cause havoc in civil society as well as in military operations.

In listing cyber warfare as a prime concern, Shelton was buttressing the warnings former CIA director John Deutsch sounded in 1996. He told Congress that "a number of countries around the world are developing the doctrine, strategies, and tools to conduct information attacks" on the computerized systems of the United States.

Besides slashing the arteries of the high-tech American military, Deutsch said, cyber attacks could devastate the civilian economy. "Day-to-day operations of U.S. banking, energy distribution, air traffic control, emergency medical services, transportation, and many other industries all depend on reliable telecommunications and an increasingly complex network of computers, information databases, and computer driven control systems," Deutsch said. "Virtually any bad actor can acquire the hardware and software needed to attack some of our critical information-based infrastructures." The then-director of the CIA said cyber attacks were "very close to the top" of the agency's threat list.

How will the armed services recruit and hold the highly skilled people needed to operate tomorrow's high-tech systems and combat attacks on them? Shelton said private industry, which can pay three times as much, will be competing for the same computer programmers, operators, and communications specialists the military will need. "I'm really concerned about our ability to attract and retain those types of skills that are going to be more and more prevalent in the military. The way we're going with high tech, your basic infantryman has to be a computer operator to operate a radio out in the field."

Shelton said he was also concerned about Congress's rushing the Defense Department to failure in national missile defense in the new century. He called for an equivalent of a cost/benefit analysis, warning that spending too much on missile defense would leave other threats uncovered. If deploying a thin missile defense should end up costing $200 billion instead of the $2 billion estimate of some of its advocates, other gaps would be bound to open up in the nation's defenses.

Besides, warned the veteran of combat in Vietnam and the Persian Gulf, "we know that all through history that every time you develop a defense, somebody develops another type of offense."

Putting himself in the place of a terrorist or enemy agent who was confronted by a U.S. missile defense, Shelton said it would be easy for him to take a mortar tube loaded with deadly chemicals aboard a civilian ship. "Sail into New York harbor," mount the mortar tube on a deserted patch of deck; "pop off ten mortar rounds," which would explode in mid-air so winds would spread the deadly gas through the city; "throw the mortar tube overboard; go back in the cabin for a drink."

Shelton, like Secretary Cohen, was getting up at 4:30 A.M. every workday to try to guide the nation's military down the right trail at a time when there were none of the markers of the cold war era, just educated guesses on which was the best way to go in the twenty-first century.

Franklin Spinney, Pentagon Heretic

The Army, Navy, Air Force, and Marine Corps will all get hurt in financial train wrecks in the twenty-first century because their civilian and military bosses ignored the warning signs flashing at them in the twentieth century.

Leaders of the military-industrial-political complex in the post–cold war period were guilty of nonfeasance and malfeasance because they had neither the will nor guts to make hard choices. They found it easier to keep planning and buying for the last war.

The victims of this nonfeasance and malfeasance will be the American taxpayers, because billions of their tax dollars will have been wasted, and the men and women who will have to fight in the twenty-first century with too few modern weapons and too many obsolete ones.

That is the scathing brief of Franklin Charles "Chuck" Spinney, the boldest and most persistent critic inside the Pentagon (if not the whole United States government) with regard to his department's own policies. Like the late J. Edgar Hoover of the FBI, Spinney had acquired too powerful a following to make it politically safe for his Pentagon bosses to fire him. A succession of vexed defense secretaries kept Spinney on under the same rationale President Lyndon B. Johnson gave when asked in 1964 why he did not fire Hoover: "I'd rather him inside the tent pissing out than outside the tent pissing in."

Spinney all through the 105th Congress and into the 106th kept raising hell in speeches, interviews, writings—especially electronic writings to a network of fellow heretics hooked together on an e-mail net called The Blaster.

Spinney's predictions may not turn out to be true. Then again they might. He bases them on solid research, experience, and feel. His views, and how he managed to keep voicing them while remaining on the Pentagon payroll as a tactical aircraft specialist in the defense secretary's Office of Program Analysis and Evaluation, are a significant part of the inside fight for defense dollars.

In one of my many visits to Spinney's crammed, nine-by-ten-foot office on the second floor of the Pentagon, I asked him to discourse on the defense budget. He struggled through the clutter to reach a file folder, chuckling in mid-reach that "I used to have a larger office but they built a wall across this end so I wouldn't contaminate the others." Inside the folder was one of his latest blasts against his Pentagon bosses. It said "defense spending is out of control and about to explode."

As I fingered the tract, Spinney said in a voice tinged with anger and disgust: "These guys have set us up for a financial train wreck. This latest defense budget is dishonest, just like all the others of the last twenty years. There's going to be a financial train wreck. But nobody seems to give a damn."

The paper itself focused on the Air Force plan for buying fighters and attack planes in the twenty-first century. The big flaws in the Air Force's procurement plan, Spinney wrote, are the assumptions that the service will be able to control the costs of buying and maintaining the planes. Costs of the F-22 fighter will shoot up so high, the paper predicted, that the Air Force will have only enough money to buy a few of them. The Air Force for want of enough new planes will have to keep older aircraft flying way past their normal retirement age, driving up maintenance costs and endangering pilots. Spinney saw the twenty-first century Air Force comprised of a few futuristic flying Porsches and a lot of dented and smoking flying Fords.

With the $86.4 billion budgeted for Air Force procurement in the eighteen fiscal years 1996 through 2013, Spinney wrote, the Air Force will be able to buy only 982 of the new F-22 and Joint Strike Fighters. Those 982 planes, even in the unlikely event their predicted costs did not turn out to be understated, would be only one quarter of the 3,952 tactical aircraft the Air Force bought with almost the same amount of money, $91.5 billion, in the eighteen-year period fiscal 1973 through 1990. Those totals are in comparable fiscal 1996 dollars.

Spinney lamented that at the same time the Air Force and other armed services were reaching out for the smartest and most expensive new weapons, with the F-22 but one example, military leaders were unwilling to stop buying and fixing the superweapons designed for the cold war. The Army, Spinney complained, was still spending billions on heavy M-1 tanks and cumbersome Crusader artillery pieces that would be difficult to transport to a distant trouble spot in a hurry; the Navy was still building

$5 billion aircraft carriers and $2 billion attack submarines; the Marine Corps was buying the $80 million a copy V-22 Osprey transport to ferry troops from ship to shore.

I told Spinney that I did not believe that black-hearted, evil men ran the Defense Department, the armed services, Congress, or the defense industry. Each segment of this military-industrial-political complex is full of hard-working, patriotic people. So, assuming you are right about train wrecks ahead, why are not all these other people seeing and reacting to the red flags you see alongside the track?

"With the military guys it borders on malfeasance because they know what's going on," Spinney replied. "The problem is that they are in a zero sum game. They think that if they cancel something like the F-22, some other service or some other part of the Air Force will take that money away from them rather than let them spend it on different aircraft. This drives them to be excessively optimistic about a program when they know better. It's part of the bureaucratic gamesmanship around here. You could call that malfeasance because it's done consciously. On the other hand, there's enormous cultural pressure driving them in that direction. It may be just weak people who are afraid to do otherwise."

I countered that the secretary of defense and other civilian executives are chartered to oversee leaders of the Army, Navy, Air Force, and Marine Corps to make sure they do not spend taxpayer dollars on the wrong things. Where are they on these programs you say are out of control?

"The level of incompetence in civilian leaders and in their staffs has grown enormously since the B-1 bomber was canceled by President Carter in the 1970s," Spinney claimed. "President Clinton allows himself to get pushed around too much by the military. I also think he's tied in too close to the defense contractors. And that's a wicked mix. He doesn't have the wherewithal to make the kind of hard decisions that are now necessary.

"[Deputy Defense Secretary John] Hamre knows what I've been saying. He hasn't made any effort to understand it. Being a congressional staffer is not good preparation for being comptroller, deputy secretary of defense, or any other high appointee in this building. As a congressional staffer, you're basically serving a baron. His interest is your interest. No ifs, ands, or buts. The staffer comes up against the military leaders of the

Army, Navy, Air Force, and Marine Corps. They've risen up through some thirty years of infighting. No matter what kind of warriors they may be, they're smart and understand the bureaucracy of the American military. Political appointees are no match for these chiefs of the services and the bureaucracies they control.

"When a new appointee reports aboard, the chiefs and we bureaucrats treat him with deference. But a standard technique is to overload him and get him to make commitments early on. I was talking to a marine colonel plugged into the front office and he was laughing, saying, 'Cohen is already captured.'

"If the generals and admirals wanted to make changes to tailor their services to the twenty-first century instead of the last war, the cold war, they don't have very competent staffs to turn to. This is particularly true of the staff under the Joint Chiefs of Staff. There's been a big change in the Joint Chiefs of Staff since the cold war ended in 1989. During the cold war the chiefs and their staffs had their act together. They may have exaggerated the threat and the need for weapons, but they had a structure which got weapons out the factory doors.

"When [Gen. Colin L.] Powell took over as chairman of the Joint Chiefs of Staff in 1989, he and Vice Chairman William Owens changed things. They threw the old structures away. But the new ones they put in were so ambiguous that the staff of the Joint Chiefs of Staff doesn't know how to operate them to achieve the efficiency of the cold war in getting weapons built.

"We're not going to go off a cliff and all of a sudden the light is going to shine on," Spinney continued. "This is like the decline and fall of the Roman Empire. It took place over a thousand years. It was a huge mountain to go down. That's essentially what's happening here. We have a huge military structure, a huge military industrial complex. It's in a state of gradual decay and dissipation. But there's a lot of room to go.

"The money needed to buy the F-22 and fix up the old planes which should have been retired, for example, will drive the Air Force to generate money by reducing personnel even more. This will happen to the other services as well as they struggle to pay for their superweapons. With fewer people left in uniform, the harder those who remain in the armed services will have to work; the more often they will have to deploy. They will be tired of overwork and being away from their families so much, so they will quit, too.

"That's what's happening in the Air Force right now," continued the former Air Force captain. "Guys are punching out or volunteering to become training pilots so they don't have to be away so much. Something unheard of in my day or my father's day in the Air Force.

"Unless someone at the top takes hold of this place and forces change, the military is going to lose its professionalism and the Defense Department is going to become like the Agriculture Department.

"A lot of people are comparing today's situation with the period between World War I and World War II. I don't buy that a bit. We had a different kind of military back then. You had guys like Patton and Marshall and Eisenhower and Bradley who were first and foremost soldiers. They studied the soldierly profession. There was a lot of dead wood in the Army, but the leaders came out of a soldierly profession. With a few exceptions, our military now is a bunch of technocrats. They've lost sight of their reason for existence because they've been swept up by these political pressures. We're not going to have the cadre to expand from if we confront a real threat. We had that cadre in World War II. I don't see that out there now.

"The taxpayer is taking a bath. There literally is no peace dividend. We've structured a situation where the post–cold war military cannot be funded properly with a cold war budget" because the armed services will not discard their "legacy systems" and the new weapons they have ordered cost too much to buy and maintain.

Congress early in the twenty-first century, Spinney predicted, will wake up to the fact the extra billions it heaped on the Pentagon in the twentieth century did not increase the military's readiness to fight significantly nor buy enough weapons to replace most of the old ones. Then, and only then, will the generals and admirals be forced to let go of some of their pet cold war weapons. Otherwise, politically popular programs such as health care and Social Security will have to go short.

"It's just sad," Spinney said, "that the politicians are going to let the Pentagon keep wasting billions of dollars before they wake up to the fact that the taxpayers were had while the contractors got rich."

The Making of a Maverick

How did the former captain Chuck Spinney, son of Air Force colonel, become so disillusioned with a military he fell in love with at an early age and still loved when we talked in 1997, 1998, and 1999?

"If it hadn't been for what I saw during the Vietnam War and right afterward, I would have retired as a gray-haired colonel nobody ever heard of," Spinney answered.

He took me back to 1968 when Second Lieutenant Spinney, a mechanical engineering graduate of Lehigh University, was a dutiful flight test engineer at Ohio's Wright Patterson Air Force Base with the boring job of calculating how much noise vibration a wing could take without cracking. His life changed suddenly when he was assigned to an Air Force team trying to figure out how the North Vietnamese with their primitive weapons were managing to shoot down so many sophisticated Air Force planes.

"We've got to get more combat data from the field to find out what's happening," Spinney, one of the youngest and brashest men on the team, said he told his superiors. His elders went along with the upstart. Once the additional data from the field were in hand, the team knew for certain that the highly publicized SA-2 Guideline missile, the flying telephone pole, was not the big threat. "It was the smaller stuff," Spinney recalled, "23 millimeter and 37 millimeter antiaircraft guns." One bullet could down an airplane by puncturing its fuel tank or a hydraulic line.

The team recommended that the effort to fill fuel tanks with pourous foam to keep them from exploding be accelerated on existing aircraft and incorporated into new designs. Air Force leaders gratefully implemented this and other recommendations. Losses declined. The lesson Second Lieutenant Spinney learned from this experience was that ground truth was to be found at ground level.

The Air Force rewarded the young Spinney for his work by sending him to the University of Central Florida in 1971 to earn a master's degree in business administration. It also promoted him to captain. A year later the Air Force assigned Captain Spinney to the Pentagon to help coordinate Air Force answers to questions from senators and representatives. A related duty was to prepare "brain books" for the generals to take with them when they testified before congressional committees. The answers to any question likely to be asked were to be inserted in the brain books and indexed so a general's aide could retrieve them easily during the hearing. Those jobs gave Captain Spinney an overview of the whole United States Air Force—the way contractors developed and produced its weapons; the way the Air Force was split into competing fiefdoms, such as fighter pilots versus bomber pilots; the behavior that got officers promoted; the cost of keeping fancy aircraft and weapons in good repair; the planning for the next war. "Nothing fit together," Spinney said he discovered. Each fiefdom within the Air Force was grabbing off what it could for itself.

Boyd's Influence

Nobody at the top of the Air Force of the Pentagon's civilian hierarchy seemed to have the knowledge, power, or desire to make the pieces fit together. These discoveries began the radicalization of Chuck Spinney. Then Air Force Col. John Boyd came into his life, accelerating Spinney's radicalization.

Boyd was a hotshot fighter pilot in the air and a break-the-mold thinker on the ground. He made generals uncomfortable because he often told them they were wrong, physically leaning into them as he fervently made his points. One time Boyd, cigar aglow, leaned so far into a general that he burned a hole in the general's tie. In 1973 reformer Boyd put would-be reformer Spinney on his team to prioritize Air Force needs. "When we started asking how the Air Force intended to use the aircraft, what weapons it needed on it to fight future wars, what were the employment strategies, no one in the Air Force research directorate knew anything," Spinney recalled. This didn't bother Boyd. He would tell the Air Force what it needed. "Fuck what everybody else thinks," Boyd told Spinney in encouraging him to be bold in thoughts and actions. Boyd fired up Spinney's sense of mission. He and others on the team did think boldly. They broke the mold of big and cumbersome two-engine fighters and championed the Air Force's highly successful, single engine, agile F-16 fighter bomber.

Shortly before Christmas 1974, Spinney went through another shaping experience. The Air Force asked him to serve on a team addressing whether the B-1 bomber was going to cost so much to produce and maintain that other worthy programs would have to be financially starved. The B-1 at the time of Spinney's assignment had just shot through the $100 million cost barrier for a single aircraft. In the Senate, Wisconsin Democrat William Proxmire was questioning the worth of this most expensive aircraft ever built. The Air Force convened a Corona, the equivalent of a summit meeting, where the service's four-star generals address a crucial question. The findings of Spinney's team were to end up in the hands of Gen. David C. Jones, Air Force chief of staff. Jones would share the findings with the Corona before deciding whether the B-1 should live or die.

"What our analysis showed," Spinney said, "was that if the Air Force kept the B-1 going under the projected budgets, it would have to cancel every major program in development, including the F-15 and F-16 fighter planes; the A-10 flying tank killer. Everything. It was going to be a nightmare."

The Chapman Incident

Captain Spinney briefed Maj. Gen. Kenneth Chapman, a leader in the Air Force's research directorate, on the team's alarming findings. Junior officer Spinney advised general officer Chapman that the B-1 would have to be canceled to keep from bankrupting other important Air Force endeavors. Chapman, a B-1 enthusiast, was horrified.

"We're not doing it this way, Captain!" thundered the two-star general, Spinney recalled. "We're going to get more money than Spinney's study projected."

"General," Spinney said he replied, "we know how much money we're going to get."

"You're going to do it my way, Captain. That's a direct order." Chapman's way was to rewrite the briefing paper under the assumption that Congress was going to give the Air Force enough money to build a fleet of 240 B-1 bombers as well as other aircraft on the Air Force's wish list in 1974.

Spinney left Chapman's office furious and disillusioned. A general, as Captain Spinney saw it, had just ordered him to lie. He sat down in his fifth floor office at the Pentagon and agonized over what to do next. He did not want to lie. He did not want to disobey an order. The tiny light of an idea beckoned from deep inside his mind: Write one brief the way Chapman had just ordered but keep your own and write two others. Give Air Force leaders those four options to choose from. This might result in Jones's getting the truth without Spinney's having to disobey Chapman's order.

"I can't take all this paper into the chief," said Lt. Gen. William "Broadway Bill" Evans, deputy chief of staff for Air Force research and development, when Spinney handed him the four papers for briefing Jones shortly before Christmas 1974. Spinney and Chapman were jammed into a cluster of officers in Evans's office. "Which one do you like, captain?" Evans asked. "This one," Spinney replied, handing his original briefing paper to Evans to take into Jones and fellow four stars convened as Corona Quest. Chapman protested and glowered at Spinney.

"Ken," Evans told Chapman. "This is the biggest problem we're ever going to have to deal with in the Air Force. We've got to give the chief the best information. We're going with the captain."

Chapman strode out of the reception room angrily, Spinney said. Spinney left the generals and climbed the stairs to his fifth floor office in the rookery of the Pentagon. He sat at his desk and pondered what had just happened. Although he had outmaneuvered a two-star general, he was not elated. He was depressed. He had grown up on glorious Air Force stories told at his family's dining room table in Severna Park, Maryland. How could a two-star general in this same Air Force he had revered as a boy order him to lie to save a pet project? "What am I doing here?" He asked himself. Spinney sought solace and advice from a brigadier general in a neighboring office whom he admired.

"You know, Chuck," Brig. Gen. Harold Confers, a B-52 pilot, said after he heard Spinney's story, "if I had seen what you've seen at your age, I would have left the Air Force years ago."

Aftermath

Confers's words hardened Spinney's idea of quitting the Air Force. Although he was heartened by Jones's decision to start backing away from the B-1 because the Air Force simply could not afford it, Spinney firmly decided to leave the service. His fears that Christmas of 1974 that bomber enthusiasts and defense contractors would get the B-1 built, no matter what, would come true once Ronald Reagan became president in 1981. Spinney resigned from the Air Force in 1975 and took a job with a defense research firm in Silver Spring, Maryland. Its sole mission was to make money. Spinney hated the narrowness of the job; missed his boat-rocking buddies at the Pentagon, especially John Boyd. So, in 1977 when Thomas Christie, chief of the tactical aircraft directorate within the Pentagon's Office of Program Analysis and Evaluation, offered to take Spinney aboard as a civilian tactical aircraft analyst, Spinney jumped at the chance.

Spinney wrote, and Christie tolerated, a steady stream of papers claiming that the Defense Department had lost control over its contractors and their costs. He predicted more B-1-style financial train wrecks. He tried to describe the engine for the train wrecks he saw ahead in a chart-studded briefing entitled "The Plans/ Reality Mismatch." Republican senator Charles E. Grassley of Iowa successfully pressed the Senate Armed Services Committee to invite Spinney to present his briefing in a public hearing in 1983. To the consternation of Defense Secretary Caspar W. Weinberger and other Pentagon leaders, the press not only covered the Friday afternoon hearing but *Time* magazine put Spinney's picture on its March 7, 1983, cover with the headline: "Are Billions Being Wasted?" The cover story opened with quotes from Spinney's two-hour briefing, including these:

"Allowing for inflation, the Army is spending the same amount of money ($2 billion in 1983 dollars) on new tanks as it did 30 years ago, toward the end of the Korean War. But the number of tanks produced has declined by 90 percent, from 6,735 to 701.

"In 1951, 6,300 fighter planes were funded by the military [the Air Force and Navy] at a cost in 1983 dollars of $7 billion. The U.S. is now spending $11 billion to build only 322 planes, 95 percent fewer than in 1951.

"The Navy is budgeting for six new ships this year. To afford them, it is mothballing 22 older ships, many of which were recently overhauled because it must cut operating and maintenance costs. For the same reason, it is reducing the sailing time of its ships by 10 percent from 1982 to 1984. With its net loss of 16 ships, the Navy would appear to be sailing full speed astern in its effort to build a 600-ship fleet."

The fundamental reason the armed services were buying fewer weapons with the same amount of money, Spinney told the senators as contractors' representatives in the audience looked on, was "a systemic tendency to underestimate future costs. Deep-seated structural problems need to be addressed." One of the biggest structural problems, he said, was the Pentagon's fallacious assumption that the cost of a weapon will decline as it moves out of one-at-a-time construction, like building a watch by hand, and into quantity production, like watches coming off a factory assembly line. Constant changes after the weapon entered production enabled the contractors to raise their original prices, eating up the projected savings from quantity production, Spinney told the lawmakers. David Chu, the director of Program Analysis and Evaluation and thus Spinney's boss, sat beside Spinney at the witness table. He and others in the Pentagon hierarchy had tried to prevent Spinney from testifying. They found they could not impugn his figures and settled for saying Spinney was talking about the past, not the new order the Reagan administration would bring to the buying of weapons.

"Those charges ignore the various steps this administration has taken . . . to deal with these problems on a systematic and decisive basis," Chu told the senators. "I urge patience." Weinberger did not bother to meet with Spinney to hear him out, dismissing his findings and warnings as "purely historical."

I asked Spinney in 1999 if anybody at the top of the Pentagon had managed to stop runaway costs since he made the cover of *Time* in 1983.

"No," he replied.

12

Summing Up

No one could spend thirty-eight years studying the process of providing for the national defense from the up-front seat of a defense reporter without reaching some conclusions about how it could be improved. I am such a student and I do have some ideas for improving the system—ideas that I will share with you now.

My first front-row seat came in 1961 when I joined *Aviation Week and Space Technology* magazine to report on congressional actions on the defense and space budgets. Because most of the readers of the magazine are connected with the aerospace industry, I had to learn the technicalities of the weapons at issue to provide these specialists with the depth of reporting they wanted and deserved. So my five years at *Aviation Week* were like earning a master's degree in aerospace technology—knowledge that stood me in good stead when I became the defense correspondent for the *Washington Post* in 1966.

In my twenty-three years at the *Post* I interviewed every secretary of defense from Robert S. McNamara onward and every chairman of the Joint Chiefs of Staffs from that time to today. I have also conversed with almost every chief of the Army, Navy, Air Force, and Marine Corps and attended countless congressional hearings and military briefings. But my richest learning experiences came from doing what military people do in the field, or at least watching them from up close.

I humped around with rifle companies in Vietnam in two combat reporting tours in 1968 and 1972; lived on an aircraft carrier for seven and a half months and flew in every airplane on the deck; followed and often slept out in the field with Army recruits as their drill sergeants turned them from boys to soldiers; chronicled the training of Navy test pilots by going to school with them for eleven months and flew many of the same flights they flew, including upside-down spins, to learn how to evaluate an aircraft; joined troopers as they patrolled remote areas of Panama and Bosnia; and accompanied a Green Beret A-Team to Venezuela to see how they train the leaders of friendly foreign armies. These and other experiences provided grist not only for my newspaper stories but for six nonfiction books about the U.S. military, including this one.

Although I was in the pilot training program of what we used to call the Navy Air Corps for some nineteen months at the tail end of World War II, I list this experience last because I learned so little about the big picture of the American military. My focus, and that of my fellow naval aviation cadets, was not to flunk out of the program. I did not flunk out but took the option of leaving the Navy when it had a surplus of aviators trained during World War II, clouding the flying future for newcomers like me.

What I Think

Having now put my credentials on the table as a student of, not an expert on, the U.S. government and how it handles defense dollars and what the armed forces do in the field, I will end my guide role and tell you what I think about what we have seen and heard in the previous eleven chapters.

My transcendent conviction is that the process of providing, apportioning, and spending defense dollars is seriously, but not fatally, flawed. The fundamental mistake civilian and military leaders made when the Berlin Wall came down in 1989, marking the end of the cold war with the Soviet bloc, was failing to make and impose hard choices about the deployment, composition, and weapons of U.S. military forces. As I write this in the fall of 1999, those choices still have not been made.

Members of the NATO alliance should have staged a victory parade right after the Berlin Wall came down. Against this backdrop, the American president could have told our European friends that the torch of defending Europe had been passed to them. The United States would keep skeleton military staffs in Europe but not one hundred thousand troops. This not-so-subtle message might have deterred European countries from slashing military budgets and impelled their leaders to prepare to defend their own neighborhood.

In this post–cold war period, no U.S. president has told Europe to grow up and protect itself and backed up his words with action, such as withdrawing more U.S. troops from Europe. Instead, U.S. forces in 1999 shouldered almost all the burden of the air war against Yugoslav president Slobodan Milosevic, even though he was committing his atrocities and "ethnic cleansing" right there in Europe's front yard.

The supposedly little war against Milosevic severely strained the Air Force and, to lesser extent, the Navy. Although the air war succeeded and no NATO troops had to fight in Kosovo, I believe the strain of the war discredited the Clinton administration's claim that the American military, despite its downsizing since the cold war, could still fight two major theater wars (MTWs) almost simultaneously. I would stop making these "two MTW" claims in official pronouncements and let a future enemy worry about what the United States armed forces could and would do if it or its vital interests were attacked.

Although most analysts inside and outside the Pentagon believe that the Persian Gulf War of 1991 was the last hurrah for huge land armies making armored sweeps a la Gen. George Patton of World War II fame, civilian leaders in the White House, Pentagon, and Congress are permitting the armed services to continue buying and/or improving weapons designed for the Gulf War and the cold war before it. Examples of this, service by service:

- **Army.** Civilian leaders allowed the Army to overbuy M-1 tanks. Army figures show the service had purchased about eight thousand of those tanks costing $5.6 million each but has no use for two thousand of that total and put them in storage. Only about twenty-five hundred M-1s are with the active Army; three thousand-plus are with Army National Guard and reserve units. Despite all the talk about the need to make the Army lighter and more mobile, the downsized Army has told the Joint Chiefs that it will need more, not fewer, transport aircraft to lift its gear from the United States to global hot spots in the twenty-first century.

• **Navy.** Civilian leaders are allowing the Navy to continue buying $2 billion-a-copy nuclear-powered attack submarines that were designed to hunt down and destroy Soviet submarines during the cold war. Officers of the surface Navy—which includes carriers, cruisers, and destroyers that would be useful in the regional wars looming in the new century—worry that they will be starved for funds to pay for the new subs. The Pentagon in its Selected Acquisition Reports cost estimates of December 31, 1998, said that the three new SSN-21 Seawolf attack submarines will cost $13.4 billion, or $4.4 billion each. It estimated that the thirty SSN-774 nuclear attack subs to follow the Seawolf will cost $65 billion, or $2.2 billion each. Submariners insist the planned fleet of fifty attack subs will be too small for their undersea missions, including covert reconnaissance off the shores of unstable or threatening nations. Civilian leaders cannot let everybody have everything when there are just so many defense dollars to go around. They are chartered to make tough choices but have not done so.

• **Air Force.** Civilian leaders have permitted the Air Force in the post–cold war era to develop and produce the F-22 fighter designed to clear European skies of Warsaw Pact aircraft that no longer exist. No potential new enemy has a fighter that can match the F-15 and F-16 fighters the Air Force already has flying. While it is prudent to keep reaching for tomorrow's airplane to maintain the U.S. edge, I believe the lack of a significant fighter threat makes it safe and sensible to buy just a handful of F-22s rather than the 341 the Air Force has in mind. The Pentagon as of December 31, 1998, estimated that the 341 F-22s would cost $62.7 billion, or $184 million each. Buying that many F-22s would siphon away too much money from other Air Force programs.

The Air Force, if allowed to proceed to the full buy, will end up sacrificing quantity of aircraft for quality while starving programs more relevant to the future threat.

- **Marine Corps.** Two secretaries of defense did make a choice and canceled the Corps' prized aircraft, the V-22 Osprey, only to be overruled by Congress. The tiltrotor V-22 takes off and lands like a helicopter but flies farther and faster like a conventional airplane. It is designed to carry twenty-four marines from a ship offshore to a battle position deep inland. The Pentagon estimated as of December 31, 1998, that the 458 V-22s the marines intended to buy would cost $36.2 billion, or $79 million each. Marine Commandant Charles C. Krulak told me repeatedly that I was dead wrong to doubt the worth of the Osprey, declaring it would revolutionize warfare and be bought by the other armed services. The marines long have been attracted to aircraft that can fly in and out of tight places. The British-design AV-8B Harrier aircraft has that capability. I was told by Krulak's predecessors that the Harrier would revolutionize warfare. It did not live up to that advance advertising, primarily because it can carry far fewer bombs than conventional tactical fighter bombers. So where's the beef? I have no doubt that the V-22 Osprey, like the Harrier before it, will be a star in air shows. But I question whether it can be bought in quantity without taking an inordinate amount of money away from more traditional and more vital marine needs. A top Army general told me that his service has no intention of buying the V-22 because "it can't carry anything."

As for the Pentagon process for buying weapons, I think it is badly in need of overhaul. Given that the United States will have no peer competitor for at least ten years and probably more, I would take military officers out of their full-time procurement jobs. They are burdened in those jobs by parochialism and by bosses who want the project at hand to continue moving forward even if reason dictates that it be stopped. I would still rely on military professionals to specify what they needed in a new plane, truck, ship, or weapon but would leave it to civilians to get prototypes built and to oversee their development. With no major threats in sight, the Pentagon has time to test prototypes against each other and choose the best one. Designing and producing weapons at the same time, called concurrency, is wasteful and unjustified in the absence of a major threat.

Although Secretary Cohen and his recent predecessors have vowed to force the Pentagon to act more like a private business when it spends tax-payer dollars, tough choices have not been made to reduce the size of the defense industry. Taxpayer money is being wasted, for example, in allowing the Lockheed Martin Corp. to spread the work of building the F-22 fighter in two different and far-apart plants: Marietta, Georgia, and Fort Worth, Texas. The F-22 could be built in a corner of either plant, saving the taxpayer millions in overhead. This move, of course, would generate protests from the politicians in the state that lost the work. Rather than take on those politicians, civilian leaders in the White House, Pentagon, and Congress have not saved defense dollars by reducing the wasteful overcapacity in the defense industry.

Greider: A Kindred Soul

William Greider, a brilliant columnist and a former editor of the *Washington Post,* spent months studying the military-industrial-political complex before writing a compelling book about it entitled *Fortress America.* I found myself agreeing with many of his keen observations in the book and several he expressed in a tape recorded interview with me, including:

"An anomaly of the cold war," Greider told me, "was that—while it consumed great fortunes and made a lot of jobs and became a great political rallying cry over two generations—it wasn't a world war. So when we came out of it, and the Soviet Union suddenly went poof, there was no visible end. No victory parades. There wasn't an end point. There was nothing forcing the American people to shake themselves and say, 'We're at peace.' The American people were not suddenly relieved of their cold war burdens because their faint-hearted leaders just kept acting like the cold war was still going.

"The cold war was an unreal episode because we did pay the freight. We did deploy troops forward. We did nurture the economics of our allies and former enemy at the same time. I think it was a great stroke of history. But I think we should have begun to unwind it twenty years ago. We should have said to the Europeans and Japanese, 'Time to be grownups. You're not poor and groveling anymore. Time to shoulder this burden of defending yourselves.'"

In contrast to U.S. government leaders who looked upon the cold war as war without end and refused to play for a different future, the defense contractors after the Berlin Wall came down began to face up to the new realities, Greider said. They were fat with fixed-price contracts placed by the Ronald Reagan administration. The contractors knew, however, that the Reagan business would run out if no new enemy emerged to replace the Warsaw Pact.

"A few contractors stared at the clouds on their horizon and saw how to extract the silver lining from them. If a fixed-price contract signed in the Reagan years required the government to pay $100 million dollars for a hundred missiles, for example, the contractor might be able to pocket most of the $50 million difference if he delivered the hundred missiles for $50 million. He could reduce his costs by merging with another contractor, using only one of the two production lines and firing thousands of workers. The executives of the merged firm would get rich; the company's stock would soar as Wall Street came to understand the play."

Enter Defense Secretary Les Aspin. The former economics professor and chairman of the House Armed Services Committee took over the Pentagon for Clinton on January 20, 1993. He kept on the job Deputy Defense Secretary William J. Perry, a veteran of both the Pentagon and the defense industry. Both knew there were too many aircraft factories and shipyards for the armed services to support in the post–cold war period. They sought to consolidate the defense facilities without dictating the move. The enticement to consolidate was held out by Perry at a dinner that became known within the military-industrial complex as the *Last Supper.* Greider describes the scene in *Fortress America:*

> In the spring of 1993, Deputy Defense Secretary William Perry, an old industry hand himself, hosted a private dinner for leading prime contractors where he predicted that half of them would probably be gone in five

years. Norm Augustine of Martin Marietta with his penchant for melo-dramatic metaphors dubbed the occasion "the Last Supper."

But Perry was actually delivering some good news to the companies: if they proceeded with a market driven consolidation, he told them, the Pentagon would reward them by sharing the benefits with their companies.

Wolfgang Demisch [a defense analyst at Bankers Trust of New York] explains: "Under defense contracting, if you put two companies together and you rationalize the production costs, the cost savings would normally go more or less 100 percent to Uncle Sam. That doesn't give managers and shareholders much incentive to eat the dirt. What Perry did was to say that as long as Uncle Sam saves more on contracts, some of the cost savings would go to the companies."

This new approach was explicitly ratified a month or so later in new procurement regulations: if companies reduced costs by restructuring and consolidating, the Pentagon would let them collect a share of the future savings up front by charging the restructuring to their existing contracts. The firms began filing claims for hundreds of millions of dollars in reim-bursements, a practice that will reach many billions if it's allowed to continue. When Congress finally figured out what was going on, critics denounced this reform as "payoffs for layoffs." It looks like a discreet sub-sidy for dumping jobs, and it is.

While the defense workers got poor, the defense executives and their stockholders who stayed in business got rich, Greider said. Because the government paid the light, water, heat, and other expenses at the plant the merged contractor had virtually abandoned, it cost the contractor next to nothing to assign just enough people to the plant to keep it alive.

"The defense industry has this peculiar state/private nature," Greider told me in an interview. "The Pentagon has this conflicting interest be-tween getting the best value for the taxpayer's dollar and keeping these companies healthy. In a sense, the government created these companies and winked at the huge profits the mergers brought them because the government was for consolidation, at least up to a point.

"What the nation's defense leaders didn't stop and say is, 'What's hap-pening to the real productive capacity of this industrial base?' If I had been czar, I would have said, 'We all know this has to happen. It's going to be painful to a lot of employees and some companies, but you've got to start shutting down assembly lines right now; turn out the lights rather than waste all this money waiting for a world war three.

" 'We'll protect you from the fallout in Congress coming from shutting down these excess defense plants. We know the politicians are going to scream bloody murder. If you think they're pissed about base closures, wait till you close down government plants at Fort Worth or Marietta, Georgia. But if we don't do that, we haven't really solved the problem. We're stuck with a lot of empty factories pretending to be alive and ready, but they're really not.

" 'So let's face the music and pay the price up front. The government will give workers and communities some help adjusting to the plant closings. Your shareholders have nothing to complain about. They have had a good ride buying into the defense industry, but that ride is over.'

"Our government leaders didn't have the guts to do that," Greider said. "So now, for example, we have this huge B-2 bomber plant in Palmdale, California, that was built only fifteen years ago but has no purpose because we're not going to build any more B-2s. But it is still open, doing a little bit of work. And the taxpayers are paying to keep open the place we no longer need. Some day they're going to have to choose between Georgia and Texas."

"Because that hasn't happened, the defense base is still operating at only 35 percent of its total capacity. That means you could eliminate one-third of our industrial base and still produce twice as many weapons as it is producing now.

"We can't keep going on like this even with budget surpluses. The military establishment and the White House are going to be driven to making choices between weapons, force size, and design. Rational argument will not be the driver but the economic and fiscal condition of the country [will be].

"The golden moment [of prosperity] is going to pass, and we're going to be back to the guns versus butter argument, very explicitly and very clearly. I don't think the American people are going to be sold on a major defense buildup in peacetime that whacks the rest of the government directly. I think that's going to play out faster than most people imagine.

"We've got a lot of national priorities, whether it's schools or infrastructure, that are being shortchanged because we haven't really faced up to the size of our defense establishment. I hear murmurings from business people and others who are trying to build a campaign along those lines. It's an argument over priorities coupled with an argument for a different kind of international system.

"We'll have a runup to the year 2000 presidential election in which the defense industry will be hounding every candidate in both parties for commitments to build the weapons and jack up the Pentagon budget. The armed services will be trying for the same thing, though less blatantly."

While the generals and admirals will keep lobbying for more super-weapons in the twenty-first century, thoughtful midgrade officers will increasingly question this choice of toys over boys, Greider predicted. In touring the country to promote his book, Greider said he heard many military people complain about the siphoning off of training, housing, and maintenance funds to pay for high-tech weapons.

"What they're beginning to realize is that they're being rolled by the industry," he said of midgrade military officers. "And that's new in politics. That's a potential split in the Iron Triangle" [of defense contractors, military leaders, and Congress].

If these midgrade officers express their concerns to Congress, "it's going to be very interesting to see which side the guys on the Hill choose," Greider said. "Are they really for the services or are they really just trying to defend the contracts?"

The contractors who are counting on budget surpluses to bring back another boom in weapons buying "will be tripped up by the economic reality." Greider in early 1999 predicted that an economic slump within the next few years would derail contractor hopes for another Reagan-style defense buildup.

It Takes a President

I told Greider during our long conversation, and now tell you, that I doubted Congress would reform itself to improve the process of appropriating and spending defense dollars. There are too many fiefdoms. The relations between the defense industry, the armed services, and the lawmakers are too cozy. I think that only the president of the United States can significantly improve the process. The president, after all, is the commander in chief of the armed forces and must act like one to build an effective military at minimum cost.

Not since Jimmy Carter, who was president from 1977 through 1980, has a president immersed himself deeply in defense issues and teamed up with his secretary of defense to force radical change on the military-industrial-complex. It was Carter and Defense Secretary Harold Brown who canceled the Air Force B-1 bomber and denied the Navy a new aircraft carrier—two monumental and controversial decisions.

Although Congress protested those and other decisions by Carter, it went along with them until President Reagan came to office in 1981 and reversed Carter. A president willing to take on the big defense issues of the day and explain his decisions to the public can prevail over congressional opponents. The ideal combination would be a president with Eisenhower's military credibility and Carter's political guts. Without such a strong and involved president, however, the military-industrial-political complex will continue to waste billions of dollars in preparing for the most recent war rather than the most likely next one.

Defense Secretary Cohen has been a consensus mechanic—and a good one. But consensus in national defense means settling for the lowest common political denominator. I do not think that is good enough in the dangerous, unstable world of the twenty-first century. I think the president has to lead; to make the hard choices and explain them to the American people; to push Congress in the president's chosen direction rather than chat by the side of the road until a compromise route is agreed upon.

Glossary

Appropriation   An appropriation is an act of Congress that enables federal agencies to spend money for specific purposes.

Authorization   An authorization is an act of Congress that establishes or continues a federal program or agency and sets forth the guidelines to which it must adhere.

Balanced Budget   A balanced budget occurs when total revenues equal total outlays for a fiscal year.

Budget Authority (BA)   Budget authority is what the law authorizes, or allows, the federal government to spend for programs, projects, or activities.

Budget Enforcement Act (BEA) of 1990   The BEA is the law that was designed to limit discretionary spending while ensuring that any new entitlement program or tax cuts did not make the deficit worse. It set annual limits on total discretionary spending and created "pay-as-you-go" rules for any changes in entitlements and taxes (see "pay-as-you-go").

Balanced Budget and Emergency Deficit Control Act of 1985   (Gramm-Rudman-Hollings, or GRH) The Balanced Budget and Emergency Deficit Control Act of 1985 was designed to end deficit spending. It set annual deficit targets for five years, declining to a balanced budget in 1991. If necessary, it required across-the-board cuts in programs to comply with the deficit targets. It was never fully implemented.

Budget Resolution   The budget resolution is the annual framework within which Congress makes its decisions about spending and taxes. This framework includes targets for total spending, total revenues, and the deficit, as well as thirty-five allocations, within the spending target, for discretionary and mandatory spending.

"Cap"   A "cap" is a legal limit on annual discretionary spending.

Deficit   The deficit is the difference produced when spending exceeds revenues in a fiscal year.

Discretionary Spending   Discretionary spending is what the president and Congress must decide to spend for the next fiscal year through thirteen annual appropriations bills. Examples include money for such activities as the FBI and the Coast Guard, housing and education, space exploration and highway construction, and defense and foreign aid.

Entitlement   An entitlement is a program that legally obligates the federal government to make payments to any person who meets the legal criteria for eligibility. Examples include Social Security, Medicare, and Medicaid.

Excise Taxes   Excise taxes apply to various products, including alcohol, tobacco, transportation fuels, and telephone service.

Federal Debt   The gross federal debt is divided into two categories: debt held by the public, and debt the government owes itself. Another category is debt subject to legal limit.

Debt Held by the Public   Debt held by the public is the total of all federal deficits, minus surplus, over the years. This is the cumulative amount of money the federal government has borrowed from the public, through the sale of notes and bonds of varying sizes and time periods.

Debt the Government Owes Itself   Debt the government owes itself is the total of all trust fund surplus over the years, like the Social Security surplus, that the law says must be invested in federal securities.

Debt Subject to Legal Limit   Debt subject to legal limit, which is roughly the same as gross federal debt, is the maximum amount of federal securities that may be legally outstanding at any time. When the limit is reached, the president and Congress must enact a law to increase it.

Fiscal Year   The fiscal year is the government's accounting period. It begins October 1 and ends on September 30. For example, fiscal 2000 ends September 30, 2000.

Gramm-Rudman-Hollings   See Balanced Budget and Emergency Deficit Control Act of 1985.

Gross Domestic Product (GDP)   GDP is the standard measurement of the size of the economy. It is the total production of goods and services within the United States.

Mandatory Spending   Mandatory spending is authorized by permanent law. An example is Social Security. The president and Congress can change the law to change the level of spending on mandatory programs—but they don't have to.

"Off-Budget"   By law, the government must distinguish "off-budget" programs separate from the budget totals. Social Security and the Postal Service are "off-budget."

Outlays   Outlays are the amount of money the government actually spends in a given fiscal year.

"Pay-As-You-Go"   Set forth by the BEA, "pay-as-you-go" refers to requirements that new spending proposals on entitlements or tax cuts must be offset by cuts in other entitlements or by other tax increases, to ensure that the deficit does not rise (see BEA).

Revenue   Revenue is money collected by the government.

Social Insurance Payroll Taxes   This tax category includes Social Security taxes, Medicare taxes, unemployment insurance taxes, and federal employee retirement payments.

Surplus   A surplus is the amount by which revenues exceed outlays.

Trust Funds   Trust funds are government accounts, set forth by law as trust funds, for revenues and spending designated for specific purposes.

Unified Federal Budget   The unified budget, the most useful display of the government's finances, is the presentation of the federal budget in which revenues from all sources and outlays to all activities are consolidated.

Source: White House Office of Management and Budget.

The Federal Government Dollar—
Where It Comes From

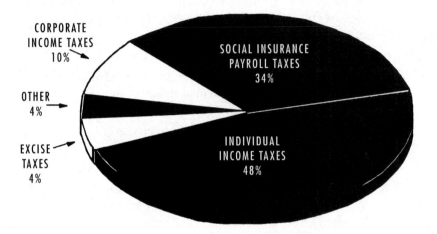

CORPORATE
INCOME TAXES
10%

OTHER
4%

EXCISE
TAXES
4%

SOCIAL INSURANCE
PAYROLL TAXES
34%

INDIVIDUAL
INCOME TAXES
48%

The money that the federal government uses to pay its bills—its revenues —comes mostly from taxes. In 1998 revenues were greater than spending, and the government was able to reduce the national debt with the difference between revenues and spending—that is, the surplus.

Revenues come from these sources:

- Individual income taxes will raise an estimated $900 billion in 2000, equal to about 10 percent of GDP.

- Social insurance payroll taxes—the fastest growing category of federal revenues—include Social Security taxes, Medicare taxes, unemployment insurance taxes, and federal employee retirement payments. This category has grown from 2 percent of GDP in 1955 to an estimated 7 percent in 2000.

- Corporate income taxes, which will raise an estimated $189 billion, have shrunk steadily as a percent of GDP, from 4.5 percent in 1955 to an estimated 2.1 percent in 2000.

Source: White House Office of Management and Budget.

Revenues by Source—Summary

($ billions)

Source	1998 Actual				Estimate		
		1999	2000	2001	2002	2003	2004
Individual income taxes	829	869	900	912	943	971	1,018
Corporate income taxes	189	182	189	197	203	212	221
Payroll taxes	572	609	637	660	686	712	739
Excise taxes	58	68	70	71	72	74	75
Estate and gift taxes	24	26	27	28	30	32	34
Customs duties	18	18	18	20	21	23	25
Miscellaneous receipts	33	35	42	45	50	52	53
TOTAL RECEIPTS	1,722	1,806	1,883	1,933	2,007	2,075	2,166

Notes: The revenues listed in this table do not include revenues from the government's business-like activities—i.e., the sale of electricity and fees at national parks. The government counts these revenues on the spending side of the budget, deducting them from other spending to calculate its outlays for the year.

Numbers may not add to the totals because of rounding.

- Excise taxes apply to various products, including alcohol, tobacco, transportation fuels, and telephone services. The government earmarks some of these taxes to support certain activities—including highways and airports and airways—and deposits others in the general fund.

- The government also collects miscellaneous revenues—e.g., customs duties, Federal Reserve earnings, fines, penalties, and forfeitures.

Source: White House Office of Management and Budget.

The Federal Government Dollar—
Where It Goes

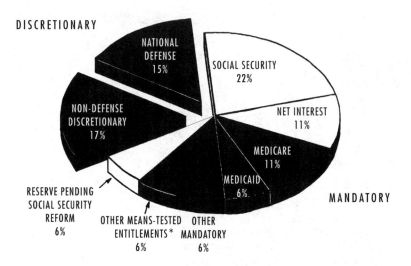

DISCRETIONARY

NATIONAL DEFENSE 15%

SOCIAL SECURITY 22%

NON-DEFENSE DISCRETIONARY 17%

NET INTEREST 11%

MEDICARE 11%

MEDICAID 6%

MANDATORY

RESERVE PENDING SOCIAL SECURITY REFORM 6%

OTHER MEANS-TESTED ENTITLEMENTS* 6%

OTHER MANDATORY 6%

* Means-tested entitlements are those for which eligibility is based on income. The Medicaid program is also a means-tested entitlement.

[1] In calculating federal spending, the government deducts collections (revenues) generated by the government's business-like activities, such as fees to national parks. These collections will total an estimated $216 billion in 2000. Without them, spending would total an estimated $2.0 trillion in 2000, not $1.8 trillion.

Spending

Federal government will spend nearly $1.8 trillion,[1] and have a surplus of over $117 billion in 2000, which we divided into nine large categories as shown in the chart above.

- The largest Federal program is Social Security, which will provide monthly benefits to nearly 45 million retired and disabled workers, their dependents, and survivors. It accounts for 22 percent of your federal dollar (or 23 percent of all Federal spending).

- Medicare, which will provide health care coverage for over almost 40 million elderly Americans and people with disabilities, consists of Part A (hospital insurance) and Part B (insurance for physician costs and other services). Since its birth in 1965, Medicare has accounted for an ever-growing share of spending. In 2000 it will comprise 11 percent of your federal dollar (or 12 percent of all federal spending).

- Medicaid, in 2000, will provide health care services to almost 34 million Americans, including the poor, people with disabilities, and senior citizens in nursing homes. Unlike Medicare, the federal government shares the costs of Medicaid with the states, paying between 50 and 83 percent of the total (depending on each state's requirements). Federal and state costs are growing rapidly. Medicaid accounts for 6 percent of your federal dollar (also 6 percent of the budget).

- Other means-tested entitlements provide benefits to people and families with incomes below certain minimum levels that vary from program to program. The major means-tested entitlements are Food Stamps and food aid to Puerto Rico, Supplemental Security Income, Child Nutrition, the Earned Income Tax Credit, and veterans' pensions. This category will account for an estimated 6 percent of your federal dollar (also 6 percent of the budget).

- The remaining mandatory spending, which mainly consists of federal retirement and insurance programs, unemployment insurance, and payments to farmers, comprises 6 percent of your federal dollar (also 6 percent of the budget).

- National defense discretionary spending will total an estimated $275 billion in 2000, comprising nearly 15 percent of your federal dollar (and 16 percent of the budget).

- Nondefense discretionary spending—a wide array of programs that include education, training, science, technology, housing, transportation, and foreign aid—has shrunk as a share of the budget from 23 percent in 1966 to an estimated 18 percent in 2000 (or 17 percent of your federal dollar).

- Interest payments, primarily the result of previous budget deficits, averaged 7 percent of federal spending in the 1960s and 1970s. But, due to the large budget deficits that began in the 1980s that share quickly doubled to 15 percent. Since the budget is now in surplus, interest payments are estimated to drop to 12 percent of the budget in 2000 (11 percent of your federal dollar).

- Six percent of your federal dollar (the budget surplus) will not be spent. The president has proposed that any surplus be reserved until a plan to save Social Security has been enacted.

Source: White House Office of Management and Budget.

Total Spending by Function
(Outlays, $ billions)

Function	1998 Actual	Estimate 1999	2000	2001	2002	2003	2004
NATIONAL DEFENSE:							
Department of Defense-Military	256	264	261	269	278	290	300
Other	12	13	13	14	14	14	14
Total, national defense	268	277	274	282	292	304	314
International affairs	13	15	16	17	18	18	18
General science, space, and technology	18	19	19	19	19	19	19
Energy	1	*	-2	-1	-1	-1	-1
Natural resources and environment	22	24	24	24	24	24	24
Agriculture	12	21	15	13	11	10	10
Commerce and housing credit	1	*	6	8	9	10	10
Transportation	40	43	46	49	50	52	53
Community and regional development	10	10	10	10	10	9	9
Education, training, employment, and social services	55	60	63	68	67	69	70
Health	131	143	152	163	173	185	197
Medicare	193	205	217	231	235	252	266
Income security	233	243	258	267	275	282	291
Social security	379	393	409	427	447	468	491
Veterans benefits and services	42	44	44	45	46	47	48
Administration of justice	23	24	28	29	28	28	28
General government	13	15	14	15	15	15	15
Net interest	243	227	215	206	195	183	173
Allowances		3	3	-27	-40	-34	-29
Undistributed offsetting receipts	-47	-40	-46	-45	-51	-47	-48
TOTAL	1,653	1,727	1,766	1,799	1,820	1,893	1,958

* $500 million or less.

Note: Spending that is shown as a minus means that receipts exceed outlays.

Numbers may not add to the totals because of rounding.

Source: White House Office of Management and Budget.

Discretionary Spending by Agency
(Outlays, $ billions)

Agency	1998 Actual	Estimate					
		1999	2000	2001	2002	2003	2004
Legislative Branch	2	2	3	3	3	3	3
Judicial Branch	3	3	4	4	4	4	4
Agriculture	16	17	16	15	15	15	15
Commerce	4	5	7	5	5	5	5
Defense-Military	258	265	262	269	279	291	301
Education	26	29	32	35	35	35	35
Energy	17	17	18	18	18	18	18
Health and Human Services	35	39	42	43	43	43	43
Housing and Urban Development	33	33	34	34	32	31	30
Interior	7	8	8	9	9	9	9
Justice	15	16	19	20	19	19	19
Labor	10	11	11	11	11	12	12
State	5	6	6	7	7	6	7
Transportation	37	40	43	46	48	49	51
Treasury	11	12	12	13	13	13	13
Veterans Affairs	18	19	19	19	19	19	19
Corps of Engineers	4	4	4	4	4	4	4
Other Defense Civil Programs	*	*	*	*	*	*	*
Environmental Protection Agency	7	7	7	8	7	7	7
Executive Office of the President	*	*	*	*	*	*	*
Federal Emergency Management Agency	3	3	3	3	2	2	2
General Services Administration	1	*	*	*	*	*	*
International Assistance Programs	11	12	12	12	13	12	12
National Aeronautics and Space Administration	14	14	13	13	13	14	14
National Science Foundation	3	3	4	4	4	4	4
Office of Personnel Management	*	*	*	*	*	*	*

Agency	1998 Actual	Estimate					
		1999	2000	2001	2002	2003	2004
Small Business Administration	1	1	1	1	1	1	1
Social Security Administration	5	6	6	6	6	6	6
Other Independent Agencies	6	6	6	6	7	7	7
Allowances		3	3	-24	-36	-29	-24
Undistributed offsetting receipts			-3	1	1	-*	-*
TOTAL	555	581	592	586	582	600	615

* $500 million or less.

Note: Discretionary spending is appropriated by the Congress each year, in contrast with mandatory spending, which is automatic under permanent law. Spending that is shown as a minus means that receipts exceed outlays.

Numbers may not add to the totals because of rounding.

Source: White House Office of Management and Budget.

Department of Defense Outlays by Service, 1945–2005 ($ millions)

	FY 45	FY 46	FY 47	FY 48	FY 49	FY 50	FY 51	FY 52	FY 53	FY 54	FY 55
Current Dollars											
Army	30,402	17,914	5,189	3,396	3,488	3,916	7,395	15,561	16,249	12,828	8,788
Navy	28,848	14,153	5,461	3,845	3,952	4,035	5,528	10,112	11,616	11,208	9,694
Air Force	17,155	8,032	2,415	2,735	3,601	3,519	6,287	12,650	15,137	15,588	16,227
Defense-wide	57	85	140	175	200	205	362	392	409	432	461
Total, Current $	76,462	40,184	13,205	10,151	11,241	11,674	19,572	38,716	43,410	40,056	35,169
Constant FY 2000 Dollars											
Army	387,416	231,228	66,252	42,595	43,638	42,795	73,004	132,896	132,614	110,039	80,611
Navy	359,922	184,197	62,147	43,602	42,866	41,981	53,294	88,083	100,132	97,141	83,022
Air Force	215,419	102,910	28,149	28,939	35,661	34,457	52,580	102,229	118,649	122,673	121,387
Defense-wide	1,162	1,478	1,861	2,197	2,472	2,640	2,901	3,163	3,267	3,686	3,722
Total, Constant $	963,918	519,813	158,409	117,333	124,636	121,872	181,779	326,371	354,662	333,539	288,742
% Real Growth											
Army		-40.3	-71.4	-35.7	2.4	-1.9	70.6	82.0	-0.2	-17.0	-26.8
Navy		-48.8	-66.3	-29.9	-1.7	-2.1	26.9	65.3	13.7	-3.0	-14.5
Air Force		-52.2	-72.7	2.8	23.2	-3.4	52.6	94.4	16.1	3.4	-1.1
Total		-46.1	-69.5	-25.9	6.2	-2.2	49.2	79.5	8.7	-6.0	-13.4

	FY 56	FY 57	FY 58	FY 59	FY 60	FY 61	FY 62	FY 63	FY 64	FY 65
Current Dollars										
Army	8,588	8,972	9,131	9,533	9,453	10,145	11,248	11,476	12,011	11,552
Navy	9,641	10,318	11,009	11,835	11,726	12,234	13,191	13,973	14,466	13,339
Air Force	16,613	18,235	18,411	19,249	19,289	19,804	20,790	20,610	20,456	18,146
Defense-wide	554	572	644	849	1,025	1,109	1,597	1,882	2,537	2,843
Total, Current $	35,396	38,098	39,194	41,467	41,494	43,292	46,826	47,941	49,470	45,880
Constant FY 2000 Dollars										
Army	73,800	74,293	70,707	69,319	68,015	70,053	77,591	77,202	77,349	73,284
Navy	79,073	80,168	80,101	83,175	82,654	83,408	89,530	94,930	93,691	84,720
Air Force	118,624	122,888	119,548	119,996	120,095	119,845	127,051	125,101	121,689	107,070
Defense-wide	4,121	4,129	4,558	5,423	6,427	7,002	9,740	11,794	15,047	16,605
Total, Constant $	275,618	281,457	274,914	277,912	277,190	280,308	303,912	309,027	307,775	281,680
% Real Growth										
Army	-8.5	0.7	-4.8	-2.0	-1.9	3.0	10.8	-0.5	0.2	-5.3
Navy	-4.8	1.4	-0.1	3.8	-0.6	0.9	7.3	6.0	-1.3	-9.6
Air Force	-2.3	3.6	-2.7	0.4	0.1	-0.2	6.0	-1.5	-2.7	-12.0
Total	-4.6	2.1	-2.3	1.1	-0.3	1.1	8.4	1.7	-0.4	-8.5

	FY 66	FY 67	FY 68	FY 69	FY 70	FY 71	FY 72	FY 73	FY 74	FY 75
Current Dollars										
Army	14,732	20,958	25,222	25,033	24,749	23,077	22,596	20,185	21,395	21,920
Navy	15,962	19,246	22,072	22,505	22,505	22,051	22,336	22,470	23,984	27,393
Air Force	20,065	22,912	25,734	25,892	24,867	23,778	23,999	23,627	23,928	25,042
Defense-wide	3,335	4,241	4,237	4,355	4,948	5,565	6,146	6,940	8,243	10,544
Total, Current $	54,093	67,357	77,266	77,785	77,070	74,472	75,076	73,223	77,550	84,900
Constant FY 2000 Dollars										
Army	85,680	113,529	129,484	124,395	114,555	101,369	91,120	76,709	75,889	70,629
Navy	93,321	105,759	115,044	113,689	105,575	97,142	90,131	85,137	83,910	86,347
Air Force	112,358	122,140	130,440	126,328	114,463	103,966	97,344	89,911	84,173	77,806
Defense-wide	18,830	22,761	22,493	22,496	23,839	24,691	25,717	27,488	29,928	33,532
Total, Constant $	310,189	364,189	397,460	386,908	358,431	327,168	304,313	279,246	273,901	268,314
% Real Growth										
Army	16.9	32.5	14.1	-3.9	-7.9	-11.5	-10.1	-15.8	-1.1	-6.9
Navy	10.2	13.3	8.8	-1.2	-7.1	-8.0	-7.2	-5.6	-1.5	2.9
Air Force	4.9	8.7	6.8	-3.2	-9.4	-9.2	-6.4	-7.6	-6.4	-7.6
Total	10.1	17.4	9.1	-2.7	-7.4	-8.7	-7.0	-8.2	-1.9	-2.0

	FY 76	FY 77	FY 78	FY 79	FY 80	FY 81	FY 82	FY 83	FY 84	FY 85
Current Dollars										
Army	21,398	23,919	26,019	28,770	32,601	37,620	45,281	51,520	55,655	66,708
Navy	28,462	30,775	33,524	37,813	42,710	50,482	59,242	67,402	70,920	84,197
Air Force	26,446	27,915	29,217	32,277	38,976	45,157	55,676	62,894	68,620	81,988
Defense-wide	11,585	12,948	14,282	16,153	18,554	22,895	24,321	23,224	25,611	12,476
Total, Current $	87,891	95,557	103,042	115,013	132,840	156,153	184,520	205,040	220,806	245,370
Constant FY 2000 Dollars										
Army	64,806	67,635	68,549	70,700	73,065	75,277	81,827	88,082	90,910	102,793
Navy	83,926	84,221	85,368	89,270	89,751	94,369	100,698	109,371	110,871	126,291
Air Force	77,335	75,658	73,998	75,449	79,666	82,136	91,426	99,536	104,699	120,444
Defense-wide	33,705	35,237	36,257	37,896	39,020	43,145	43,239	39,751	42,115	19,154
Total, Constant $	259,772	262,750	264,171	273,315	281,502	294,928	317,190	336,740	348,595	368,682
% Real Growth										
Army	-8.3	4.4	1.4	3.1	3.3	3.0	8.7	7.6	3.2	13.1
Navy	-2.8	0.4	1.4	4.6	0.5	5.1	6.7	8.6	1.4	13.9
Air Force	-0.6	-2.2	-2.2	2.0	5.6	3.1	11.3	8.9	5.2	15.0
Total	-3.2	1.1	0.5	3.5	3.0	4.8	7.5	6.2	3.5	5.8

	FY 86	FY 87	FY 88	FY 89	FY 90	FY 91	FY 92	FY 93	FY 94	FY 95
Current Dollars										
Army	71,107	73,808	77,315	79,973	78,017	90,360	79,228	72,233	64,999	63,692
Navy	88,492	90,813	94,570	101,171	97,725	102,180	96,858	94,914	85,927	85,910
Air Force	91,188	91,144	93,060	94,676	93,546	94,510	85,019	83,802	80,289	76,799
Defense-wide	14,848	18,241	16,990	19,060	20,468	-24,661	25,526	27,626	37,420	34,207
Total, Current $	265,636	274,007	281,935	294,880	289,755	262,389	286,632	278,574	268,635	260,608
Constant FY 2000 Dollars										
Army	106,306	107,255	108,136	107,360	101,919	111,998	96,344	84,826	74,889	71,826
Navy	129,476	129,070	130,208	133,586	125,295	124,148	115,170	109,684	96,740	94,840
Air Force	131,027	127,688	126,762	123,903	118,774	112,820	100,532	96,021	90,033	84,906
Defense-wide	22,067	26,018	23,481	25,099	25,838	-28,013	29,784	31,570	41,625	37,372
Total, Constant $	388,876	390,031	388,586	389,949	371,827	320,953	341,830	322,102	303,288	288,945
% Real Growth										
Army	3.4	0.9	0.8	-0.7	-5.1	9.9	-14.0	-12.0	-11.7	-4.1
Navy	2.5	-0.3	0.9	2.6	-6.2	-0.9	-7.2	-4.8	-11.8	-2.0
Air Force	8.8	-2.6	-0.7	-2.3	-4.1	-5.0	-10.9	-4.5	-6.2	-5.7
Total	5.5	0.3	-0.4	0.4	-4.7	-13.7	6.5	-5.8	-5.9	-4.7

	FY 96	FY 97	FY 98	FY 99	FY 00	FY 01	FY 02	FY 03	FY 04	FY 05
Current Dollars										
Army	61,183	64,346	64,586	64,415	66,628	67,770	71,703	74,531	77,366	81,580
Navy	79,587	82,098	78,047	83,043	80,878	83,273	86,865	90,236	92,894	96,677
Air Force	75,378	76,622	77,906	77,505	76,302	80,266	83,782	87,156	90,688	94,136
Defense-wide	37,109	35,364	35,597	38,593	37,026	37,255	35,973	38,326	39,038	45,228
Total, Current $	253,258	258,330	256,136	263,555	260,834	268,564	278,323	290,247	299,985	317,620
Constant FY 2000 Dollars										
Army	67,534	69,146	67,916	66,236	66,628	65,931	67,948	68,797	69,387	71,145
Navy	86,132	86,911	81,073	84,890	80,878	81,134	82,581	83,737	83,870	84,953
Air Force	81,532	80,897	80,634	78,983	76,302	78,275	79,828	81,170	82,293	83,223
Defense-wide	39,652	36,947	36,844	39,348	37,026	36,510	34,538	36,083	35,880	40,675
Total, Constant $	274,849	273,900	266,467	269,457	260,834	261,850	264,895	269,788	271,431	279,996
% Real Growth										
Army	-6.0	2.4	-1.8	-2.5	0.6	-1.1	3.1	1.3	0.9	2.5
Navy	-9.2	0.9	-6.7	4.7	-4.7	0.3	1.8	1.4	0.2	1.3
Air Force	-4.0	-0.8	-0.3	-2.1	-3.4	2.6	2.0	1.7	1.4	1.1
Total	-4.9	-0.4	-2.7	1.1	-3.2	0.4	1.2	1.8	0.6	3.2

Source: Defense Department.

Department of Defense Manpower,
1940–2001 (end strength in thousands)

	ACTIVE DUTY MILITARY						CIVILIAN WORKFORCE							
Fiscal Year	Army	Navy	Marine Corps	Air Force	Full Time Gd&Res	Total Military	Army	Navy including Marines	Air Force	Defense Agencies & Other	Total Civilians	Total DoD Manpower	Defense Related Employment in Industry	Total Defense Related Manpower
1940	218	161	28	51	–	458	137	119	–	–	256	714	314	1,028
1941	1,310	284	54	152	–	1,801	329	227	–	–	556	2,357	2,500	4,857
1942	2,311	641	143	764	–	3,859	852	432	–	–	1,284	5,143	10,000	15,143
1943	4,797	1,742	309	2,197	–	9,045	1,545	648	–	–	2,193	11,238	13,361	24,599
1944	5,622	2,981	476	2,372	–	11,452	1,503	736	–	–	2,239	13,691	12,600	26,291
1945	5,984	3,320	470	2,282	–	12,056	1,881	747	–	–	2,628	14,684	11,000	25,684
1946	1,435	978	156	456	–	3,025	927	489	–	–	1,416	4,441	1,168	5,609
1947	685	498	93	306	–	1,582	503	356	–	–	859	2,441	786	3,227
1948	554	418	85	388	–	1,444	303	347	152	1	804	2,248	958	3,206
1949	660	448	86	419	–	1,614	310	343	166	2	821	2,434	732	3,166
1950	593	381	74	411	–	1,459	261	293	154	2	710	2,170	713	2,883
1951	1,532	737	193	788	–	3,249	487	452	261	2	1,201	4,551	2,400	6,851
1952	1,596	824	232	983	–	3,636	515	481	310	2	1,308	4,944	3,600	8,544
1953	1,534	794	249	978	–	3,555	884	470	382	2	1,738	5,293	4,118	9,411
1954	1,405	726	224	948	–	3,302	720	433	371	2	1,527	4,829	2,975	7,804

	ACTIVE DUTY MILITARY						CIVILIAN WORKFORCE							
Fiscal Year	Army	Navy	Marine Corps	Air Force	Full Time Gd&Res	Total Military	Army	Navy including Marines	Air Force	Defense Agencies & Other	Total Civilians	Total DoD Manpower	Defense Related Employment in Industry	Total Defense Related Manpower
1955	1,109	661	205	960	—	2,935	651	433	397	2	1,483	4,419	2,500	6,919
1956	1,026	670	201	910	—	2,806	592	416	333	2	1,443	4,249	2,500	6,749
1957	998	676	201	920	—	2,795	571	411	417	2	1,400	4,195	2,850	7,045
1958	899	640	189	871	—	2,600	530	381	373	2	1,286	3,885	2,800	6,685
1959	862	626	176	840	—	2,504	497	375	364	2	1,238	3,741	2,700	6,441
1960	873	617	171	815	—	2,475	473	365	355	2	1,195	3,671	2,460	6,131
1961	859	626	177	821	—	2,483	472	363	346	2	1,183	3,665	2,600	6,265
1962	1,066	666	191	885	*	2,808	476	365	349	20	1,210	4,018	2,725	6,743
1963	976	665	189	870	*	2,700	459	360	337	32	1,188	3,888	2,550	6,438
1964	973	668	189	857	*	2,688	430	347	322	38	1,137	3,825	2,280	6,105
1965	969	672	190	825	*	2,656	414	343	317	42	1,116	3,771	2,125	5,896
1966	1,200	745	261	887	*	3,094	450	367	336	69	1,222	4,316	2,640	6,956
1967	1,442	751	285	897	*	3,377	516	416	349	76	1,357	4,733	3,100	7,833
1968	1,570	765	307	905	*	3,548	510	429	339	75	1,352	4,900	3,174	8,074
1969	1,512	776	310	862	*	3,460	531	438	349	72	1,390	4,849	2,916	7,765

	ACTIVE DUTY MILITARY						CIVILIAN WORKFORCE							
Fiscal Year	Army	Navy	Marine Corps	Air Force	Full Time Gd&Res	Total Military	Army	Navy including Marines	Air Force	Defense Agencies & Other	Total Civilians	Total DoD Manpower	Defense Related Employment in Industry	Total Defense Related Manpower
1970	1,322	692	260	791	1	3,066	480	388	328	68	1,264	4,330	2,399	6,729
1971	1,123	623	212	755	1	2,715	452	362	313	63	1,189	3,904	2,031	5,935
1972	811	588	198	726	1	2,323	446	353	300	60	1,159	3,482	1,985	5,467
1973	801	564	196	691	1	2,253	406	334	288	72	1,099	3,352	1,850	5,202
1974	783	546	189	644	1	2,162	409	335	289	75	1,108	3,270	1,860	5,130
1975	784	535	196	613	1	2,128	401	326	278	73	1,078	3,206	1,800	5,006
1976	779	524	192	585	1	2,082	390	321	262	72	1,045	3,127	1,690	4,817
1977	782	530	192	570	1	2,074	372	318	255	77	1,022	3,096	1,730	4,826
1978	771	530	191	569	1	2,062	371	317	251	77	1,016	3,078	1,765	4,843
1979	758	522	185	559	7	2,031	359	310	245	77	991	3,022	1,860	4,882
1980	777	527	188	558	13	2,063	361	309	244	77	990	3,053	1,990	5,043
1981	781	540	191	570	19	2,101	372	321	246	80	1,019	3,121	2,085	5,206
1982	780	553	192	583	22	2,130	378	319	248	82	1,028	3,158	2,290	5,448
1983	780	558	194	592	39	2,162	391	339	251	83	1,064	3,226	2,415	5,641
1984	780	565	196	597	46	2,184	403	342	253	87	1,085	3,270	2,735	6,005

	ACTIVE DUTY MILITARY						CIVILIAN WORKFORCE							
Fiscal Year	Army	Navy	Marine Corps	Air Force	Full Time Gd&Res	Total Military	Army	Navy including Marines	Air Force	Defense Agencies & Other	Total Civilians	Total DoD Manpower	Defense Related Employment in Industry	Total Defense Related Manpower
1985	781	571	198	602	55	2,206	420	353	264	92	1,129	3,335	2,980	6,315
1986	781	581	199	608	64	2,233	413	342	263	94	1,112	3,345	3,315	6,660
1987	781	587	200	607	69	2,243	418	353	264	98	1,133	3,376	3,625	7,002
1988	772	593	197	576	71	2,209	393	348	253	96	1,090	3,299	3,430	6,729
1989	770	593	197	571	72	2,202	403	354	261	99	1,117	3,319	3,275	6,595
1990	751	583	197	539	74	2,143	380	341	249	103	1,073	3,216	3,115	6,332
1991	725	571	195	511	75	2,077	365	329	233	117	1,045	3,122	3,045	6,166
1992	611	542	185	470	72	1,880	334	309	214	149	1,006	2,886	2,840	5,726
1993	572	510	178	444	71	1,776	294	285	202	156	937	2,713	2,620	5,332
1994	541	469	174	426	68	1,678	280	269	196	156	901	2,579	2,460	5,039
1995	509	435	174	400	65	1,583	267	249	186	147	849	2,432	2,315	4,747
1996	491	417	175	389	66	1,538	259	240	183	138	819	2,356	2,210	4,568
1997	492	396	174	378	64	1,504	247	223	180	136	786	2,290	2,215	4,505
1998	484	382	173	367	64	1,470	237	210	174	126	747	2,217	2,190	4,407

ACTIVE DUTY MILITARY / CIVILIAN WORKFORCE

Fiscal Year	Army	Navy	Marine Corps	Air Force	Full Time Gd&Res	Total Military	Army	Navy including Marines	Air Force	Defense Agencies & Other	Total Civilians	Total DoD Manpower	Defense Related Employment in Industry	Total Defense Related Manpower
1999	480	372	172	366	64	1,454	226	207	169	123	725	2,179	2,210	4,389
2000	480	372	172	361	64	1,449	220	199	163	118	700	2,149	2,185	4,334
2001	480	371	172	354	64	1,441	216	192	162	114	684	2,125	2,200	4,325

* Indicates less than 500 full-time National Guardsmen and Reservists. Data prior to 1962 not available.

Notes: Air Force civil service employment is included in the Army prior to 1948 and identified separately thereafter. Beginning in 1953, the civilian work force figures include both U.S. and foreign national direct hires and the foreign national indirect hire employees that support U.S. forces overseas. Beginning with FY 1996, all the federal civilian work force are measured in Full-time Equivalents (FTE) on this table. Navy reserve personnel on active duty for Training and Administration of Reserves (TARS) are included in the active Navy prior to FY 1980 and in the Full-Time Guard and Reserve thereafter. Active Duty Military includes the activation of 25,652 National Guard and Reservists in FY 1990 pursuant to sections 673b, Title 10 U.S.C., 17,059 National Guard and Reservists in FY 1991 and 954 National Guard and Reservists in FY 1992 pursuant to sections 672 and 673, Title 10 U.S.C., to support Operation Desert Shield/Desert Storm.

Source: Defense Department.

Military Force Trends

	Cold War (1990)	2000	QDR Target
ARMY:			
Divisions (active/National Guard)	18/10	10[1]/8[2]	10[1]/8[2]
AIR FORCE:			
Fighter wings (active/reserve)	24/12	13/7	12+/8
NAVY:			
Aircraft carriers (active/reserve)	15/1	11/1	11/1
Air wings (active/reserve)	13/2	10/1	10/1
Total battle force ships[3]	546	314	306
MARINE CORPS:			
Divisions (active/reserve)	3/1	3/1	3/1
Wings (active/reserve)	3/1	3/1	3/1
STRATEGIC NUCLEAR FORCES:			
Intercontinental ballistic missiles/warheads	1,000/2,450	550/2,000	500/500[4]
Ballistic missile submarines	31	18	14[4]
Sea-launched ballistic missiles/warheads	568/4,864	432/3,456	336/not over 1,750[4]
Heavy bombers	324	90[5]	92[5]
MILITARY PERSONNEL:			
Active	2,069,000	1,384,806	1,363,000
Selected reserve	1,128,000	865,298	835,000

[1]Plus two armored cavalry regiments.

[2]Plus 18 separate brigades (15 of which are at enhanced readiness levels).

[3]Includes active and reserve ships of the following types: aircraft carriers, surface combatants, submaries, amphibious warfare ships, mine warfare ships, combat logistics force, and other support ships.

[4]Upon entry-into-force of START II.

[5]Does not include 95 B-1 bombers dedicated to conventional missions.

Source: White House Office of Management and Budget.

Department of Defense Budget Authority by Service, 1996–2005 ($ billions)

	FY 99	FY 00	FY 01	FY 02	FY 03	FY 04	FY 05
Army	65.3	67.2	71.3	73.6	76.4	78.9	82.3
Navy/Marine Corps	81.9	83.3	91.4	89.2	93.1	96.2	100.3
Air Force	76.9	79.1	84.8	86.7	89.2	92.3	95.1
Defensewide	38.5	37.6	38.9	38.8	40.0	40.3	41.2
Total DoD	262.6	267.2	286.4	288.3	298.7	307.6	318.9

Source: Defense Department.

Department of Defense Budget Authority by Title, 1996–2005 ($ billions)

	FY 99	FY 00	FY 01	FY 02	FY 03	FY 04	FY 05
Military Personnel	70.9	73.7	76.3	78.4	80.9	83.7	86.7
O & M*	98.1	103.5	103.8	105.0	107.8	111.2	114.4
Procurement	49.0	53.0	61.8	62.3	66.6	69.2	75.1
RDT&E**	36.6	34.4	34.3	34.7	34.5	35.0	34.2
Military Construction	5.1	2.3	7.1	4.2	4.3	4.5	4.8
Family Housing	3.6	3.1	3.8	3.6	3.7	3.9	3.9
Funds & Other	-0.7	-2.8	-0.7	—	0.9	0.1	-0.3
Total DoD	262.6	267.2	286.4	288.3	298.7	307.6	318.9

*Operations and maintenance
**Research, development, testing, and engineering.

Source: Defense Department.

Where Military Dollars Are Spent
($ thousands)

	PERSONNEL COMPENSATION					PRIME CONTRACT AWARDS		
State	Civilian Pay	Military Active Duty Pay	Reserve & National Guard Pay	Retired Military Pay	Total Compensation	Civil Functions Contracts	Military Functions Contracts	Total Contracts
Alabama	762,214	523,820	172,458	724,278	2,182,770	43,136	1,795,140	1,838,276
Alaska	170,795	605,440	15,526	87,234	878,995	23,685	541,205	564,890
Arizona	312,349	719,643	55,375	777,137	1,864,504	12,506	2,898,429	2,910,935
Arkansas	127,063	184,586	68,093	350,686	730,388	43,965	205,316	249,281
California	3,627,760	4,952,715	307,102	3,444,074	12,331,651	208,369	18,021,355	18,229,724
Colorado	477,315	834,590	92,750	752,741	2,157,396	26,702	2,016,374	2,045,076
Connecticut	169,284	254,212	32,895	156,707	613,098	53,228	2,585,032	2,638,260
Delaware	56,470	149,915	31,008	94,158	331,551	3,397	98,157	101,554
District of Columbia	636,175	512,417	28,112	60,087	1,236,791	39,223	1,443,450	1,482,673
Florida	1,157,936	2,379,839	149,865	2,981,955	6,669,585	84,578	5,778,061	5,862,639
Georgia	1,109,939	1,988,127	192,757	1,041,260	4,332,083	41,873	3,923,850	3,965,723
Hawaii	713,844	1,338,345	44,043	234,275	2,330,507	11,151	917,329	928,480
Idaho	51,129	130,509	25,338	139,348	346,324	22,011	110,506	132,517
Illinois	8,541.676	873,397	134,215	438,859	1,988,147	117,374	1,138,636	1,256,010
Indiana	554,332	46,315	152,296	268,692	1,021,635	17,433	1,534,579	1,552,012
Iowa	50,057	13,527	62,827	117,943	244,354	18,523	352,094	370,617
Kansas	197,139	543,881	60,733	277,684	1,079,437	9,269	753,324	762,593
Kentucky	379,708	974,595	59,219	309,485	1,723,007	36,221	837,873	874,094
Louisiana	290,561	532,259	108,812	401,425	1,333,057	162,588	915,281	1,077,869
Maine	234,643	109,056	25,401	155,436	524,538	942	796,282	797,224
Maryland	1,490,012	954,076	114,804	705,903	3,264,795	39,111	4,097,674	4,136,785
Massachusetts	348,417	123,971	90,982	279,525	842,895	36,973	4,637,674	4,674,647
Michigan	326,365	50,416	91,860	294,951	763,592	20,566	1,220,770	1,241,336
Minnesota	93,840	29,783	94,401	175,394	393,418	58,411	901,950	960,361
Mississippi	374,560	503,396	93,659	329,204	1,300,819	76,932	1,835,174	1,912,106
Missouri	592,320	444,460	158,756	434,837	1,630,373	55,938	7,037,071	7,093,009
Montana	41,247	133,490	24,237	98,592	297,566	3,573	87,038	90,611

229

	PERSONNEL COMPENSATION					PRIME CONTRACT AWARDS		
State	Civilian Pay	Military Active Duty Pay	Reserve & National Guard Pay	Retired Military Pay	Total Compensation	Civil Functions Contracts	Military Functions Contracts	Total Contracts
Nebraska	125,678	365,766	31,840	188,010	711,294	14,157	307,880	322,037
Nevada	81,536	304,873	16,231	374,329	776,969	2,164	283,098	285,262
New Hampshire	50,575	24,742	18,794	145,798	239,909	199	567,693	567,892
New Jersey	705,028	318,030	84,944	310,679	1,418,681	95,056	2,469,210	2,564,266
New Mexico	301,576	526,874	29,052	310,569	1,168,071	6,064	670,327	675,381
New York	485,232	635,461	171,141	395,777	1,687,611	64,365	3,436,648	3,501,013
North Carolina	629,739	2,504,484	101,144	1,024,094	4,259,461	111,857	1,309,214	1,421,071
North Dakota	57,624	311,020	25,175	44,682	438,501	2,726	103,363	106,089
Ohio	1,267,431	407,404	124,773	536,932	2,336,540	39,060	2,693,688	2,732,748
Oklahoma	675,660	957,126	76,497	462,708	2,171,991	17,254	753,978	771,232
Oregon	100,291	35,730	57,053	288,122	481,196	60,109	142,754	202,863
Pennsylvania	1,292,216	125,959	185,425	614,645	2,218,245	54,426	3,632,931	3,687,357
Rhode Island	194,197	132,192	19,282	91,572	437,243	4,909	329,060	333,969
South Carolina	408,134	1,003,978	95,167	755,558	2,262,837	24,430	988,067	1,012,497
South Dakota	42,107	120,517	23,242	71,861	257,727	22,414	87,555	109,969
Tennessee	186,075	181,744	98,176	605,614	1,071,609	56,164	1,081,068	1,137,232
Texas	1,820,640	3,675,335	268,482	2,618,063	8,382,520	150,039	8,669,057	8,819,098
Utah	498,055	184,119	61,356	171,978	915,508	1,504	393,174	394,678
Vermont	18,815	5,986	21,633	43,366	89,800	243	225,183	225,426
Virginia	4,145,269	4,885,942	106,778	2,217,749	11,355,738	109,123	9,453,855	9,562,978
Washington	1,052,614	1,608,031	109,540	1,042,655	3,812,840	83,403	2,299,014	2,382,417
West Virginia	59,277	18,084	43,116	121,214	241,691	98,714	100,610	199,324
Wisconsin	111,554	23,834	86,828	190,333	412,549	18,295	532,981	551,276
Wyoming	33,935	125,468	14,153	58,978	232,534	2,781	88,732	91,513
Total U.S.	29,230,408	38,389,459	4,357,346	27,817,136	99,794,349	2,309,134	107,098,784	109,407,898
Guam	129,086	219,738	2,797	25,972	377,593	0	129,315	129,315
Puerto Rico	97,485	75,712	92,501	71,748	337,446	12,178	261,834	274,012
Other U.S. Possessions	26,654	55,423	283	9,586	91,946	17,665	330,002	347,667
Total U.S. Possessions	253,225	350,873	85,581	107,306	806,985	29,843	721,151	750,954

Source: Defense Department.

Procurement Dollars

($ in millions)

		FY 1996	FY1997	FY1998	FY 1999 Estimate
ARMY					
	Aircraft	1,539	1,346	1,162	1,240
	Missiles	839	1,038	1,178	1,541
	Weapons, Tracked	1,454	1,468	1,066	1,475
	Ammunition	1,052	1,126	891	976
	Other	2,698	3,177	2,455	3,140
	Total	7,586	8,156	6,752	8,373
NAVY					
	Aircraft	4,454	6,873	6,086	7,669
	Weapons	1,541	1,358	1,136	1,436
	Ammunitions (Navy & Marine Corps)	392	284	337	503
	Shipbuilding & Conversion	6,548	5,492	7,438	5,958
	Other	2,427	2,892	2,825	4,185
	Marine Corps	442	580	374	695
	Total	15,805	17,479	18,197	20,447
AIR FORCE					
	Aircraft	7,149	6,485	5,818	8,080
	Ammunition	336	316	404	456
	Missiles	2,743	2,269	2,558	2,892
	Other	6,513	6,026	6,561	6,755
	Total	16,742	15,096	15,341	18,183
OTHER					
	Defense-Wide	2,153	2,063	1,695	2,616
	National Guard & Reserve Equipment	767	717	—	—
	Chemical Agents & Munitions Destruction	656	758	621	1,094
	Defense Export Loan Guarantees	—	.5	.5	.5
	Total DOD Procurement	43,709	44,269	42,606	50,714

Source: Defense Department.

The Pentagon

The Pentagon, headquarters of the Department of Defense, is one of the world's largest office buildings. Virtually a city in itself, the building houses more than 23,000 people. It was built in the remarkably short time of sixteen months and was completed in January 15, 1943, at an approximate cost of $83 million. It consolidated seventeen buildings of the War Department.

STATS:

Total land area	280 acres
Original land cost	$2,245,000
Area covered by Pentagon building	29 acres
Parking space	67 acres
Capacity (vehicles)	10,329
Gross floor area	6,546,360 square feet
Net space for offices, concessions, and storage	3,900,533 square feet
Length of each outer wall	921 feet
Height of building	71 feet 3.5 inches
Total length of corridors	17.5 miles

Source: Defense Department.

Index

Ralston, Gen. Joseph W. (JCS vice chairman), 25, 53, 72, 130, 171
Readiness. *See* Military readiness
Reimer, Gen. Dennis J., 64, 95, 96
Rescue forces
    O'Grady rescue mission, 59–60
    TRAP (Tactical Recovery Aircraft and Personnel), 59
    in Vietnam War, 46–47
Revere, Paul, 12
Ricks, Thomas E., 22
Rivers, L. Mendel (D-S.C.), 32
Robyn, Dorothy (White House special asst. for economic policy), 157, 158, 159, 164
Rodriguez, Ciro D. (D-Texas), 165
Russell, Richard B. (D-Ga.), 120
Ryan, Gen. Michael E. (Air Force chief of staff), 95, 96

Secretary of defense. *See* Defense secretary
Senate
    Appropriations Committee, 23, 120–122
    Armed Services Committee
    defense budget hearings, 7–8, 22–24, 135–136
    dysfunctional nature of, 120
    military readiness hearings, 91–97
    QDR report hearings, 29
    Big Four meeting on emergency appropriations, 105–106, 107
    Budget Committee, 8, 23, 108–109, 119–122
Shalikashvili, Gen. John M. (JCS chairman)
    QDR criticism rebuttal, 72–74
    QDR report endorsement, 7, 25, 28–29, 34, 36, 129
    QDR strategy review, 39–40
    U.S. military involvement, 14
Shelton, Gen. Hugh H. (JCS chairman), 9, 94–97, 105, 107, 129–138, 171, 178–181
Shuster, Bud (R-Pa.), 77
Skelton, Ike (D-Mo.), 31, 77, 87, 107, 140
Social Security Trust Fund, 81, 82
Somalia, U.S. involvement, 17
Spence, Floyd (R-S.C.)
    BRAC closings, 153–154, 161, 166

defense budget ceilings, 81, 84–88
defense budget for FY 2000, 139–140
emergency appropriations bills, 107
QDR report, 30–32
Spinney, Franklin C. "Chuck," 34–36, 67, 182–192
Spratt, John M., Jr. (D-S.C.), 76, 77
Stevens, Ted (R-Alaska), 88, 89, 103, 105–106, 107
Stuart, Sandy, 101

Terrorist groups
    bombing of Air Force barracks (Saudi Arabia), 43
    cyber terrorism, 175–176, 180–181
    and homeland defense, 174–177
    rogue countries, 174, 176
Thurmond, Strom (R-S.C.), 91–92, 94
"Trigger pullers," 48–49
Two-MRC (major regional contingencies) strategy, 27, 35–36, 74, 195

Urban warrior experiments, 61–62

Vietnam War, 32, 45–47, 67–72
Vinson, Carl (D-Ga.), 120

Warner, John W. (R-Va.), 104, 106, 107, 116
Warner, Ted, 40, 41
Warren, James, 12
Warsaw Pact, 5, 63, 65–66, 120, 196, 199
Watts, J. C. (R-Okla.), 155, 156, 164
Weapons development. *See also* Aircraft; Modernization program
    the Army Big Five, 50
    Army M-1 tanks, 51, 73, 96, 183, 195–196
    and defense budget, 14
    Hawk antiaircraft missile, 63
    Marine Corps, 197
    MLRS (multiple launch rocket system), 63
    Navy attack submarine, 96
    Pentagon procurement process, 197–198
Weinberger, Caspar W. (defense secretary), 11, 191, 192
Weldon, Curt (R-Pa.), 168
White, John (deputy defense secretary), 148, 162, 163, 166